Analyzing
INEQUALITIES

Analyzing INEQUALITIES

An
Introduction to
**Race, Class,
Gender, and
Sexuality**
Using the
General Social Survey

CATHERINE E. HARNOIS
Wake Forest University

Los Angeles | London | New Delhi
Singapore | Washington DC | Melbourne

FOR INFORMATION

SAGE Publications, Inc.
2455 Teller Road
Thousand Oaks, California 91320
E-mail: order@sagepub.com

SAGE Publications Ltd.
1 Oliver's Yard
55 City Road
London, EC1Y 1SP
United Kingdom

SAGE Publications India Pvt. Ltd.
B 1/I 1 Mohan Cooperative Industrial Area
Mathura Road, New Delhi 110 044
India

SAGE Publications Asia-Pacific Pte. Ltd.
3 Church Street
#10–04 Samsung Hub
Singapore 049483

Library of Congress Cataloging-in-Publication Data

Names: Harnois, Catherine E., author.

Title: Analyzing inequalities : an introduction to race, class, gender, and sexuality using the general social survey / Catherine E. Harnois, Wake Forest University.

Description: Los Angeles : SAGE, [2018] | Includes bibliographical references.

Identifiers: LCCN 2016036593 | ISBN 9781506304113 (pbk. : alk. paper)

Subjects: LCSH: Social surveys—United States—Evaluation. | Equality—United States—Statistics. | Social indicators—United States. | Social sciences—Research—Methodology.

Classification: LCC HN90.S67 H37 2018 | DDC 300.72/3—dc23 LC record available at https://lccn.loc.gov/2016036593

This book is printed on acid-free paper.

SFI Certified Sourcing
www.sfiprogram.org
SFI-00453

Acquisitions Editor: Jeff Lasser
Editorial Assistant: Adeline Wilson
eLearning Editor: Gabrielle Piccininni
Production Editor: Kelly DeRosa
Copy Editor: Rachel Keith
Typesetter: Hurix Systems Pvt. Ltd.
Proofreader: Theresa Kay
Cover Designer: Janet Kiesel
Marketing Manager: Kara Kindstrom

17 18 19 20 21 10 9 8 7 6 5 4 3 2 1

CONTENTS

CHAPTER 3 • Analyzing Gender With the GSS 43

CHAPTER 4 • Analyzing Race and Ethnicity With the GSS 65

PREFACE

This book seeks to provide students and faculty with a resource for connecting sociological issues with real-world data analysis in the context of introductory-level courses. It is not meant to be a comprehensive guide to social statistics, nor is it meant to provide statistical findings concerning every single issue related to inequality—clearly an impossible task! Rather, the goal is to provide readers with (1) an introduction to secondary data analysis in the social sciences, (2) an overview of the range of questions included in the General Social Survey (GSS) that are related to social inequalities, and (3) some basic techniques for analyzing this data online. Though the analytic techniques covered are basic, it is hoped that through active engagement with online data analysis, readers will gain a better understanding of social science research and will be better positioned to ask and answer the questions that are of most interest them.

The first two chapters provide students with an introduction to social science survey research and an overview of data-related concepts. Chapter 1 addresses the importance of survey research for issues related to social inequality and the benefits and limitations of using survey research to address social inequalities. It outlines four key themes in social justice statistics: power and inequality, socially constructed differences, links between the individual and the broader society, and intersecting inequalities. These themes are carried through the remainder of the book. Chapter 2 introduces students to the GSS and SDA (the Computer-Assisted Survey Methods Program's Survey Documentation and Analysis website) as well as basic concepts in data analysis, including level of measurement and measures of central tendency. While this is a lot of information to be covered in a single chapter, these concepts are then reinforced throughout the remaining chapters. In this book, unlike traditional statistics textbooks, students do not need to master all the concepts presented in Chapter 2 before proceeding to subsequent chapters. Rather, the book is designed in such a way that readers master these concepts *as they progress* through the subsequent chapters.

Chapters 3 through 6 focus on gender, race and ethnicity, class, and sexuality. Because this book is meant to be used alongside a more substantive introductory text, Chapters 3 through 6 are designed to be read in any order. It is expected that an instructor might assign only two or three of these chapters and pair them with more qualitative or theoretical readings. Thus, in *Analyzing Inequalities*, in contrast to traditional social science statistics books, the statistical concepts and techniques do not build on each other from chapter to chapter. Instead, the basic tools of data analysis (e.g., finding variables, producing and interpreting univariate descriptive statistics, crosstabs, creating charts and graphs, selecting cases) are reinforced in each chapter. Taken together, these chapters provide students multiple opportunities to practice basic data analysis using a variety of variables and to investigate a wide range of issues related to social inequality.

While Chapters 3 through 6 focus primarily on individual systems of inequality, Chapters 7 through 9 take a more intersectional approach, highlighting the interplay of multiple systems of inequality within social institutions. Chapter 7 focuses on family, Chapter 8 on education, and Chapter 9 on work. The analyses presented in these chapters are exploratory, and the goal is to provide neither a comprehensive overview of these topics nor the "final word" on any of the research questions presented. It is my hope that readers will see limitations in all the analyses and exercises presented here, and that this will then entice some to examine these issues with greater theoretical and methodological complexity.

Instructors, sign in at study.sagepub.com/harnois for the following instructor resources:

- Answers to end of chapter multiple choice questions;
- Guided answers for in-text essay questions; and
- Bonus multiple choice test bank questions for each chapter.

ACKNOWLEDGMENTS

Writing this book has taken several years and would not have been possible without a supportive network of colleagues, friends, and family. At Wake Forest University, I have benefited from working with a number of generous colleagues. I am grateful to Joseph Soares, Ana Wahl, Catherine Ross, and Saylor Breckenridge, each of whom gave me valuable feedback. I am particularly indebted to Steve Gunkel, who reviewed the entire manuscript—several chapters twice!—with a fine-tooth comb, and whose insights and attention to detail have improved literally every page of the book. It is difficult for me to imagine a more generous friend and colleague.

Over the duration of this project, I had the good fortune of working with three undergraduate research assistants: Sydni Williams, Ann Nguyen, and Ashley Mitchell. In addition to providing me with feedback about the book, they have helped me to think through issues of education, family, and intellectual activism.

In the process of writing this book, I participated in a panel on intersectional pedagogy at the 2015 annual meeting of the Southern Sociological Society. The comments and discussion that this panel generated were both insightful and motivating, and I am grateful to the organizers of this panel, Marni Brown and Cameron Lippard, for creating a place for this dialogue. In addition, this book has benefited from the insights of João Luiz Bastos, who has taught me much and has helped me to think more clearly about intersectionality, social statistics, and the relationship between the two.

Jeff Lasser at Sage has guided me through the publication process, and it has been a wonderful experience to work with and learn from him. I am also grateful to the individual reviewers who took the time to carefully read and evaluate the book proposal and manuscript. In particular, I would like to thank Robert S. Bausch, Cameron University; Jennifer Roebuck Bulanda, Miami University; Fareeda Griffith, Denison University; Peter Meiksins, Cleveland State University; Kerry Strand, Hood College; Esther Isabelle Wilder, Lehman College and The Graduate Center, The City University of New York (CUNY); Cari Beecham-Bautista, College of DuPage; Jason Lee Crockett, Kutztown University of Pennsylvania; Geoff Harkness, Morningside College; Lorien Lake-Corral, University of Maine at Augusta; William A. Mirola, Marian University; Julia Nevarez, Kean University; Thomas Piñeros Shields, University of Massachusetts Lowell; and Maura Ryan, Georgia State University. Their feedback has been invaluable.

In this and other projects, I am deeply indebted to Robin W. Simon, Barbara Risman, and Brian Powell for their continued mentorship and support. I am especially grateful to Joe Harrington, who has provided me with a constant stream of encouragement and patience for the past decade and who has, among other things, helped me to see the beauty of short, clear sentences (unlike this one). To the extent that they appear here, credit is his. My thanks also go to Toni and Tom Merfeld, Charlie Harrington, Jo Cox, Sandya Hewamanne, Neil DeVotta, Kim Babon, and Mark Ashley and my parents, Jim and Sheila, all of whom have helped me to see this project from start to finish.

Finally, my deep appreciation goes to the Computer-Assisted Survey Methods Program (CSM), which develops and maintains the outstanding Survey Documentation and Analysis (SDA) package. CSM was originally part of the University of California, Berkeley, and is now part of the Institute for Scientific Analysis. I thank the individuals and institutions responsible for creating the General Social Survey (GSS) and for maintaining and enhancing it for nearly 50 years. The GSS is a project of the independent research organization NORC at the University of Chicago, with principal funding from the National Science Foundation. At the time of this writing, more than 25,000 scholarly articles, chapters, books, and presentations have used data from the GSS to advance knowledge about American society—44 years of extremely high-quality survey data pertaining to a range of inequalities and available for free to students, researchers, and anyone else who may be interested. This is something from which we can all benefit and for which we might all be grateful.

CHAPTER 1

AN INTRODUCTION TO ANALYZING INEQUALITIES

In the United States (US), almost 3% of Black men were imprisoned on December 31, 2013, compared to 0.5% of white men. In other words, Black men were imprisoned at approximately six times the rate of white men. On this same date, Black women in the US were imprisoned at more than twice the rate of white women.

Bureau of Justice Statistics' National Prisoner Statistics Program[1]

Across the world, approximately 781 million people age 15 and over are functionally illiterate. Nearly two thirds of them are women, a proportion that has remained unchanged for two decades. Illiteracy rates are highest among older people and are higher among women than men. At age 65 and over, 30% of women and 19% of men are illiterate.

United Nations Statistics Division[2]

In the US, almost 1 in 5 women (18.3%) reported experiencing rape at some time in their lives, compared to 1 in 71 men (1.4%).[3] In response to a 2011 survey of US high school students, "11.8% of girls and 4.5% of boys from grades 9–12 reported that they were forced to have sexual intercourse at some time in their lives."[4]

US Centers for Disease Control and Prevention[5]

When, in 2014, a survey asked adults in the US about a "hypothetical emergency expense" that would cost $400, nearly half of all respondents (47%) said that this expense would represent a significant financial hardship for them. Fourteen percent said they simply could not cover the expense; another 10% of respondents indicated that they

Learning Objectives

By the end of this chapter, you should be able to:

1. Explain how statistical research can play a role in documenting and addressing a range of social inequalities.

2. Describe the key themes involved in doing "social justice statistics."

3. Describe the major benefits and limitations of using existing survey data in the context of social justice work.

4. Explain the difference between correlation and causation.

5. Explain the difference between dependent and independent variables.

would need to sell something to cover the expense; others would need to borrow funds from friends or family or charge the expense to a credit card that they knew they would be unable to pay off.

Federal Reserve Board's Division of Consumer and Community Affairs' 2014 Survey of Household Economics and Decisionmaking[6]

Nearly half the world's population, 2.8 billion people, survive on less than $2 a day. About 20% of the world's population, 1.2 billion people, live on less than $1 a day, and 1 billion people do not have access to safe water.

Food and Agriculture Organization of the United Nations[7]

INTRODUCTION

Consider a social justice issue that is important to you: inequalities of income and wealth; racial and ethnic inequalities; gender inequalities; inequalities of sexual orientation; inequalities of health and well-being; transnational inequalities stemming from patterns of cultural and economic globalization, legacies of colonialism, and global climate change. Broadly understood, social justice refers to the recognition of systemic inequalities and a commitment to dismantling these inequalities as they occur within the institutional, interactional, and attitudinal dynamics of society.[8] This book provides an introduction to statistical analyses in pursuit of social justice, using data from the General Social Survey.

Much of what we know about social justice issues comes from surveys and statistics. Social scientists, health researchers, governmental organizations, and nonprofit nongovernmental organizations (NGOs) routinely design surveys focused on social justice issues and use the information collected in these surveys to understand and address a wide range of inequalities. Many of the most important facts and figures we have about racial inequality in the US criminal justice system—for example, the extent of racial/ethnic inequality in incarceration rates, how these inequalities have changed over time, and how racial/ethnic inequalities intersect with inequalities of class and gender—stem from data collected by the US Bureau of Justice Statistics (BJS). The BJS collects this information on a regular basis, and social scientists who work for the BJS analyze this information using a variety of statistical techniques. In addition, the BJS produces reports summarizing this information and makes these reports available to the public—at no cost—on its website (www.bjs.gov). Other branches of the US government, including the Centers for Disease Control and Prevention (CDC), the Census Bureau, the Bureau of Labor Statistics, the Department of Education, and many others, also conduct surveys, analyze the resulting data, create reports based on their findings, and share these findings with the public. Activists, organizations, and researchers in pursuit of social justice often turn to these sources of data to document their claims and to strengthen their arguments.

Statistical research has also been a vital tool for keeping track of gender inequality in the United States. The US Census Bureau's Current Population Survey (CPS), for example, showed that in March 1964, the weekly wages of full-time, year-round women workers ages 25 to 64 were 58% of what full-time, year-round men workers of the same age group earned.[9] More than four decades later, the Census Bureau reported that women's earnings had improved relative to men's, but they noted that a significant wage gap remains. In 2014, women in the United States who worked full time year-round earned only 79% of what full-time, year-round men workers earned.[10] A recent report from the US Bureau of Labor Statistics shows that the gender gap in earnings remains at every level of educational attainment. In 2014, median usual weekly earnings for full-time wage and salary workers age 25 years and older was $517 for men who had achieved less than a high school education. For women, the corresponding figure was $409—roughly 79% that of men's earnings. For men and women with a bachelor's degree or higher, the weekly earnings for full-time workers were $1,385 and $1,049, respectively—a gender gap of 76%.[11]

Beyond the US context, international organizations such as the World Bank, the International Monetary Fund, the European Union, and the United Nations (UN) also conduct surveys on a variety of social justice issues and often make their data, and the reports summarizing these data, available to the public at no cost. The World Bank, for example, collects data on a variety of social and economic indicators in countries around the world, including the percentage of the population with access to electricity, the prevalence of HIV among men and women, illiteracy rates for men and women, and men's and women's life expectancies. It also maintains a website where anyone can access and analyze these data for free (http://data.worldbank.org/data-catalog/world-development-indicators).

High-quality survey research, along with the statistical analyses based on these data, have played a vital role in social justice movements historically, and in our increasingly data-driven society, this trend will certainly continue into the future. Statistical research is also of the utmost importance for democracy. As explained in the United Nations' Fundamental Principles of Official Statistics, "official statistics provide an indispensable element in the information system of a democratic society, serving the Government, the economy and the public with data about the economic, demographic, social and environmental situation."[12] Within any particular country, statistical information provides a window into multiple dimensions of social and economic inequality and mobility. Social statistics allow us to assess how well we, as a society, are living up to our values and ideals. International survey data are crucial for assessing inequalities at a more global level.

SOCIAL JUSTICE STATISTICS

As discussed above, survey research, and statistical analyses of quantitative data more generally, have played an important role in a variety of social justice movements. It is also true, however, that statistical research has been used to perpetuate inequalities.

In the United States, statistical research has been used in the context of the eugenics movement, to justify discriminatory immigration policies, and to reduce social welfare programs for the poor.[13] Statistical analyses of survey research have also been used recently by opponents of same-sex marriage and opponents of LGBT adoption rights.[14] The complex history of statistics and social justice underscores the importance of thinking critically about the relationship between the two. Social statistics can and have been used to advance social justice, but they also have been used to advance privilege, domination, and oppression.

A critical question to consider, then, is this: How and under what circumstances can social statistics be a resource for social justice projects?[15] There is no single answer to this question, but social justice statistics tend to emphasize four key themes. First, social justice statistical analyses acknowledge the existence of socially patterned inequalities as well as the role of power and privilege in maintaining these inequalities. A second feature of social justice statistics is that they tend to highlight the social context in which surveys and other research tools are created and the socially constructed categories upon which they rely. Social justice statistics also frequently emphasize the relationships between individuals and the institutions that organize their world—in other words, between the micro and macro levels of society. Finally, social justice statistics increasingly recognize the interplay of multiple systems of inequality, taking an "intersectional" approach to analyzing inequalities.

Power and Inequality

At their best, social justice statistical analyses keep issues of power and inequality at the forefront.[16] This means that researchers are attentive to power and inequality at every step of the research process. When formulating a research question, a social justice approach asks: Whose interest does this research serve? Why is it important to have this question answered? Who benefits from having this question answered, and how? When considering research design, such an approach asks us to consider questions such as: How and to what extent were inequalities challenged or reproduced in the data collection process? Which social groups are represented in this research sample and which are excluded? When interpreting findings, a social justice framework draws our attention to how the findings might actually be used. It urges consideration of multiple perspectives and interpretations. It emphasizes commonalities as well as differences across social groups. Finally, when communicating the results, a social justice framework asks us to consider how the results might be disseminated in such a way as to reach the widest possible audience, including not only policy makers and academics but also the everyday people and social groups who are often at the heart of the analysis.

Socially Constructed Differences

A second feature of social justice statistics is that this approach tends to view difference and inequalities as largely, and in some cases entirely, socially created.

Some people believe that gender, race, class, and sexual orientation are naturally occurring phenomena: stable across time and space and representing "objective categories of real difference among people."[17] In the media, racial, gender, and sexual identities are often presented as if they were clear and uncontested properties of individuals—identities that stem from an agreed-upon set of physical and biological markers and which are only somewhat influenced by social and cultural processes. This way of thinking about difference and inequality is known as an **"essentialist"** perspective. As Karen Rosenblum and Toni-Michelle Travis put it, "essentialists tend to view categories of people as 'essentially' different in some important way."[18]

In contrast to an essentialist perspective, a **"social constructionist"** perspective views gender, race, class, and sexual orientation as categories of difference that are socially created: intertwined with history and culture, taking on different forms and meanings at different times and in different societies. While an essentialist might equate men with males and women with females, a social constructionist is likely to emphasize that the social expectations for men and women differ across time and space and also across particular situations. The social expectations of middle-class women in Victorian England were different, for example, from the social expectations of middle-class women in the contemporary United States. Similarly, a social constructionist perspective on race rejects the idea that racial categories stem from natural biological or genetic differences. Most social scientists now recognize that racial categories, and the hierarchies that emerge from them, are socially created. The racial groups that we recognize today in the United States are different from the racial groups that Americans recognized a century ago and also different from the racial categories recognized in other countries around the world today.[19] Like gender-, class-, and sexuality-based inequalities, the extent of inequality among racial groups is historically rooted and perpetuated by social structures and social institutions, such as governmental policies, the media, and the criminal justice system.

Data from social surveys can be interpreted from a variety of perspectives, including essentialist and social constructionist perspectives. Most social justice projects, however, rely on a social constructionist perspective. In other words, social justice projects that use statistics do not generally seek to uncover "fundamental differences" between men and women, between African Americans and whites, and between those who are poor and those who are wealthy. Social justice researchers use statistics to highlight how and to what extent inequalities organize our society, and to understand the circumstances under which these inequalities become more or less severe. Where an essentialist might ask, "Do poor people tend to have less motivation than wealthy people?" a social constructionist is more likely to ask, "What are the long-term psychological consequences of living in poverty?" or "How do the myths of meritocracy and the 'American dream' affect the self-esteem of those at the top and bottom of the socioeconomic ladder?"

When gender is assessed with a single survey question such as "What is your sex: male or female?" or race is assessed with a question like "What is your race: Black, white, or something else?" it is easy to see how surveys can feed into an essentialistic understanding of difference and inequality. Survey questions can also be interpreted from a social constructionist perspective, however. An analysis of gender arrangements and gender ideology over the past four decades can, for example, draw attention to gender as a socially constructed and historically changing hierarchy.[20] Even an analysis of gender based on the categories of "men" and "women" can be used to underscore the variation among women and among men, for example, as well as to highlight the similarities between men and women. In this way, survey research based on these categories can be used to disrupt essentialistic notions of gender and to challenge gender-based stereotypes.

Links Between the Individual and the Broader Society

In addition to conceptualizing inequalities as socially created and maintained, social justice statistics emphasize links between individuals and the society in which they live. A key insight of sociology is that what individuals believe, how individuals behave, and even what individuals feel are all to some extent shaped by the broader society. In addition, the social statuses and identities that individuals hold, including those based on gender, race, class, sexuality, age, religion, and dis/ability, further influence individuals' attitudes, beliefs, behaviors, and feelings.

Social surveys like the General Social Survey pose questions to individual people, and when analyzing the data from these surveys it is easy to focus on individual characteristics. An analysis of gender and work in the US, for example, might show that working women tend to work fewer hours than working men. An analysis of racial/ethnic differences in education in the US might reveal that, on average, non-Hispanic whites are more likely to graduate from college than are African Americans or Latinos/Latinas. Often in news stories and governmental reports, findings such as these are reported without considering the social context.

A social justice approach asks us to interpret these results in the broader social context, with attention to the role of history, culture, social institutions, and governmental policies in creating these inequalities. How might ideals about motherhood, fatherhood, femininity, and masculinity; the availability and affordability of child care and elder care; the presence of gender discrimination and sexual harassment in the workforce; and public policies concerning parental leave all work together to influence the hours that men and women spend at work? How do racial/ethnic segregation in housing and schools; school-funding policies at the local, state, and federal levels; the persistence of racial/ethnic prejudice and discrimination; and the increasing cost of college tuition work together to influence racial/ethnic differences in educational attainment?

While social surveys provide a crucial source of data for understanding these issues, interpreting the results of statistical analyses always requires a careful and critical interpretation of the data and attention to the ways in which individuals are situated within the broader social context. Reading the existing literature on social inequalities—including research that is qualitative, historical, comparative, and theoretical—is one of the best ways to clarify the connections between the micro (individual) and macro (societal) levels.

Intersecting Inequalities

In addition to drawing connections between individuals and the broader society and highlighting the ways in which inequalities are socially created and maintained, social justice statistics are at their best when they recognize the ways in which inequalities intersect. **Intersectionality** is the theoretical framework that draws attention to the ways in which social inequalities (such as race, gender, class, sexuality, age, dis/ability, nation, and citizenship status) work with and through one another at multiple levels of society.[21]

Inequalities intersect at the level of the individual, where "people experience race, class, gender, and sexuality differently depending upon their social location in the structures of race, class, gender, and sexuality."[22] Consider your own recent experiences—for example, in school, at home, at work, and around your neighborhood. Even if you didn't recognize it at the time, chances are that your experiences were influenced not just by one social status, such as your gender, but also by your age, your social class, your racial/ethnic identity, and your status as someone with or without a disability.

Inequalities also intersect at the macro levels of society, where, for example, systems of race, gender, class, and sexuality are each built into our economic, political, and cultural institutions. Consider the school you attended most recently and the faculty, staff, and administration who worked there. Chances are that gender, race, and social class all worked—at least to some extent—to structure which people held which positions and which people took which classes. You might also consider the neighborhood in which you grew up. Chances are that there were patterns in terms of who lived where and that these patterns had something to do with race, ethnicity, gender, and class. Consider the public spaces in this neighborhood, such as parks, basketball courts, playgrounds, and sidewalks. Chances are that in your neighborhood, people congregate in different areas and at different times depending on their class, race, gender, disability status, and age.[23] Intersectionality emphasizes that, at the macro level, social institutions and social spaces are often organized on the basis not of a single inequality but of multiple, intersecting inequalities.

Intersectionality draws attention to the ways in which systems of inequality work together to structure the experiences of individuals and groups, including those that are socially disadvantaged as well as those that are privileged. Social justice statistics can highlight the intersecting inequalities in a number of ways. At the individual level, social justice statistics can show how race, class, gender, and sexuality combine to shape the behavior and experiences of individuals. At the more macro level, social justice statistics can be used to show how these and other inequalities help to structure social institutions.

SOCIAL JUSTICE STATISTICS: CRITIQUES AND LIMITATIONS

Social Constructionist Critiques

Many feminist, anti-racist, queer, and intersectional scholars argue that quantitative analyses of social surveys work to essentialize and naturalize socially constructed differences. Even in high-quality surveys, gender is often equated with "sex"—an overly simplistic categorical variable with just two categories: male and female. When surveys represent gender in this way, the research based on these surveys risks losing sight of the processes through which gender is socially constructed and maintained. A further risk is that attention is drawn away from how gender operates as a social institution—the ways in which gender "establishes the patterns of expectations for individuals" and "orders the social processes of everyday life."[24]

A similar process occurs with survey representations of race and ethnicity. As sociologist Tukufu Zuberi writes, "when we discuss the 'effect of race [in statistical models],' we are less mindful of the larger social world in which the path to success or failure is influenced."[25] Within the context of social surveys, race is often represented as if it were a never-changing, naturally occurring property of individuals. As such, researchers analyzing these data risk losing sight of the dynamic social processes that create racial groups and maintain differences among them. In addition, those analyzing and interpreting the results of survey data risk ignoring the institutional dimensions of racial inequality.[26] Sexuality-based identities—when included at all in large-scale surveys—are often problematic in similar ways.

Beyond drawing attention to essentialist interpretations of survey data, the social constructionist perspective makes two additional critiques. First is that social surveys—like all research methods—are a product of the society in which they are created. No existing survey is entirely objective, free from values or bias. Decisions about who to include in the survey sample, which questions to include in the survey, how these questions are phrased, and what response categories are provided for each question are all guided to some extent by subjective factors.[27] A second contribution of the social constructionist critique is that it highlights the importance of distinguishing between survey data on the one hand and the interpretation of survey data on the other. It is true that many researchers fall into the trap of interpreting survey data in essentialistic ways. As discussed above, however, and as shown in subsequent chapters, it is entirely possible to interpret survey data in a way that is consistent with a social constructionist perspective.

Limitations of Secondary Data Analysis

In situations where someone is designing a small-scale survey from scratch and has a great deal of control over who will be given the opportunity to take the survey, which questions will be included, how these questions will be worded, and so forth, it is possible to craft surveys that easily fit within a social justice framework. Researchers can design questions that capture the nuances of a particular set of inequalities, respondents' attitudes and beliefs about these inequalities, and a particular set of identities. In other circumstances, however, individual researchers have a lot less control over the data collection process. When analyzing existing data—whether those data are from the Bureau of Justice Statistics, the United Nations, the World Bank, or the General Social Survey—researchers are limited to working with the data that are available.

Working with the large-scale datasets from these organizations has many limitations but also many benefits. First and foremost, the data are available at no cost, making them a very important source of information for those with limited resources. The large-scale datasets produced by these organizations are generally of very high quality, with great care given to issues of sampling and question wording. Large-scale surveys are also especially valuable for assessing the experiences, beliefs, and identities of minority populations. In a small-scale survey of 200 people, for example, there may be very few people who identify as racial/ethnic, sexual, or religious minorities, making it difficult to say much about these groups. Large-scale surveys with thousands of respondents can provide more information about how minority groups differ from majority groups and, just as importantly, can also highlight diversity within minority groups. Finally, large-scale surveys such as the General Social Survey have in many cases been administered over multiple decades, making it possible for researchers to analyze the extent to which inequalities have changed over time.

Correlation and Causation

In statistical analyses, **correlation** describes the extent to which two variables are related to each other. A positive correlation is one in which an increase in one variable is associated with an increase in another variable. Think about education and income, for example. Individuals with high levels of education tend to have higher personal incomes and vice versa, indicating a positive correlation between education and personal income. A negative correlation is one in which an increase in one variable is associated with a decrease in another variable. Here we might think about education and chronic depression. Individuals with higher educational attainment have a lower incidence of depression, which indicates a negative correlation between education and likelihood of depression.[28] Statistical analyses are invaluable for assessing not only the direction of a correlation but also the strength of a correlation—the extent to which the relationship between two variables is strong or weak. A perfect positive relationship—the strongest positive relationship—has a correlation of 1.0, and a perfect negative relationship—the strongest negative relationship—has a correlation of –1.0.

The ability to assess the relationship between two or more variables is perhaps the most important contribution of statistics to social justice projects. One of the most important limitations of statistical analyses of survey research, however, is their inability to prove causation. A **causal relationship** is one in which one variable has a direct effect on another variable. In a causal relationship, the variable doing the causing is termed the **independent** variable and the variable that is affected is the **dependent** variable. In other words, the dependent variable is thought to depend on the independent variable. Think back to education and personal income. Not only is there a positive correlation between these two variables, but there is also a causal relationship, where educational attainment (the independent variable) has a direct effect on personal income (the dependent variable).

You may have heard the phrase "correlation does not imply causation." This is a very important phrase and worth remembering! Sometimes a correlation between two variables is due simply to chance. In other cases, a correlation between two variables exists because both variables are influenced by a third variable. In cases like this, where the correlation between two variables, variables A and B, is actually driven by a third variable, variable C, the relationship between variables A and B can be described as **spurious**.

Tyler Vigen provides many examples of spurious relationships on his website (http://tylervigen.com/spurious-correlations). One such example shows the relationship between cheese consumption in the US and the number of people in the US who die each year as a result of becoming tangled in their bedsheets (see Figure 1.1).

The data in Vigen's analysis come from reliable sources: the US Department of Agriculture and the CDC. There appears to be a clear relationship between these

Figure 1.1 Per Capita Cheese Consumption Correlates With Number of People Who Die by Becoming Tangled in Their Bedsheets

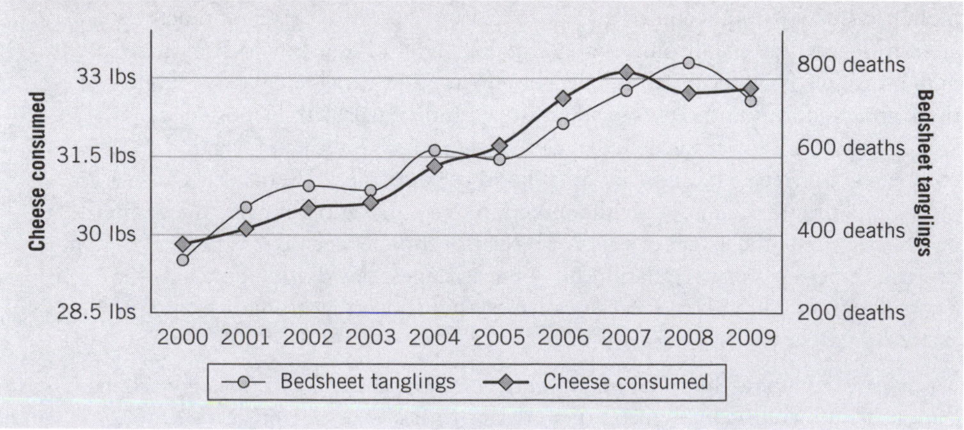

two variables: Over time, the number of bedsheet tanglings tracks almost perfectly with cheese consumption. Statistically speaking, the correlation between these two variables is extremely high: 0.947. And yet, it is very unlikely that per capita cheese consumption in the US has anything to do with the number of deaths due to becoming tangled in bedsheets. While there is a correlation between these variables, this correlation does not imply a causal relationship.

When interpreting the findings from statistical analyses, it is crucial to remember that a correlation between two variables—even a very strong correlation—does not always indicate a causal relationship. To argue effectively that a correlation represents a causal relationship, it is often necessary to consult existing research, including research that is qualitative, historical, comparative, and theoretical.

Social Surveys and Telling "the Truth"

Finally, when analyzing data from any social survey, it is important to remember that participants' responses don't always represent "the truth." When respondents are asked about events that occurred in the past, for example, their memory of these events may be unreliable. In other situations, respondents may not understand the question being asked of them and so may unintentionally provide answers that are inaccurate. In still other situations, respondents may answer questions without fully thinking about the answer. In what's known as **satisficing**, survey respondents might provide what they think will be a reasonable answer to the interviewer without giving their answer a significant amount of thought.[29] Chances are, if you've been asked to participate in a survey and you care little about the questions being asked, the survey takes longer than you expected, and you just want to be done with it, you will start satisficing with your responses.

An equally important problem, particularly when analyzing issues related to inequality, is the issue of **social desirability**. When survey participants are asked about sensitive or difficult issues, they sometimes provide answers that they think will be viewed favorably by others. Some respondents might emphasize "good behavior" in their answers. When asked about their financial contributions to charities or how much they love their mother, for example, respondents might exaggerate their answers upward, making themselves look more generous and loving than they actually are. In other circumstances, respondents might downplay what they perceive to be "bad behaviors," such as underage drinking, substance abuse, or participation in criminal activities. Attitudinal questions can also be affected by social desirability. Respondents who hold negative beliefs about women, poor people, or particular religious groups, for example, might not reveal these beliefs if they perceive that their views are unpopular.

Finally, when analyzing survey data that include questions about respondents' beliefs, it is important to remember that respondents' beliefs are just that: beliefs. Just because the majority of respondents believe a particular thing is true doesn't mean that this thing is "true." In recent years, for example, the General Social Survey has included a question that asks respondents about the origins of the universe. The variable BIGBANG corresponds to the following survey question:

> Now, I would like to ask you a few short questions like those you might see on a television game show. For each statement that I read, please tell me if it is true or false. If you don't know or aren't sure, just tell me so, and we will skip to the next question. Remember true, false, or don't know. "The universe began with a huge explosion. Is that true or false?"

More than 4,000 people were asked this question from 2006 to 2014, and a slight majority (50.4%) answered that this statement was false. Questions like these that ask respondents about what is true are not included to determine what is actually true. Rather, these sorts of questions give researchers the opportunity to examine what factors affect the likelihood of respondents' believing a particular thing. How might respondents' religion and political party, for example, shape beliefs about the origins of the universe? And do men versus women respondents or younger versus older respondents differ in their beliefs?

Another example from the General Social Survey is the variable FEFAM, which corresponds to the following survey question:

> Please tell me whether you strongly agree, agree, disagree, or strongly disagree . . . It is much better for everyone involved if the man is the achiever outside the home and the woman takes care of the home and family.

In 1977, the first year in which this question was included in the General Social Survey, the majority of respondents (66%) either agreed or strongly agreed with this idea. Just because the majority of respondents agreed with this idea doesn't mean that the breadwinner/homemaker model works better for everyone. Again, survey questions like this are meant to assess respondents' beliefs. When interpreting data based on these questions, be careful not to confuse respondents' beliefs about the truth with the "real truth."

CONCLUSION

No single survey is able to fully and accurately capture the complex experiences of individuals and groups, and no single statistical analysis is able to fully represent the complex, dynamic, intersecting inequalities that organize society. It is the contention of this book that, despite these limitations, social surveys and quantitative data analysis can play an extremely important role in the fight for social justice. Statistical research—when done in a way that is attentive to (1) issues of power and inequality, (2) the social processes through which difference and inequality are created and maintained, (3) the relationship between individual identities and macro-level social structures, and (4) the intersection of multiple systems of inequality—is an important tool for social justice work. Statistical research is vital for evaluating the effectiveness—and often the unintended consequences—of public policies, such as the War on Drugs, California's "three-strikes" law, and federal welfare reform. Statistics can also highlight diversity, dismantle stereotypes, and provide a way to challenge problematic representations of disadvantaged groups.

Statistical analyses should always be interpreted with a critical eye, however, as there are limitations to every statistical analysis. Even when people agree on the statistical results, they might interpret these results through different worldviews and come to very different conclusions about what the results mean. Thus, rather than viewing statistical analysis as the "final word" on any particular issue, it is more useful to think of statistical analysis as an important voice in an ongoing conversation.

Organization of the Book

This book provides an introduction to analyzing inequalities with an eye toward social justice. It makes use of one large-scale social survey, the US General Social Survey (GSS), which has been conducted just about every other year since 1972. The GSS is described in greater detail in Chapter 2, but it is worth noting here that the survey includes questions pertaining to not only a wide range of social justice issues, including race, gender, class, and sexuality, but also issues of citizenship, multiculturalism, health and well-being, politics, science, religion, and media.

Throughout the book, there are tables and images that show the results of analyses produced with the Survey Documentation and Analysis (SDA) website, and all of these tables can be replicated using this website.

Before analyzing data from the GSS or any other social survey, it is imperative to have at least a basic understanding of social surveys and the types of information they can produce. Chapter 2 provides an overview of some of the most important concepts in survey research and data analysis, including issues of samples and populations, levels of measurement, and measures of central tendency.

Chapters 3 through 6 build on the information presented in Chapters 1 and 2 and can be read in any order. Each chapter highlights a particular form of inequality and a particular statistical technique. Chapter 3 focuses on gender and provides an overview of producing and interpreting cross-tabulations (also called cross-tabs). Chapter 4 examines race, ethnicity, and multiculturalism using cross-tabs but also shows how to use "Filters" and "Control Variables" to analyze GSS data. Because their focus is on creating and interpreting cross-tabs, Chapters 3 and 4 rely on categorical and ordinal-level variables— variables that typically have a small number of categories that can easily be represented in a table. Chapter 5, which focuses on social class, introduces a statistical technique called "comparisons of means," and describes how to recode variables using the SDA website. Chapter 6, which focuses on issues of sexuality, also describes the process of recoding variables but couples this with a discussion of how and why to use Filters.

Throughout Chapters 3 through 6, you will see that some skills and concepts are repeated, and this repetition is intentional. If you mastered the concept and skill of using Filters in Chapter 4, for example, feel free to skim over the presentation of Filters in Chapter 6. Some readers will benefit from reading the discussion a second time. Other readers—due to the structure of their course syllabus—will likely read Chapter 6 before Chapter 4, or read Chapter 5 before reading Chapter 3. In conjunction with Chapters 1 and 2, the repetition in Chapters 3 through 6 ensures that each chapter contains the information required to complete the analyses in that chapter.

While Chapters 3 through 6 focus on individual systems of inequality, Chapters 7 through 9 highlight the interplay of multiple systems of inequality within particular social institutions. Chapter 7 focuses on families, Chapter 8 on education, and Chapter 9 on the economy and work. Chapters 7 through 9 use a combination of the statistical techniques introduced in the preceding chapters and show how these techniques can be used in combination to produce a more comprehensive and intersectional analysis.

EXERCISES

1. A researcher who is interested in beliefs about gun control believes that men and women are likely to hold different views on the subject. Analyzing data from the General Social Survey, she finds that men are in fact much more likely to support the selling of semi-automatic weapons to the general public. This researcher is using respondents' gender as the:

    a. independent variable.

    b. control variable.

    c. dependent variable.

    d. intervening variable.

2. In the above example, the researcher is using support for selling semi-automatic weapons to the general public as the:

    a. independent variable.

    b. control variable.

    c. dependent variable.

    d. intervening variable.

3. A researcher analyzed two variables from the General Social Survey, RINCOM06

(respondents' personal income) and HAPPY ("Taken all together, how would you say things are these days—would you say that you are very happy, pretty happy, or not too happy?"), and found that higher levels of personal income are associated with higher levels of personal happiness. Based on this finding, the relationship between personal income and happiness is best described as having:

a. a positive correlation.

b. a negative correlation.

c. no real correlation.

4. A person who believes that men and women are inherently different, so much so that men, by nature, are not able to care for others as much as women can, can be described as holding a(n) _____ perspective on gender differences.

a. social constructionist

b. essentialist

c. intersectional

d. statistical

5. A person who believes that the differences we see between men and women in the US are largely a result of social processes, such as socialization and gendered social institutions, can be described as holding a(n)_____ perspective on gender differences.

   a. social constructionist

   b. essentialist

   c. intersectional

6. A researcher is interested in how race-, gender-, and class-based statuses work together to influence individuals' perceptions of social inequality. In this situation, the researcher is using perceptions of social inequality as the:

   a. independent variable.

   b. control variable.

   c. dependent variable.

   d. intervening variable.

7. The theoretical perspective that most closely aligns with the above research question is:

   a. social constructionist.

   b. essentialist.

   c. intersectional.

8. Which of the following is true of social statistics and survey research?

   a. Social statistics and survey research can be used only to advance social justice.

   b. Social statistics and survey research can be used only to promote inequality.

   c. Social statistics and survey research can be used either to advance social justice or to promote inequality.

9. Analyzing statistical data, a research team finds that at times when people eat a lot of ice cream, the number of deaths by drowning also tends to increase.[30] The team releases a press release stating that eating ice cream increases the likelihood of death by drowning. In this situation, the researcher is using ice cream consumption as the:

   a. independent variable.

   b. control variable.

   c. dependent variable.

   d. intervening variable.

10. A critic of the study argues that there is no direct relationship between ice cream consumption and death by drowning, but rather that the summer season is really at the root of this relationship. In warmer months, people are more likely to eat ice cream and also more likely to swim, and thus more likely to die by drowning. According to the above study's critic, the relationship between ice cream consumption and death by drowning is best described as:

    a. a spurious relationship.

    b. a negative correlation.

    c. a socially constructed relationship.

    d. an intersectional relationship.

ANALYSES & ESSAYS

1. In your own words, describe the key themes of "social justice statistics."

2. What are the major benefits and limitations of using existing survey data in the context of social justice work?

3. In your own words, explain the difference between correlation and causation.

4. Visit the Bureau of Justice Statistics website (www.BJS.gov) and take a moment to browse through their research. Find one report that is of interest to you and explain how the findings from this report might be used to advance social justice.

5. Visit the website of one of the four social justice organizations listed below. Find one example where this organization is effectively using statistics in pursuit of social justice. Explain what you think makes this a particularly effective example.

   • **INCITE!** is a "nation-wide network of radical feminists of color working to end violence against women, gender non-conforming, and trans people of color, and our communities." See more at http://www.incite-national.org/.

- **The Human Rights Campaign** is "the largest national lesbian, gay, bisexual, transgender and queer civil rights organization[.] HRC envisions a world where LGBTQ people are ensured of their basic equal rights, and can be open, honest and safe at home, at work and in the community." See more at http://www.hrc.org.

- **The National Coalition for the Homeless** is "a national network of people who are currently experiencing or who have experienced homelessness, activists and advocates, community-based and faith-based service providers, and others committed to a single mission: To prevent and end homelessness while ensuring the immediate needs of those experiencing homelessness are met and their civil rights protected." See more at http://www.nationalhomeless.org/.

- **The African American Policy Forum** is "an innovative think tank that connects academics, activists and policy-makers to promote efforts to dismantle structural inequality." The forum "promote[s] frameworks and strategies that address a vision of racial justice that embraces the intersections of race, gender, class, and the array of barriers that disempower those who are marginalized in society. AAPF is dedicated to advancing and expanding racial justice, gender equality, and the indivisibility of all human rights, both in the U.S. and internationally." See more at http://www.aapf.org.

NOTES

1. Carson, E. Ann. 2014. *Prisoners in 2013.* NCJ 247282. US Department of Justice, Office of Justice Programs, Bureau of Justice Statistics. Retrieved August 9, 2016 (http://www.bjs.gov/content/pub/pdf/p13.pdf).

2. United Nations Statistics Division. *The World's Women 2015.* Retrieved May 8, 2016 (http://unstats.un.org/unsd/gender/chapter3/chapter3.html).

3. Black, Michele C., Kathleen C. Basile, Matthew J. Breiding, Sharon G. Smith, Mikel L. Walters, Melissa T. Merrick, Jieru Chen, and Mark R. Stevens. 2011. *The National Intimate Partner and Sexual Violence Survey (NISVS): 2010 Summary Report.* Atlanta, GA: Centers for Disease Control and Prevention, National Center for Injury Prevention and Control.

4. Centers for Disease Control and Prevention. "1991–2011 High School Youth Risk Behavior Survey Data." Retrieved August 24, 2012 (http://apps.nccd.cdc.gov/youthonline).

5. Centers for Disease Control and Prevention. 2012. "Sexual Violence: Facts at a Glance." Retrieved May 19, 2016 (http://www.cdc.gov/ViolencePrevention/pdf/SV-DataSheet-a.pdf).

6. Board of Governors of the Federal Reserve System. 2015. *Report on the Economic Well-Being of U.S. Households in 2014.* Retrieved May 8, 2016 (http://www.federalreserve.gov/econresdata/2014-report-economic-well-being-us-households-201505.pdf).

7. Food and Agriculture Organization of the United Nations. Economic and Social Development Department. 2010. "Global Hunger Declining, but Still Unacceptably High." Retrieved May 8, 2016 (http://www.fao.org/docrep/012/al390e/al390e00.pdf).

8. Adapted from Arrigo, Bruce A. 1998. *Social Justice/Criminal Justice: The Maturation of Critical Theory in Law, Crime, and Deviance.* Boston, MA: Wadsworth, pp. 55–59, 122; and Fuller, John R. 1998. *Criminal Justice: A Peacemaking Perspective.* Needham Heights, MA: Allyn & Bacon, pp. 9–10, 260.

9. Based on calculations from the March 1964 Current Population Survey (Bureau of the Census), as reported in: White House. Council of Economic Advisers. 1998. "Explaining Trends in the Gender Wage Gap." Retrieved August 15, 2016 (https://clinton4.nara.gov/WH/EOP/CEA/html/gendergap.html).

10. White House. Council of Economic Advisers. 2016. "The Gender Pay Gap on the Anniversary of the Lilly Ledbetter Fair Pay Act." Retrieved

August 15, 2016 (https://www.whitehouse.gov/sites/default/files/docs/20160201_cea_gender_pay_gap_issue_brief_final.pdf).

11. US Bureau of Labor Statistics. 2015. "Highlights of Women's Earnings in 2014." BLS Report 1058. Retrieved May 8, 2016 (http://www.bls.gov/opub/reports/womens-earnings/archive/highlights-of-womens-earnings-in-2014.pdf), Table 19. These figures are adjusted for inflation.

12. United Nations Social and Economic Council. 2013. "Resolution Adopted by the Economic and Social Council on 24 July 2013." Retrieved May 8, 2016 (http://unstats.un.org/unsd/dnss/gp/FP-Rev2013-E.pdf).

13. Zuberi, Tukufu, and Eduardo Bonilla-Silva, eds. 2008. *White Logic, White Methods: Racism and Methodology.* Lanham, MD: Rowman & Littlefield.

14. For a recent example, read the *Washington Post*'s coverage on a study by sociologist Mark Regnerus: https://www.washingtonpost.com/news/volokh-conspiracy/wp/2015/05/10/new-criticism-of-regnerus-study-on-parenting-study/.

15. In asking this question, I am drawing from Sandra Harding, a feminist philosopher of science. In her work *Feminism and Methodology* (Bloomington, IN: Indiana University Press, 1987), Harding rejects the idea that there is a "distinctive feminist method of research." She encourages us to ask instead, "What are the characteristics that distinguish the most illuminating examples of feminist research?" (p. 6). In the same way, I am suggesting here that there is no distinctive approach to "social justice statistics." We might look to the many social justice projects that have used statistics in positive ways, however, and make note of commonalities and guiding themes.

16. In my description of social justice statistics, I am drawing from Maxine Baca Zinn and Bonnie Thornton Dill's (1996) conceptualization of multiracial feminism ("Theorizing Difference from Multiracial Feminism," *Feminist Studies* 2:321–31).

17. Rosenblum, Karen E., and Toni-Michelle C. Travis. 2006. *The Meaning of Difference: American Constructions of Race, Sex and Gender, Social Class, and Sexual Orientation.* 4th ed. New York: McGraw-Hill, p. 3.

18. Ibid., p. 5.

19. Nobles, Muriel. 2000. "History Counts: A Comparative Analysis of Racial/Color Categorization in US and Brazilian Censuses." *American Journal of Public Health* 90:1738–45; Omi, Michael, and Howard Winant. 1994. *Racial Formations in the United States.* New York: Routledge; Sáenz, Rogelio, David G. Embrick, and Néstor P. Rodríguez, eds. 2015. *The International Handbook of the Demography of Race and Ethnicity.* New York: Springer; Telles, Edward E. 2004. *Race in Another America: The Significance of Skin Color in Brazil.* Princeton, NJ: Princeton University Press.

20. Harnois, Catherine E. 2014. "Complexity Within and Similarity Across: Interpreting Black Men's Support of Gender Justice, Amidst Cultural Representations That Suggest Otherwise." Pp. 85–89 in *Hyper Sexual, Hyper Masculine? Gender, Race and Sexuality in the Identities of Contemporary Black Men*, edited by B. Slatton and K. Spates. Farnham, England: Ashgate.

21. Baca Zinn, Maxine, and Bonnie Thornton Dill. 1996. "Theorizing Difference from Multiracial Feminism." *Feminist Studies* 2:321–31; Berger, Michele Tracy, and Kathleen Guidroz, eds. 2009. *The Intersectional Approach: Transforming the Academy through Race, Class, and Gender.* Chapel Hill, NC: University of North Carolina Press; Collins, Patricia Hill. 2000. *Black Feminist Thought.* New York: Routledge; Crenshaw, Kimberlé W. 1989. "Demarginalizing the Intersection of Race and Sex: A Black Feminist Critique of Antidiscrimination Doctrine, Feminist Theory and Antiracist Politics." *University of Chicago Legal Forum* 139:139–67; Crenshaw, Kimberlé W. 1991. "Mapping the Margins: Intersectionality, Identity Politics, and Violence against Women of Color." *Stanford Law Review* 43:1241–99.

22. Baca Zinn and Thornton Dill, "Theorizing Difference," p. 326–327.

23. Hobson, Katherine. 2016. "Girls and Older Adults Are Missing Out on Parks for Recreation." *NPR*, May 18. Retrieved May 18, 2016 (http://www.npr.org/sections/health-shots/2016/05/18/478402956/girls-and-older-adults-are-missing-out-on-parks-for-recreation).

24. Lorber, Judith. 1994. *Paradoxes of Gender.* New Haven, CT: Yale University Press, p. 1.

25. Zuberi and Bonilla-Silva, *White Logic, White Methods*, "Introduction," p. 6.

26. Pager, Devah, and Hana Shepherd. 2008. "The Sociology of Discrimination: Racial Discrimination in Employment, Housing, Credit, and Consumer Markets." *Annual Review of Sociology* 34:181–209; Zuberi, Tukufu. 2002. *Thicker Than Blood: How Racial Statistics Lie.* Minneapolis, MN: University of Minnesota Press.

27. Individuals who are homeless or who are residing in institutions such as prisons or mental health facilities are routinely excluded from large-scale social surveys in the US, for example, as are individuals who can speak neither English nor Spanish.

28. Lorant, Vincent, Denise Deliège, William W. Eaton, Annie Robert, Pierre Philippot, and Marc Ansseau. 2003. "Socioeconomic Inequalities in Depression: A Meta-analysis." *American Journal of Epidemiology* 157:98–112.

29. Krosnick, Jon A. 1999. "Survey Research." *Annual Review of Psychology* 50: 537–67, p. 548.

30. This example comes from Moore, David S. 2007. *The Basic Practice of Statistics.* New York: W. H. Freeman.

CHAPTER 2

UNDERSTANDING DATA: CRITICAL CONCEPTS

Before analyzing inequalities with survey data, it is important to be familiar with some of the basic concepts in survey research and data analysis. This chapter begins with an introduction to the General Social Survey (GSS), which is one of the most widely analyzed surveys in the United States. Following this introduction, the chapter presents some basic techniques for finding and interpreting variables in the GSS.

Data from the 1972–2014 General Social Surveys can be easily accessed and analyzed through the Institute for Scientific Analysis's Survey Documentation and Analysis (SDA) website (http://sda.berkeley.edu/sdaweb/analysis/?dataset=gss14). You can also access this same page using this link: http://tinyurl.com/GSS72to14. The SDA is free for anyone to use and can be used on any computer, tablet, or mobile device.

OVERVIEW OF THE GSS[1]

The General Social Survey is a national survey of adults in the United States that has been conducted regularly since 1972. From 1972 to 1993, the survey was administered almost annually, and it contained approximately 1,400 interviews each year. From 1994 on, the survey has been conducted every other year. It contains numerous questions about respondents' sociodemographic characteristics (e.g., respondents' age, sex, income, and occupation); a range of questions about respondents' behaviors (e.g., whether respondents voted in the last election, whether they participate in voluntary organizations, how frequently they use email, and how frequently they attend religious services);

Learning Objectives

By the end of this chapter, you should be able to:

1. Describe the General Social Survey.

2. Use the SDA website to identify variables of interest to you.

3. Use the SDA website to identify the mode and, where applicable, the median and mean of each variable.

4. Describe a range of variables, including the survey question associated with each variable, the response categories for each variable, and level of measurement.

5. Interpret a univariate frequency table.

and events that may have occurred in respondents' lives (e.g., if they have been arrested, if they are married or divorced, and if they have experienced discrimination).

The GSS also includes a number of questions about what respondents believe (e.g., if they believe the government should spend more money to help the poor, or if they believe abortion should be legal under all circumstances). It also includes questions designed to tap respondents' knowledge—there is a small vocabulary test, and recent surveys have included questions assessing respondents' knowledge of science and perceptions of scientific careers (e.g., "Did the universe begin with a big bang?" "Is astrology a science?" and "If you had a daughter, how would you feel if she wanted to be a scientist?"). There are also a range of questions concerning respondents' physical health, psychological health, and feelings (e.g., how often respondents feel in poor mental health; how often respondents feel in poor physical health; how happy respondents are; and—for those who are married—how happy their marriages are).

Some of the GSS questions (such as respondents' age, marital status, and educational attainment) are asked every year to all respondents. Other survey questions are included in only a handful of years, and still others are included in only one or two years and are asked to a randomly selected subsample of respondents. For this reason, whenever analyzing data from the GSS, it is important to make sure you understand when the survey questions you are analyzing were included in the survey. When sharing your results in a paper, presentation, or other type of project, you should be sure to explain this to your audience.

Who Is Included in the GSS Sample?

The GSS includes respondents who are 18 years of age or older and living in households at the time of the survey. It includes both citizens and noncitizens of the US. The requirement that people be living in households means that individuals who live in institutions such as college dorms, nursing homes, prisons, or jails, and also those who are homeless, are not included in the GSS sample. From 1972 to 2004, the GSS included only individuals who were able to speak English. Since 2006, the GSS has been administered in Spanish also, so now both Spanish and English speakers are represented in the survey.

How Are the Data Collected?

As described on its website, the GSS relies primarily on face-to-face interviews, though in some cases, when it is difficult to arrange an in-person interview, interviews are conducted by telephone. All interviewers undergo extensive training before conducting any interviews.

What Are Variable Weights?

Throughout this book, data will be analyzed using variable weights. In brief, variable weights are values assigned to each observation (in the GSS, each person who takes the survey can be thought of as an "observation"), and the use of these weights helps to ensure that the sample of respondents matches the overall population from which the sample was drawn. For example, during the years 1975 to 2002, the GSS used a sampling design that gave each household in the US an equal probability of being included in the GSS. Because only one adult per household is allowed to be interviewed, those who live in larger households had a slightly lower probability of being included in the GSS sample. Weights are used to adjust for this small discrepancy. In the 1982 and 1987 surveys, the sample included an "oversample" of Black respondents. Survey designers often deliberately include oversamples of minority groups so that they can be sure to have a sufficient number of minority respondents in the final sample. If one were to analyze data from these years without using variable weights, the responses of Black respondents would be disproportionately represented. Using the variable weights is an easy way to adjust for the disproportionately higher number of Black respondents or other groups that are oversampled in particular years.

In this book, all analyses are conducted using the weighting variable COMPWT, which is the default selection in the Survey Documentation and Analysis (SDA) program. For the most part, if you were to perform basic analyses of data with and without this weight, the results would be similar. Below is an example of the variable HAPPY, which corresponds to the survey question "Taken all together, how would you say things are these days—would you say that you are very happy, pretty happy, or not too happy?" Figure 2.1 shows the frequency distribution for this variable when no weights are used. Figure 2.2 shows the frequency distribution using the weight COMPWT.

Figure 2.1

Un-Weighted Frequency Distribution (HAPPY)	
Cells contain: **-Column percent** **-N of cases**	**Distribution**
1: VERY HAPPY	**31.6** 17,316
2: PRETTY HAPPY	**55.9** 30,655
3: NOT TOO HAPPY	**12.5** 6,880
COL TOTAL	**100.0** 54,851

Figure 2.2

Weighted Frequency Distribution (Happy)	
Cells contain: -Column percent -Weighted N	Distribution
1: VERY HAPPY	**33.2** 18,253.3
2: PRETTY HAPPY	**55.4** 30,416.8
3: NOT TOO HAPPY	**11.4** 6,247.3
COL TOTAL	*100.0* *54,917.4*

In both figures, the top number in each cell represents the percentage of respondents who select each response. Without the weights (Figure 2.1), it appears that 31.6% of respondents describe themselves as "very happy." With the weights (Figure 2.2), we see that 33.2% of respondents describe themselves as "very happy." The bottom number in each cell corresponds to the number of cases in each category of the variable. In Figure 2.1, for example, we see that 6,880 people described themselves as "not too happy" (corresponding to 12.5% of respondents who provided valid answers to the survey question). In Figure 2.2, the bottom number in each cell still represents the number of observations that fall into each category of the variable, but rather than the *raw number of cases*, the weighted frequency distribution produces a *weighted number of cases*. When interpreting the 6,247.3, we could say that "about 6,247 people reported being 'not too happy.'" An even better interpretation would be "11.4% of respondents reported being 'not too happy,' which corresponds to approximately 6,247 people." More information on constructing and interpreting frequency distributions is provided in the latter part of this chapter and throughout the rest of this book.

FINDING DATA IN THE GSS

Searching for Variables

Starting from the homepage of the GSS SDA website, click on the "Search" button toward the top of the screen. This brings us to a new screen with a prominent field on the right for entering search terms. Capitalization doesn't matter here, so don't worry about that. When searching for variables, you can also use * and ? as "wildcard characters." As shown in Figure 2.3, typing in WOM?N will produce a search for all variables that include the words *woman* or *women*, for example. Typing in WOMEN*, on the other hand, will produce a search for all variables that include the term *women* or *women's* but won't search for variables that simply use the singular *woman*.

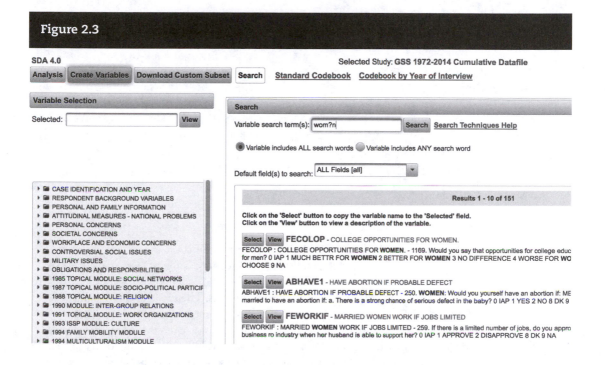

Figure 2.3

To get started, type *gender* in the "Variable search term(s)" box, and then click the "Search" button. The results appear on the bottom portion of the screen and show us that our search produced 25 hits. These results show us that, since 1972, there have been 25 unique variables that have used the term *gender* somewhere. The term *gender* might appear in the variable name itself, in the wording of the question asked to the respondent, or in the response categories.

To get more information about any of the 25 variables, simply click on the "View" button next to the variable that interests you. If we look at the variable WKSEXISM, for example, clicking on the "View" button brings up a new screen that shows us the precise wording of the survey question: "Do you feel in any way discriminated against on your job because of your gender?"

"Viewing" a variable in this way also produces a frequency table—a table displaying the response categories for each variable as well as the number of responses that fall into each category. To exit this screen and to return to the search results, simply click outside the pop-up window. Alternatively, click on the small "x" in the bottom right-hand corner of the pop-up window. More information on interpreting a frequency table is provided under "Viewing the Survey Question, Response Categories, and Variable Distribution" below.

SEARCH TIP

When searching for variables, remember that the search engine does not recognize slang, abbreviations, acronyms, or texting language!

– Avoid abbreviations and acronyms.
  • For example, type out VETERANS rather than VETS.
  • Search for GAY, LESBIAN, HOMOSEXUAL, or BISEXUAL rather than LGBT.
– Try to use more formal words like CHILDREN and MOTHER rather than KIDS and MOM.

• If searching for variables about respondents' sexual behaviors, for example, search for SEX or even CASUAL SEX rather than HOOK-UP.
• When searching for variables about the number of children a respondent has or would like to have, type in NUMBER OF CHILDREN rather than # OF KIDS.

Browsing for Variables

In addition to searching for variables with the search function, a good resource for identifying variables related to gender or any other issue is the SDA virtual codebook, located in the left-hand side of the SDA interface. The codebook is a topical tree, where headings are used to group variables on similar topics. The first subject heading is "Case Identification and Year." The next is "Respondent Background Variables," which includes a range of information on respondents' race, sex, age, socioeconomic status, and other topics. Clicking on the small triangle to the left of "Respondent Background Variables" will expand the topic and show a list of subheadings. Clicking again on the small triangle to the left of any of these subheadings (e.g., "Education") will finally bring us to a list of variables, as shown in Figure 2.4.

Each variable name is presented in capital letters and is followed by a brief description of the variable. For example, the variable EDUC is described as "highest year of school completed"; DEGREE is the respondent's highest degree (RS is an abbreviation for *respondent's*); and the variable MAEDUC is described as "highest year school completed, mother."

In addition to browsing for variables using the topical tree, you can browse for variables using the "Standard Codebook," the link to which is appears in blue text at the top of the SDA page.

Viewing the Survey Question, Response Categories, and Variable Distribution

To gain more precise information about the meaning of a variable, you can easily view the variable in one of two ways. Double-clicking on either the name or short description of a variable inside the topical tree will add the variable name into the "Variable Selection" box in the upper left-hand corner of the screen. Alternatively, you can simply type the name of the variable into this field. Capitalization doesn't

Figure 2.4

```
▸ 📁 CASE IDENTIFICATION AND YEAR
▾ 📂 RESPONDENT BACKGROUND VARIABLES
   ▸ 📁 Age, Gender, Race, and Ethnicity
   ▾ 📂 Education
         📄 EDUC - HIGHEST YEAR OF SCHOOL COMPLETED
         📄 PAEDUC - HIGHEST YEAR SCHOOL COMPLETED, FATHER
         📄 MAEDUC - HIGHEST YEAR SCHOOL COMPLETED, MOTHER
         📄 SPEDUC - HIGHEST YEAR SCHOOL COMPLETED, SPOUSE
         📄 DEGREE - RS HIGHEST DEGREE
         📄 PADEG - FATHERS HIGHEST DEGREE
         📄 MADEG - MOTHERS HIGHEST DEGREE
         📄 SPDEG - SPOUSES HIGHEST DEGREE
   ▸ 📁 2012 CORE
   ▸ 📁 Military Service
   ▸ 📁 Respondent and Spouse Work Week
   ▸ 📁 Respondent's Dwelling
   ▸ 📁 Word Association
   ▸ 📁 R's Activities
   ▸ 📁 Religious Attendance and Identity
   ▸ 📁 Respondent's Household Composition
   ▸ 📁 Socio-Economic and Status Indicators
   ▸ 📁 Other Respondent Background Variables
▸ 📁 PERSONAL AND FAMILY INFORMATION
▸ 📁 ATTITUDINAL MEASURES - NATIONAL PROBLEMS
▸ 📁 PERSONAL CONCERNS
▸ 📁 SOCIETAL CONCERNS
```

matter, but spelling does, so be sure to spell it correctly! Regardless of how you get the variable name to appear in the "Variable Selection" field, once you do, clicking the "View" button will open up a new window with detailed information about the variable you selected. You can find the variable HRS1 in the topical tree under "Personal and Family Information," under the subheading for "Respondent's Employment." Viewing the variable HRS1 tells us that this variable corresponds to the question "If working, full or part time: how many hours did you work last week, at all jobs?" Viewing the variable in this way tells us that this question was asked only to those respondents who indicated (previously in the survey) that they were currently working either full or part time.

Toward the end of the codebook are a series of "Topical Modules" that correspond to variables included in specific years of the GSS—for example, "2000 Topical Module: Health Status" and "2002 Topical Module: Quality of Working Life." As explained earlier, some of the variables included in the GSS (e.g., AGE, SEX) have been included in every year of the survey, but other variables have been included only one or two years. The topical modules that appear in the bottom portion of the SDA codebook include variables that are not asked every year. The date of the topical module indicates the first year in which these survey questions were asked. *It does not necessarily mean that these survey questions were asked only in this year, however.* The "2002 Topical Module: Quality of Working Life," for example, includes the variable *WKHARSEX*, which corresponds to the question "In the last 12 months, were you sexually harassed by anyone while you were on the job?" As we shall see below, this question was asked to a subset of respondents in four years of the GSS: 2002, 2006, 2010, and 2014.

IN WHICH YEARS WAS THIS VARIABLE INCLUDED IN THE GSS?

When "viewing," "searching," and "browsing" for variables in the SDA, the results are pooled from across the more than four decades in which the GSS has been administered (1972–present). When analyzing survey data, it is always important for the researcher to understand when the data that she or he is analyzing was collected.

The easiest way to determine the years in which a particular variable was included in the GSS is to make a cross-tab of the variable of interest with the variable YEAR.

To do this, first make sure you are on the "Analysis" tab, which is on the top left of the SDA page, and the "Tables" tab, which is on the right portion of the page. Then, type the name of the variable that you are curious about (e.g., WKSEXISM) in the "Row" field, and the variable YEAR in the "Column" field. The resulting cross-tab will show you the frequency distribution for the variable WKSEXISM within each year for which there are data (in this case, 2002, 2006, 2010, and 2014). Producing and interpreting cross-tabs is covered at greater length in Chapters 3 and 4.

PRODUCING AND INTERPRETING A FREQUENCY TABLE

In addition to showing the wording of the survey question, "viewing" a variable also produces a frequency table showing the distribution of responses for the variable. Here it is important to remember that, when we examine a variable using the "View" option, we are examining the totality of information about this variable since the beginning of the GSS. In other words, the data that we see when "viewing" a variable are the aggregated data from 1972 to 2014. As explained in later chapters, in many cases we may want to look at a smaller subset of data, and there are easy ways to do this using the "Filter" option.

Figure 2.5 shows the frequency table for the variable WKSEXISM, which assesses whether respondents feel in any way discriminated against in their workplace because of their gender. Focusing on the middle portion of the table and reading from right to left, the "Label" heading tells us the names of the different categories for the variable. In this case, respondents are asked if they feel discriminated against on the job because of their gender, and they are offered two options: yes, they have felt discriminated against, or no, they haven't.

Figure 2.5			
WKSEXISM	R FEELS DISCRIMINATED BECAUSE OF GENDER		
Description of the Variable			
902. Do you feel in any way discriminated against on your job because of your gender?			
Percent	N	Value	Label
6.2	365	1	YES
93.8	5,528	2	NO
	53,632	0	IAP
	15	8	DONT KNOW
	59	9	NO ANSWER
100.0	59,599		Total
Properties			
Data type:	numeric		
Missing-data codes:	0,8,9		
Mean:	1.94		
Std Dev:	.24		
Record/column:	1/3820		

Missing-Data and "Invalid" Responses: IAP, DK, NA

The values of "Inapplicable" (IAP), "Don't know" (DK), and "No answer" (NA) are all considered to be invalid responses and are examples of "missing data." While analyzing patterns of missing data can be both important and insightful, social scientists generally focus only on data with valid responses and disregard cases with missing data.[2]

"Don't know" means that the respondent indicated that she or he wasn't sure or didn't know if they felt discriminated against on the basis of their gender, and "No answer" means that the respondent didn't provide an answer—not even an answer of "I don't know." "Inapplicable" means that this question was not included as part of the survey for some respondents. Recall that the "View" screen is showing us an overall picture of the combined data from 1972 to 2014 and that not every question is included every year. In addition, in some years the GSS uses a "split-ballot" design, where some questions are asked to a randomly selected group of respondents but not to others. If respondents were not given the opportunity to provide a response to a question because it was not included in the survey they were administered, then their responses are coded as "IAP."

The response categories for each variable are always assigned a number. Taken together, the "Value" and "Label" headings show us which response corresponds to which number. So, here, "Yes" corresponds to the number 1 and "No" corresponds to the number 2.[3] Missing-data categories are also given numbers: In this case, 0 is IAP, 8 is DK, and 9 is NA.

The heading "N" refers to the number of respondents whose answers fell into each category of the variable. Again, in Figure 2.5, we see that 365 respondents indicated that yes, they had perceived gender discrimination on the job, and 5,528 respondents indicated that no, they hadn't perceived gender discrimination. The majority of responses (53,632) fall into the "IAP" category, suggesting that WKSEXISM is a question that has not been included regularly in the GSS. The total number, 59,599 refers to the number of respondents who took the survey from 1972 to 2014. This number will be the same for any variable you view.

The "Percent" column tells us the percentage of valid responses that fell into each category of the variable. When calculating the percentages, the SDA program takes into consideration only those cases where respondents provided "valid" data. The 6.2% in the top line is calculated by dividing the number of respondents who answered "Yes, I have felt discriminated against at work on the basis of my gender" (N = 365) by the total number of respondents who provided valid data for this question, and then multiplying this number by 100. In this case, a total of 5,893 respondents provided valid answers (365 + 5528 = 5893). The percentage is calculated as follows:

$$(365/5893) * 100 = 6.2\%$$

Taken as a whole, the frequency table tells us that most individuals (93.8%) who answered the survey question responded that they had not felt discriminated against at work on the basis of their gender. But this table likely raises more questions for you than it answers. In what year or years was WKSEXISM included in the survey?

Are these data from 2014, 1972, or somewhere in between? Is this a question that is asked to all respondents, or is it asked only to women? And is it asked only to individuals who are currently working for pay? Finally, what factors might influence the likelihood of individuals perceiving gender discrimination at work? Are men and women equally likely to perceive gender discrimination at work? What about women with various levels of education, women of different racial and ethnic groups, and women working in different occupations? These questions are easily answered with the GSS data and will be addressed in later chapters.

DESCRIBING VARIABLES: LEVELS OF MEASUREMENT

In addition to knowing the precise wording of the survey question and the year in which the data were collected, it is also important to know the level of measurement for each variable. When analyzing data from the GSS, it is useful to consider three levels: nominal, ordinal, and interval-ratio.[4]

Nominal-Level Variables

Nominal-level variables, also known as categorical variables, are variables that have no meaningful order to their categories. With nominal-level variables, it is impossible to speak of "high" or "low" values, because there is no order to the values. The variable categories would make just as much sense if they were completely reordered. Examples include RELIG, which corresponds to respondents' religious preference; SEX, which corresponds to respondents' gender; RACEIISP, which is one of many variables describing respondents' racial/ethnic group; DWELLING, which represents the type of situation in which the respondent lives (e.g., a trailer, an apartment, a single-family house); and MARITAL, which corresponds to respondents' marital status (i.e., whether they are currently married, widowed, divorced, never married, etc.).

Let's look more closely at the variable RELIG. By viewing the variable RELIG, you should see a chart identical to that in Figure 2.6 below. Respondents are asked, "What is your religious preference? Is it Protestant, Catholic, Jewish, some other religion, or no religion?" You can also see that, when respondents answer this question, their responses are put into one of 13 categories. A person who answers "Protestant" will be assigned a 1 on this variable, someone who responds "Catholic" will be assigned a 2, someone who answers "Jewish" will be assigned a 3, and so forth.

What makes RELIG a nominal-level variable is that the ordering of the religious categories is arbitrary. The variable would make just as much sense if the categories were put in a different order and each religious group was associated with a different number.

Someone who describes themselves as "Orthodox-Christian" scores a 10 on this variable, and someone who describes themselves as "Catholic" scores a 2, but this does not mean that Orthodox-Christians are five times as religious, or have five times

Figure 2.6

RELIG	RS RELIGIOUS PREFERENCE		
Description of the Variable			
104. What is your religious preference? Is it Protestant, Catholic, Jewish, some other religion, or no religion?			
Percent	**N**	**Value**	**Label**
58.3	34,596	**1**	PROTESTANT
24.5	14,532	**2**	CATHOLIC
2.0	1,195	**3**	JEWISH
11.2	6,635	**4**	NONE
1.7	1,025	**5**	OTHER
0.3	156	**6**	BUDDHISM
0.1	76	**7**	HINDUISM
0.1	34	**8**	OTHER EASTERN
0.2	117	**9**	MOSLEM/ISLAM
0.2	105	**10**	ORTHODOX-CHRISTIAN
1.2	723	**11**	CHRISTIAN
0.0	26	**12**	NATIVE AMERICAN
0.2	128	**13**	INTER-NONDENOMINATIONAL
	23	**98**	DK
	228	**99**	NA
100.0	**59,599**		**Total**

Properties	
Data type:	numeric
Missing-data codes:	0,98,99
Mean:	1.90
Std Dev:	1.67
Record/columns:	1/480-481

more religious preference than Catholics. It doesn't even mean that "Orthodox-Christians" have a "higher" level of religiosity than Catholics. While the variable categories themselves have meaning, the ordering of the categories does not.

INTERPRETING A MEAN OR STANDARD DEVIATION FOR NOMINAL-LEVEL DATA

Note that, when viewing a variable in SDA, the bottom portion of the resulting chart provides a mean and standard deviation. For the variable RELIG, for example, the mean is 1.90 and the standard deviation (abbreviated "Std Dev") is 1.67. As explained below, the mean and standard deviation for nominal-level variables is nonsensical. Because the ordering of the categories as well as the number associated with each category is arbitrary, both the mean and the standard deviation are meaningless. It makes no sense to talk about an average religious preference of 1.90. Even though the SDA reports this mean, you should pay it no attention when analyzing a nominal-level variable.

Dummy Variables

Dummy variables are a special kind of nominal-level variable, where responses are coded into just two categories. The variable SEX (1 = male, 2 = female) is a dummy variable, as is the variable CITIZEN, based on the question "Are you a citizen of America?" (1 = yes, 2 = no). Other examples include XMOVIE, the variable that corresponds to the question "Have you seen an X-rated movie in the last year?" (1 = yes, 2 = no); WKRACISM, "Do you feel in any way discriminated against on your job because of your race or ethnic origin?" (1 = yes, 2 = no); and CONVICTD, "Not counting minor traffic offenses, have you ever been convicted of a crime?" (1 = yes, 2 = no).

Ordinal-Level Variables

Ordinal-level variables have a meaningful order to their response categories. Unlike interval-ratio-level variables (discussed below), however, the number associated with each category doesn't provide a meaningful indication of relative distance between each category. In other words, in ordinal-level variables, the interval between categories is undefined. The size of the categories themselves is often uneven.

The variable DEGREE provides a good example.[5] This variable represents respondents' highest educational degree and is shown in Figure 2.7. We see that respondents who have less than a high school education ("LT High School") score a 0 on this variable and that those who have a high school degree—but no degree beyond that—score a 1. Those whose highest degree is an associate's degree would score a 2, and those with a bachelor's degree would score a 3.

The categories of this variable clearly have an underlying order to them. Higher scores on this variable represent higher levels of education. But the categories themselves are uneven and the distance between them is undefined. A score of 0 could represent someone with 0 to 11 years of education, but a score of 1 likely represents someone who has between 12 and 13 years of education. Someone who scores a 4 on this variable could have a one-year master's degree, a three-year law degree (JD), or a master's and a doctoral degree.

With ordinal-level variables, caution must be used when making claims about the categories in relation to one another. It would be appropriate to say that those who score a 4 on this variable report having a higher degree than those who score a 2 on this variable. It would not, however, be accurate to say that someone who scores a 4 on this variable has twice as much education, or twice as high a degree, as someone who scores a 2.

Figure 2.7

DEGREE	RS HIGHEST DEGREE		
Description of the Variable			
19. If finished 9th-12th grade: Did you ever get a high school diploma or a GED certificate?			
Percent	N	Value	Label
21.9	12,997	0	LT HIGH SCHOOL
51.4	30,556	1	HIGH SCHOOL
5.5	3,256	2	JUNIOR COLLEGE
14.3	8,474	3	BACHELOR
7.0	4,151	4	GRADUATE
	30	8	DK
	135	9	NA
100.0	59,599		Total

Properties	
Data type:	numeric
Missing-data codes:	7,8,9
Mean:	1.33
Std Dev:	1.17
Record/column:	1/152

The GSS contains hundreds of ordinal-level variables. Respondents' personal income (as measured by the variable RINCOM06) and respondents' family income (as measured by the variable INCOME06) are both good examples of ordinal-level variables. Examples also include all of the attitudinal and opinion questions involving Likert scales, such as ETHIGNOR and RESPECT:

> ETHIGNOR: Here are some opinions some people have expressed in connection with ethnic issues in the United States. To what extent do you agree or disagree with each one? a. Harmony in the United States is best achieved by down-playing or ignoring ethnic differences. (1 = strongly agree, 2 = agree, 3 = neither agree nor disagree, 4 = disagree, 5 = strongly disagree)

> RESPECT: Now I'm going to read you a list of statements that might or might not describe your main job. Please tell me whether you strongly agree, agree, disagree, or strongly disagree with each of these statements . . . At the place where I work, I am treated with respect. (1 = strongly agree, 2 = agree, 3 = disagree, 4 = strongly disagree)

The GSS also includes some "feeling thermometer" variables, and these too are measured at the ordinal level. Examples include FEELBLKS ("In general, how warm or cool do you feel towards African Americans?") and FEELWHTS ("In general, how warm or cool do you feel towards white or Caucasian Americans?"). Both variables have nine categories, where scores of 1 indicate feeling "very warm" toward the group and scores of 9 indicate feeling "very cool" toward the group. Respondents who score a 1 on the variable RESPECT strongly agree with the notion that they are treated with respect at work. Higher numeric scores on this variable (such as a 2, 3, or 4) are associated with increased disagreement. Similarly, on the variable FEELBLKS, we can say that low scores indicate respondents who report having "very warm" feelings toward African Americans, and higher scores represent increasingly cool feelings.

Interval-Ratio-Level Variables

Like ordinal variables, **interval-ratio variables** have an intrinsic order to the variable response categories. Unlike ordinal variables, however, interval-ratio variables have a defined space between the categories, which is uniform throughout the range of the variable. Variables like AGE (respondent's age in years), HRS1(the number of hours the respondent worked last week), and SIBS (respondent's number of brothers and siblings) are all interval-ratio variables. Not only are the categories ordered (for example, someone who scores a 4 on the variable SIBS has more siblings than someone who scores a 1), but the interval between the categories is constant: each one-unit increase in the variable SIBS represents an additional sibling. Similarly, in the variable HRS1, each one-unit increase represents an additional hour worked last week.

INTERVAL-RATIO VARIABLES AND CROSS-TABS

Interval-ratio level variables often have a high number of response categories. For example, SIBS ranges from 0 to 68, AGE ranges from 18 to 89 (89 indicates respondents who are 89 and older), and EDUC (years of formal schooling) ranges from 0 to 20. With so many categories, interval-ratio variables can be difficult to analyze using cross-tabs unless the variables are recoded into a smaller number of categories. Recoding variables is easy in SDA and is discussed in detail in Chapters 5 and 6.

DESCRIBING VARIABLES: MEASURES OF CENTRAL TENDENCY

As discussed above, the first steps in analyzing survey data are (1) determining what the variable of interest to you actually measures (that is, identifying the survey question from which the variable was created) and (2) determining what the variable categories represent (that is, understanding what the response categories are and determining whether the variable is a categorical, ordinal, or interval-ratio level variable). After doing so, the next logical step is to take a look at how respondents actually answered the question. Researchers are often interested to see if there is a particular response or range of responses that are given more frequently than others.

The Mode

The mode of the variable is the response category with the highest number of responses. For example, in Figure 2.7, we see that in the variable DEGREE, the category for "high school degree" has 30,556 responses—more than any other response category. Figure 2.6 provides the distribution for the variable RELIG and shows that 34,596 people described themselves as Protestants. Because the number of people who describe their religious preference as Protestant is greater than the number of people who select any other religion, we can say that the mode of the variable RELIG is Protestant. While the mode can be found for any variable, whether categorical, ordinal, or interval-ratio, it is most meaningful for interpreting categorical-level and ordinal-level variables.

The Median

When a variable is an ordinal or interval-ratio level, it is often useful to determine the median. To find the median for a particular variable, the individual responses first are arranged from greatest to smallest, or smallest to greatest. Once they are so arranged, the median is simply the value of the middle observation. More specifically, in situations where there is an odd number of observations, the median is the value of the middle observation. When there are an even number of cases and thus no single middle observation, the median is found by taking the average of the two most middle observations. The median also corresponds to the 50th percentile.

Figure 2.8, for example, shows the distribution for the variable IMMCULT, which was first asked in the 2014 survey. The variable corresponds to a survey question that asks, "How much do you agree or disagree with the following statements? American culture is generally undermined by immigrants." In total, 1,207 (36 + 184 + 267 + 606 + 114 = 1207) people provided valid responses to this question. Imagine asking these 1,207 people to line themselves up so that people who strongly agree that American culture is generally undermined by immigrants were on the left and people who strongly disagreed with this sentiment were on the right. Because the people were lined up in order, we would know that, moving from left to right, we would first see 36 people who "strongly agree," then 184 people who "agree," and then 267 people who "neither agree nor disagree." Taken together, there would be 487 people in these first three categories. The next 606 people would be people who responded "disagree," and finally there would be 114 people who "strongly disagree." The person standing in the exact center of this line would have 603 people on her or his left and 603 people on her or his right. The middle person, the 604th person, is someone who "disagrees" with this survey question.

Figure 2.8			
IMMCULT	**IMMIGRANTS UNDERMINE AMERICAN CULTURE**		
Description of the Variable			
How much do you agree or disagree with the following statements? B. American culture is generally undermined by immigrants.			
Percent	**N**	**Value**	**Label**
3.0	36	1	Agree Strongly
15.2	184	2	Agree
22.1	267	3	Neither Agree nor Disagree
50.2	606	4	Disagree
9.4	114	5	Strongly disagree
	58,325	0	IAP
	64	8	Don't know
	3	9	No answer
100.0	**59,599**		**Total**

Because an underlying order to the response categories is necessary to identify the median, it is not possible to calculate a meaningful median for categorical-level data. Again, for categorical data, the best measure of central tendency is the mode.

The Mean

The mean of a variable is the arithmetic average, calculated by adding up all the scores and dividing that sum by the number of observations. Consider the example below, which examines a random sample of 10 respondents from the 2014 GSS, and their responses for the variable COLSCINM. The survey first asks respondents, "Have you ever taken any college-level science courses?" Those who respond that they *have* taken a college-level science course are then asked, "How many college-level science courses have you taken?" COLSCINM is an interval-ratio level variable with responses ranging from 1 to 90 (those who have taken no courses are not asked the question).

Figure 2.9	
	COLSCINM: How many college-level science courses have you taken?
Respondent #1	1
Respondent #2	2
Respondent #3	3
Respondent #4	2
Respondent #5	8
Respondent #6	4
Respondent #7	2
Respondent #8	1
Respondent #9	2
Respondent #10	1

To calculate the mean for this variable, using this small sample of 10 respondents, simply add up the individual responses and then divide by the number of observations (which in this case is 10):

$$\text{Mean number of science courses} = \frac{1 + 2 + 3 + 2 + 8 + 4 + 2 + 1 + 2 + 1}{10} = 2.6$$

To interpret this number, we can say that in our sample, which includes only those who have taken at least one college-level science course, the mean number of courses taken is 2.6. The modal number of science courses is 2, since 2 is the number of science courses that occurs most frequently among this sample of respondents.

The median number of science courses from this small sample is calculated by ordering the responses from smallest to largest (ordering them largest to smallest will also work) and by then identifying the most central observation. When put into order, the responses are:

$$1, \quad 1, \quad 1, \quad 2, \quad 2, \quad 2, \quad 2, \quad 3, \quad 4, \quad 8$$

With an even number of responses, there is no one single central value. In this case, the fifth and sixth responses represent the middle-most values. Since they are both 2, we can say that the median is 2. If the values were different from each other, the median would be calculated by taking the average of the fifth and sixth responses.

PRODUCING THE MEAN, MEDIAN, AND MODE IN SDA

Using the SDA, it is easy to find the mean, median, and modes for any variable. On the "Analysis" page, simply type the variable name into the "Row" field. Underneath, click on "Output Options," and under "Other Options" click the box for "Summary Statistics." When you run the table, a new window will open that shows you the frequency table for your variable, and beneath that will be a table of summary statistics, as shown in Figure 2.10.

Figure 2.10 Summary Statistics for COLSCINM		
Mean =6.07	Std Dev =8.85	Coef var =1.46
Median =3.00	Variance =78.29	Min =1.00
Mode =2.00	Skewness =3.50	Max =90.00
Sum =15,303.67	Kurtosis =15.69	Range =89.00

When examining means, medians, and modes in this way, the default in SDA is to provide these measures for all cases, for all years in which the question was asked. If you would prefer to see the mean, median, and mode for a subgroup of cases, then you can use the "Filter" field to restrict the cases included in the analysis. By typing YEAR (2010-2014) in the "Filter" field and then running the table, the median, mean, and mode presented will be calculated by including only those cases included in the 2010, 2012, and 2014 surveys. More information on using the "Filter" option is included in Chapters 4 and 6.

Note: SDA and other computer programs like SPSS and STATA will often provide a median and mean for categorical-level data, but it is important for you, the researcher, to be able to determine when this value is meaningful and when it isn't. Because the variable for the number of science courses taken is an interval-ratio level variable, the mean, the median, and the mode all have meaning. Notice in Figure 2.6, however, that SDA provides the mean for the variable RELIG—a categorical-level variable assessing respondents' preference. The mean provided by SDA is 1.90, but since the numbers assigned to each religious preference are entirely arbitrary and there is no underlying order to the response categories, this number is completely meaningless!

MEASURES OF CENTRAL TENDENCY AND MISSING DATA

Missing-data and "invalid" responses such as "Don't know," "No answer," and "Inapplicable" should not be included when calculating means, medians, and modes. The SDA program will automatically exclude these values.

CONCLUSION

After reading this chapter, you should have a sense of how the General Social Survey has been conducted, including who has been eligible for inclusion in the sample, and the broader population to which the results from analysis of the GSS can be generalized. The GSS website contains a much more in-depth discussion of survey design as well as of how and why this design has changed over time.

This chapter also served as an introduction to the Survey Documentation and Analysis (SDA) website. SDA provides an easy way to identify and analyze data from the GSS. After reading this chapter, you should have a good sense of how to search and browse for variables using the SDA website. You should also feel comfortable viewing variables to determine the precise wording of individual survey questions.

Finally, this chapter provided an introduction to describing variables. Before analyzing any variable, it is crucial to determine its level of measurement: Is it categorical, ordinal, or interval-ratio? It is also important to consider the number of valid responses for each variable and the extent of missing data. After determining the variable's level of measurement and examining the extent of missing data, it is useful to examine the central tendency of the variable: the modal category if the variable is nominal level, or the median and mean if the variable is ordinal or interval-ratio level.

The following chapters use the concepts and techniques presented in this chapter, along with the concepts presented in Chapter 1, to analyze a range of inequalities.

So far, we have focused on univariate statistics—that is, statistics about a single variable. The next several chapters focus on assessing the relationship between two variables—bivariate analyses—using cross-tabulations and comparisons of means. In addition, these chapters introduce filters and control variables, with which it is possible to show even more complex relationships and to highlight the intersection of multiple inequalities.

EXERCISES

1. View the variable CLASS. What, precisely, does this variable assess?

   a. respondent's perception of herself or himself as a member of the lower class, the working class, the middle class, or the upper class

   b. respondent's occupational status

   c. respondent's level of wealth

   d. respondent's beliefs about class inequality

2. View the variable SPEDUC. What, precisely, does this variable assess?

   a. respondent's formal education, measured in years

   b. respondent's formal education, measured in terms of highest degree earned

   c. respondent's spouse's formal education, measured in years

   d. respondent's spouse's formal education, measured in terms of highest degree earned

3. View the variable SPPOORKD. In what year was this variable included in the GSS?

   a. 1980

   b. 1990

   c. 2000

   d. 2010

4. View the variable UNEMP. This variable is best described as:

   a. a dummy variable.

   b. an ordinal-level variable.

   c. an interval-ratio-level variable.

5. View the variable SPANKING. This variable is best described as:

   a. a nominal-level variable.

   b. a dummy variable.

   c. an ordinal-level variable.

   d. an interval-ratio-level variable.

6. View the variable ETHNIC. This variable is best described as:

   a. a nominal-level variable.

   b. a dummy variable.

   c. an ordinal-level variable.

   d. an interval-ratio-level variable.

7. View the variable NUMPROBS. This variable is best described as:

   a. a nominal-level variable.

   b. a dummy variable.

   c. an ordinal-level variable.

   d. an interval-ratio-level variable.

8. In what year was the variable NUMPROBS included in the GSS?

   a. 2012

   b. 2002

   c. 1992

   d. 1982

9. Using the variable NUMPROBS, approximately what percentage of respondents reported having no close friends?

   a. 4

   b. 8

c. 12

d. 25

10. Using the summary statistics for the variable NUMPROBS, what is the mean number of close friends that respondents report having? Be sure to keep the default of COMPWT in the "Weight" field.

a. 8.17

b. 11.01

c. 5

d. 2

ANALYSES & ESSAYS

1. Identify two variables related to inequalities of race or ethnicity. For each variable, identify the precise wording of the survey question, the level of measurement, and the response categories. How might analyzing these variables help to advance a social justice project?

2. Identify two variables related to inequalities of gender or sexuality. For each variable, identify the precise wording of the survey question, the level of measurement, and the response categories. How might analyzing these variables help to advance a social justice project?

For questions 3, 4, and 5 below, choose a specific social justice issue that is important to you and find three variables in the GSS that are related to this issue.

3. View each of these variables (separately) and identify the precise wording of the survey question, the level of measurement, and the response categories. Then, describe the resulting univariate frequency tables, including the extent of missing data.

4. For each of these variables, identify the most appropriate measure of central tendency. Explain why you chose the measure of central tendency you did.

5. Describe how an analysis of these three variables could contribute to a better understanding of the social justice issue you have chosen.

NOTES

1. Much of this information comes from the GSS website (http://www3.norc.org/GSS+Website/) and from the FAQs about the GSS (http://www3.norc.org/GSS+Website/FAQs/). More detailed information, including a complete description of the survey methodology, can be found here as well.

2. One major exception here is when survey questions have a high percentage of "Don't know" or "No answer" responses. Particularly when there are patterns to the missing data, this can result in biased findings. A classic example here concerns missing data related to income. If people with high levels of education, for example, are less likely than people with low levels of education to provide information about their income, then analyses that simply disregard cases with missing values on education will result in an analytic sample that is biased with respect to both education and income. In other words, the conclusions that we draw from our analyses could be incorrect.

3. Because the variable WKSEXISM is nominal level (also called a categorical variable), the decision to assign the value of 1 to "Yes" and 2 to "No" is completely arbitrary.

4. In using the term "interval-ratio" level variables, I am drawing from Frankfort-Nachmias and Leon-Guerrero (2015), who include "interval"- and "ratio"-level variables as a single category

for purposes of learning the basics of social statistics. (Frankfort-Nachmias, Chava, and Anna Leon-Guerrero. 2015. *Social Statistics for a Diverse Society*. 7th ed. Thousand Oaks, CA: SAGE.)

5. As discussed in Chapter 5, "viewing" in SDA almost always shows the precise wording of the survey question that was asked to respondents. DEGREE is one of the exceptions. In the survey, respondents are asked a number of questions about their educational attainment, and their answers provide information that is later combined into the variable DEGREE. In other words, while viewing DEGREE seems to suggest that this variable is associated with the question "If finished 9th–12th grade: Did you ever get a high school diploma or a GED certificate?" the variable draws from multiple survey questions.

CHAPTER 3

ANALYZING GENDER WITH THE GSS

INTRODUCTION: KEY CONCEPTS IN GENDER

In popular discourse, the term *gender* is often used to describe a characteristic of individuals ("I'm a woman" or "He's a man"). In everyday settings, the term *gender* is also often used interchangeably with the term *sex*. In the US today, most people in most situations think of sex and gender as being one and the same.

In contrast to the popular understanding of sex and gender, sociologists often draw a distinction between the two terms. *Sex* is used to describe individuals' status as male, female, or intersex. *Gender* is used to describe the socially constructed statuses of man, woman, boy, girl, and transgender. By focusing on gender statuses rather than simply sex categories, we highlight the ways in which society shapes—and in many cases produces—social differences between men and women.[1]

As discussed in Chapter 1, a social constructionist perspective emphasizes the ways in which gender differences and inequalities are created, reproduced, and contested in society. A sociological understanding of gender highlights the fact that gender is learned through gender socialization and gendered social control. Gender socialization is the process through which individuals learn the norms appropriate for different gender groups. Gendered social control refers to the ways in which our society rewards those who enact gender norms "appropriately" and punishes, stigmatizes, and disadvantages those who deviate from gender norms.[2] Sometimes we are told things directly: "John,

Learning Objectives

By the end of this chapter, you should be able to:

1. Identify variables related to gender.

2. Produce and interpret a univariate frequency table.

3. Produce a meaningful bivariate table, also called a *cross-tab.*

4. Interpret these analyses within a social justice framework.

stop crying. Man up!" or "Lisa, stop being so bossy!" At other times, the lesson is more subtle. Boys and girls are often given "gender-appropriate" toys. Boys might be given footballs, action figures, building blocks, microscopes, and chemistry sets. Girls might be given baby dolls, tea sets, princess dresses, easy-bake ovens, and aprons. Gender socialization can be further reinforced by the activities in which girls and boys participate: dance lessons for girls, football for boys; Girl Scouts and cookie sales for girls, Boy Scouts and box-car derbies for boys.

In addition to highlighting the processes through which individuals learn gender, sociologists underscore the importance of understanding gender as social institution. Gender is not just a characteristic of individuals and is not merely a collection of learned social expectations. Rather, gender operates more at the more macro level as an organizing structure of society.[3] As Judith Lorber explains, ideas about gender are built into the major social organizations of society, such as religion, culture, the economy, the family, and politics. But gender can also be seen as an institution in and of itself. Gender "establishes patterns of expectations for individuals" and "orders the social processes of everyday life."[4] Gender not only shapes which toys are given to children and the activities in which children participate but also organizes the work, family, emotional, and sexual lives of women and men alike.

The social institution of gender is reinforced by gender ideology, an interconnected system of attitudes and beliefs that supports and justifies gender differences and inequality. In the Victorian era, for example, it was commonly believed that too much physical exercise might cause women's organs (particularly the reproductive organs) to become dislodged and wander around the body.[5] This belief worked to justify limiting women's activities and opportunities—keeping them in the home "for their own safety." Fortunately, this is a less commonly held belief today! Many people continue to believe that men are naturally more logical than women, however. Some people still believe that women are ill suited to political and religious leadership positions, and even more believe that the breadwinner/homemaker model of family life is best for all involved. Gender ideology is such an entrenched part of our worldview that we often treat gender as if it were natural, inevitable, and unchangeable, despite a significant body of evidence to the contrary.[6]

As discussed in Chapter 1, most existing survey instruments conceptualize gender statuses as if gender were a clear-cut binary. Unfortunately, the General Social Survey (GSS) is no exception. In the GSS, at this point in time, the only indication of respondents' sex or gender status is the variable SEX. Like many other large-scale surveys, the GSS asks interviewers to record the interviewees' sex without actually asking the respondent how they themselves describe their sex or gender identity. At the time of this writing, there is no option for people who identify as transgender or gender-queer to make this known within the survey.[7]

Despite these significant limitations, the GSS remains an excellent resource for analyzing many aspects of gender inequality. As shown in the remainder of this chapter, data from the GSS can be analyzed to document the extent to which gender ideology and gendered work and family arrangements have changed over time. These types of analyses can draw attention to changes in gender at the macro level and, in so doing, can reveal the socially constructed nature of gender difference and inequality. In addition, individuals' gender statuses can be analyzed in conjunction with individuals' racial/ethnic-, sexuality-, and class-based identities to highlight diversity among women and men. In this way, an analysis of GSS data can help to demonstrate the importance of intersectionality.

How does an understanding of gender as a social construct help to explain the persistence of gender difference and inequality? And how might an empirical analysis of the GSS shed light on the dimensions of gender inequality in the contemporary US? For the past four decades, the GSS has asked a range of survey questions about gender. Some of these questions focus on gender as a characteristic of individuals, and some can be used to assess mechanisms of gender socialization. The majority of questions directly related to gender focus on individuals' gender attitudes and beliefs as well as their experiences. Analyzing the extent to which individuals' experiences differ for men and women provides a window into gender as an organizing mechanism of society. In other words, it allows us to assess the strength of gender as a social institution.

This chapter provides an introduction to analyzing gender in the General Social Survey, with a focus on the dimensions of gender described above.

IDENTIFYING VARIABLES RELATED TO GENDER

Chapter 2 presented an overview of how to search for variables using the SDA website. The following section builds on that overview and presents more detailed information for analyses focusing on gender.

Searching for Gender Variables

The first step in identifying variables related to gender is to brainstorm possible key words. When searching for data related to gender in the GSS, it is important to remember that the survey uses the terms *sex* and *gender* interchangeably. *Sex* and *gender* are good key words to start with, but consider some others: *mother, father, women, woman, men, man, girl, boy, sister, brother, spouse, daughter, son, child*.

Searching for the key word *mother*, for example, will result in dozens of questions related to gender, including beliefs about parenting as well as sociodemographic information concerning the respondent's living arrangements when she or he was growing up. The variable MAWRKGRW, for example, corresponds to the survey question "Did your mother ever work for pay for as long as a year while you were growing up?"

WHOSE GENDER?

If you search for variables using the key word *gender*, you will come across variables such as GENDER3, "gender of third person," and GENDER12, "gender of 12th person (visitor)." These variables do not correspond to the gender of the respondent! This group of variables concerns the composition of the respondent's household. Similarly, the variable INTSEX is a variable recording the gender of the interviewer, not the interviewee.

In most cases, when you want to analyze gender differences in experiences, behaviors, attitudes, or beliefs, you will want to use the variable SEX, which represents the respondent's gender status.

Browsing for Gender Variables

One of the best features of the SDA website is the online codebook (on the left-hand side of the SDA) that allows users to easily identify clusters of variables about specific topics, such as gender. There are several headings that deal specifically with gender-related issues (for example, "2012 ISSP Module: Gender"), but many of the other sections include gender-related questions too.

If you are interested in browsing for variables related to gender, you may find the following subject headings and subheadings to be particularly useful:

- Respondent Background Variables
  - Respondent and Spouse Work Week
  - Respondent's Household Composition

- Personal and Family Information
  - Respondent's Employment
  - Marital Status
  - Family Composition
  - Respondent's Background and Childhood

- Controversial Social Issues
  - Gender Issues
  - Abortion
  - Family Planning, Sex, and Contraception
  - Pornography
  - Abortion Part Two
  - Women's Rights
  - 2002 Topical Module: Quality of Working Life
  - 2012 ISSP Module: Gender

Keep in mind that there are many variables related to gender that occur outside the subject headings mentioned above. By browsing through the codebook and searching for terms related to gender, you should be able to find many dozens of survey questions directly related to gender.

Viewing a Variable

Once you have identified potential variables to analyze, the next step is to "view" the variable so that you can determine what exactly the variable represents. Viewing a variable in SDA is easy, as discussed in detail in Chapter 2. From the GSS SDA homepage, simply type the variable name into the "Variable Selection" field (this is in the upper left corner) and then click "View." A new window will open, in which you will find the exact wording of the question as well as the frequency distribution of the responses.

Remember that when you view a variable in this way, the resulting frequency distribution shows the combined responses from *all* survey years in which the question was asked. Viewing the variable doesn't tell us about when this variable was included in the GSS. To determine when the data were collected, it is necessary to construct a bivariate table, which is discussed below.

PRODUCING AND INTERPRETING A BIVARIATE TABLE OR "CROSS-TAB"

Background

The ability to produce and accurately interpret a meaningful bivariate table is perhaps the single most important tool of data analysis. Bivariate simply means "two variables," and bivariate tables are used to explore the relationship between two variables. If we were interested in knowing whether married men and women reported similar or different levels of happiness in marriages, for example, we could use the variables HAPMAR and SEX to explore this relationship with a bivariate table. We could also examine the extent to which individuals in different generations had similar or different ideas about the ideal organization of work and family life using the variables FEFAM and AGE.

Before creating a bivariate table, it is useful to consider whether you believe the relationship you are investigating is a causal relationship or if the relationship would be better understood as a correlation. (See Chapter 1 for a more in-depth discussion of causation and correlation.) In a causal relationship, the variable doing the causing is termed the independent variable and the variable that is affected is the dependent variable. In other words, the dependent variable is thought to depend on the independent variable.

An analysis of gender differences in full-time and part-time work, for example, would use respondents' gender as the independent variable and work status as the dependent variable. To the extent that a correlation exists, it is gender that influences work status. Someone's status as a man or woman isn't generally changed as a result of participation in the labor force. Another example is that in the US, men tend to take more college-level science courses than women. We can be pretty sure that it is respondents' gender (along with the social institution of gender) that is affecting individuals' course selection and not the other way around. Again, in this case, gender would be the independent variable, and the number of science courses taken would be the dependent variable.

When testing for gender differences in experiences, beliefs, attitudes, identities, and other social phenomena, gender will usually be the independent variable. The experiences, beliefs, attitudes, and identities that you believe will differ for men and women, or boys and girls, will be dependent variables.

Creating a Cross-Tab in SDA

To produce a cross-tab in SDA, first make sure that you are on the "Analysis" section of the SDA website. In the upper left corner of the SDA page, click on the "Analysis" button. The screen should look like Figure 3.1.

The left-hand side of the screen shows the codebook, discussed above, and the right side is used to conduct the analysis. In cases where you believe there is a causal relationship, enter the name of your dependent variable in the "Row" field and the name of your independent variable in the "Column" field.

Figure 3.1

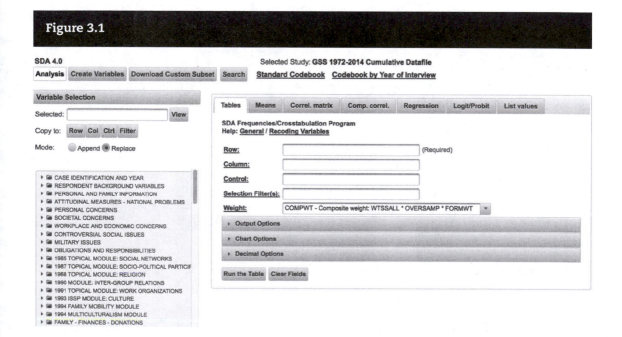

Let's use the example of gender differences in workforce status to get us going. Workforce status can be assessed with the variable WRKSTAT: "Last week were you working full-time, part-time, going to school, keeping house, or what?" If we are interested to know whether workforce participation differs for men and women, then WRKSTAT is the dependent variable and SEX is the independent variable.

In the "Weight" field, you will see that the default setting for weights is "COMPWT - Composite weight WTSSALL *OVERSAMP* FORMWT." To replicate the analyses as presented in this chapter, keep this selection as is.[8]

Once you have entered your dependent variable, WRKSTAT, in the "Row" field and your independent variable, SEX, in the "Column" field, click the "Run the Table" button. A new window will appear that presents the cross-tab, shown in Figure 3.2.

Interpreting a Cross-Tab

The window that appears contains three main parts. First is a description of the variables used in the analysis (labeled "Variables"), followed by the cross-tab (labeled "Frequency Distribution"). Below the cross-tab is a chart that gives a visual representation of the information presented in the cross-tab.

The "Variables" section, at the top, presents a summary of the analysis that follows, including variable names, short variable descriptions (variable labels), the range of valid response categories ("Range"), and the response categories that correspond to nonvalid values (MD or "Missing Data"). This summative information is especially useful when using recoded variables, filters, and/or control variables to produce cross-tabs.

The "Frequency Distribution" section shows your bivariate table. In the upper left corner of the frequency distribution chart, we see that the cells contain "column percents" and the number of cases (N) in each cell. Let's first look at the cells that are red or blue. The dark red cell in the upper left corner contains two numbers: 63.0 and 17,190.9. The N of 17,190.9 indicates that about 17,191 respondents in the GSS were men who reported that they were working full time. To the immediate right, we see a cell that contains the numbers 39.5 and 12,774.8. This tells us that about 12,775 respondents in the GSS were women who reported that they were working full time. Comparing the two Ns, we can see that more men were working full time than women.

In addition to the number of cases in each cell (N), the cross-tab provides the column percents for each cell. **Column percents** are calculated by dividing the number of cases in a given cell by the total number of cases in each column, and then multiplying the resulting proportion by 100. So in the upper left corner, the column percent of 63.0 is calculated in the following way:

$$(17{,}190.9 \, / \, 27{,}281.0) * 100 = 63.0\%$$

Figure 3.2

Variables					
Role	**Name**	**Label**	**Range**	**MD**	**Dataset**
Row	**WRKSTAT**	LABOR FORCE STATUS	1-8	0,9	1
Column	**SEX**	RESPONDENTS SEX	1-2	0	1
Weight	**COMPWT**	Composite weight = WTSSALL * OVERSAMP * FORMWT	.1913-11.1261		1

Frequency Distribution				
Cells contain:		**SEX**		
-**Column percent**		1 MALE	2 FEMALE	*ROW TOTAL*
-Weighted N				
WRKSTAT	1: WORKING FULLTIME	**63.0** 17,190.9	**39.5** 12,774.8	*50.3* *29,965.7*
	2: WORKING PARTTIME	**8.0** 2,174.5	**13.4** 4,343.0	*10.9* *6,517.5*
	3: TEMP NOT WORKING	**2.3** 620.4	**2.1** 693.2	*2.2* *1,313.5*
	4: UNEMPL, LAID OFF	**5.0** 1,355.0	**2.1** 686.4	*3.4* *2,041.4*
	5: RETIRED	**14.6** 3,970.6	**9.2** 2,975.9	*11.7* *6,946.6*
	6: SCHOOL	**3.8** 1,030.4	**3.6** 1,170.8	*3.7* *2,201.2*
	7: KEEPING HOUSE	**1.4** 377.4	**28.3** 9,139.0	*16.0* *9,516.4*
	8: OTHER	**2.1** 561.9	**1.7** 558.3	*1.9* *1,120.2*
	COL TOTAL	*100.0* *27,281.0*	*100.0* *32,341.3*	*100.0* *59,622.3*

The column percent tells us the percentage of individuals in each category of the column variable who fall into each category of the row variable. In this case, 63.0% of men who provided a "valid response" to the question about their work status reported that they were working full time. The cell to the right indicates that about 12,775 women respondents indicated that they were working full time, and this corresponds to 39.5% of women respondents:

$$(12,774.8 / 32,341.3) * 100 = 39.5\%$$

Looking at the data for the men in the sample, we see that 63% answered that they were working full time, 8% were working part time, 2.3% were temporarily not working, 5% were unemployed or had been laid off, 14.6% were retired, and so forth. The column percents add up to approximately 100% (due to rounding) as you go down the column.

$$63.0\% + 8.0\% + 2.3\% + 5.0\% + 14.6\%$$
$$+ 3.8\% + 1.4\% + 2.1\% = 100.2\%$$

The **row totals** at the far right-hand side of the table tell us the overall distribution of the row variable (WRKSTAT). Taken on the whole, including both men and women, approximately 29,966 respondents indicated that they were working full time, and this number corresponds to 50.3% of the total number of respondents:

$$(29,965.7 / 59,622.3) * 100 = 50.3\%$$

The **column totals** in the bottom row of the table tell us the overall distribution of the variable in the column (SEX). Reading across the bottom row of the table, we see that 27,281 respondents were men and about 32,341 were women.

The bottom right-hand corner of the table shows a percentage of 100 and an N of approximately 59,622. This number corresponds to the total number of respondents represented in the table. *Because we have not specified any specific time period for this analysis, the resulting bivariate table is drawing from all available data from 1972 to 2014.* If we wanted to focus on a specific time period, we could use the "Filter" option in SDA, which is discussed in Chapters 4 and 6.

By examining the percentages in the top row of the cross-tab, we can immediately see some big differences. While 63% of men responded that they were working full time, only 39.5% of women were working full time. On the other hand, women were much more likely than men respondents to report they were working part time.

The cross-tab shows us that there are gender differences in who is likely to work full time, but it shows us much more than that, too. Women are much more likely than men to be working part time and are also much more likely to be "keeping house." More than a quarter of the women who responded (28.3%) indicated that

WHAT DO THE COLORS IN A BIVARIATE TABLE MEAN?

When you produce a cross-tab on the SDA website, you will notice that the cells are different shades of blue and red. These colors, represented here in shades of gray, are meant to help you identify patterns in the data and can be used as a shorthand way to assess the statistical significance of the relationship between two variables. The color of each cell reflects the Z-statistic, which shows whether the frequencies in a cell are greater or fewer than we would expect if there were no relationship between the variables in the general population. The color coding also takes into account the total number of cases in the table. In analyses that contain a relatively small number of respondents, the deviations from the expected values will not be as significant as when there are a large number of respondents in the analysis.[9]

For example, in the example of gender differences in men and women working full time, we see a difference of 23.5 percentage points (63.0 – 36.5 = 23.5). If, in the overall population, there were no relationship between gender and workforce participation, we would expect the percentage of men who were working full time to be approximately equal to the percentage of women who were working full time. A difference of 23.5 percentage points is very large for social science research!

Since the cross-tab includes a very large number of cases (N = 59,622), we can be pretty sure that the differences are meaningful. The dark red and dark blue colors indicate that we can be *at least* 95% confident that, in the general population, there is a difference in the percentage of men and women who are working full time.

they were "keeping house," compared to only 1.4% of men. As we have seen, men are more likely to be employed full time, but men are also more likely than women to be "unemployed/temporarily laid off" and more likely to answer that they are "retired."

While informative, this cross-tab likely also raises some unanswered questions for you:

- This table shows data aggregated from 1972 to 2014. If we looked only at more recent data, would gender differences be this large?

- This table shows us data from individuals aged 18 and older. How, if at all, would these patterns change if we looked at only one age group, for example, respondents aged 30 and higher?

- This table includes information from adults with children and without children. If we looked only at nonparents, would we see similar results?

- What other factors in addition to respondents' gender might be influencing workforce participation?

As explained in subsequent chapters, all of these questions can be answered using SDA. Chapter 9 focuses on gender, race, and class as they intersect and organize the world of work and demonstrates techniques for analyzing the interplay among multiple inequalities.

APPLICATION: HOW HAVE BELIEFS ABOUT GENDER ROLES CHANGED OVER THE PAST FOUR DECADES?

As explained previously, the GSS is an excellent resource for analyzing gender ideology. New questions about gender beliefs, gender arrangements, and gendered experiences are introduced regularly. For example, an entire module on gender, work, and family was included in the 2012 survey. To assess how beliefs about gender have changed over time, however, it is necessary to focus on those questions that have been asked repeatedly over the past few decades. These questions tend to focus on work and family. This application focuses on three variables, FEFAM, FECHLD, and FEPRES, each of which examines beliefs about gender roles and responsibilities.

Step 1. Restate the research question and identify the independent and dependent variables.

In this application, the research question is "How have GSS respondents' beliefs about gender roles changed over the past four decades?" The independent variable is YEAR, and the three dependent variables are FEFAM, FECHLD, and FEPRES.

Step 2. View each variable to make sure it means what you think it means. Viewing the variable shows the precise wording of the survey question that corresponds to the variable.

By viewing FEFAM, we can see that the variable corresponds to the following survey question:

> Now I'm going to read several more statements. As I read each one, please tell me whether you strongly agree, agree, disagree, or strongly disagree with it . . . It is much better for everyone involved if the man is the achiever outside the home and the woman takes care of the home and family.

By viewing FECHLD, we can see that respondents were asked the following question:

> Now I'm going to read several more statements. As I read each one, please tell me whether you strongly agree, agree, disagree, or strongly disagree with it . . . A working mother can establish just as warm and secure a relationship with her children as a mother who does not work.

Figure 3.3

Cells contain:
- Column percent
- Weighted N

Distribution

		YEAR																			ROW TOTAL
		1977	1985	1986	1988	1989	1990	1991	1993	1994	1996	1998	2000	2002	2004	2006	2008	2010	2012	2014	
FEFAM	1: STRONGLY AGREE	19.0 / 285.1	9.7 / 146.4	8.8 / 127.4	9.0 / 86.1	9.6 / 95.0	6.6 / 60.6	7.6 / 74.9	5.5 / 58.1	6.4 / 121.8	7.4 / 176.0	6.8 / 125.3	11.1 / 199.9	10.3 / 91.5	8.7 / 76.7	9.1 / 178.6	8.2 / 108.6	6.8 / 96.9	6.5 / 84.0	6.3 / 104.4	8.6 / 2,297.2
	2: AGREE	47.0 / 706.1	38.7 / 581.8	38.3 / 551.9	32.0 / 307.6	30.6 / 302.4	32.5 / 297.5	33.3 / 328.2	29.4 / 311.8	27.7 / 528.2	30.5 / 723.5	27.2 / 458.9	28.9 / 522.4	28.8 / 257.1	28.0 / 247.8	26.2 / 516.6	27.0 / 355.9	28.6 / 405.7	25.2 / 327.2	24.7 / 405.3	30.6 / 8,179.2
	3: DISAGREE	28.2 / 423.4	39.3 / 590.8	40.1 / 579.1	43.3 / 416.0	43.1 / 425.4	46.5 / 425.1	42.0 / 413.7	47.5 / 502.6	47.9 / 912.5	44.6 / 1,058.7	47.2 / 865.8	40.7 / 735.7	42.9 / 382.6	45.9 / 406.3	47.4 / 933.8	47.2 / 621.7	43.5 / 617.3	48.3 / 626.8	48.1 / 795.4	43.9 / 11,730.4
	4: STRONGLY DISAGREE	5.9 / 88.4	12.3 / 185.8	12.8 / 184.3	15.8 / 151.4	16.7 / 165.0	14.4 / 131.8	17.1 / 168.9	17.6 / 186.6	18.1 / 344.2	17.4 / 413.9	18.7 / 343.2	19.3 / 345.7	18.0 / 160.6	17.5 / 155.2	17.3 / 341.3	17.5 / 230.4	21.2 / 300.4	20.0 / 260.0	20.9 / 345.2	16.9 / 4,505.3
	COL TOTAL	100.0 / 1,503.0	100.0 / 1,504.7	100.0 / 1,442.8	100.0 / 961.2	100.0 / 987.8	100.0 / 915.0	100.0 / 985.7	100.0 / 1,059.2	100.0 / 1,906.8	100.0 / 2,372.1	100.0 / 1,833.3	100.0 / 1,804.7	100.0 / 891.9	100.0 / 885.8	100.0 / 1,970.4	100.0 / 1,316.6	100.0 / 1,420.4	100.0 / 1,297.5	100.0 / 1,653.3	100.0 / 26,712.0

Figure 3.4

Cells contain:
- Column percent
- Weighted N

Frequency Distribution

		YEAR																			ROW TOTAL
		1977	1985	1986	1988	1989	1990	1991	1993	1994	1996	1998	2000	2002	2004	2006	2008	2010	2012	2014	
FECHLD	1: STRONGLY AGREE	15.4 / 232.2	20.5 / 313.4	22.4 / 326.3	22.4 / 217.8	20.7 / 207.9	22.0 / 206.2	19.9 / 199.1	20.8 / 222.5	23.4 / 453.0	24.0 / 579.0	22.1 / 409.8	20.3 / 374.5	23.4 / 209.7	21.9 / 195.1	23.4 / 462.6	26.3 / 350.1	28.8 / 411.6	25.0 / 326.8	30.1 / 500.9	22.9 / 6,198.6
	2: AGREE	33.5 / 503.5	39.0 / 594.9	40.1 / 584.7	40.1 / 390.5	43.8 / 439.2	41.5 / 388.9	46.1 / 460.4	46.9 / 501.1	46.9 / 907.7	42.2 / 1,019.0	45.8 / 849.8	41.4 / 763.9	39.9 / 357.0	42.7 / 380.9	43.5 / 858.6	46.0 / 612.4	46.0 / 656.0	46.7 / 609.6	46.3 / 769.3	43.1 / 11,647.5
	3: DISAGREE	33.8 / 509.4	30.3 / 462.0	29.6 / 432.1	28.4 / 276.8	28.1 / 281.9	29.3 / 274.7	27.9 / 278.8	25.9 / 277.0	25.0 / 484.9	26.1 / 631.2	25.2 / 466.9	29.4 / 543.2	26.5 / 237.1	28.3 / 252.9	27.3 / 538.4	22.2 / 295.3	20.1 / 286.6	23.1 / 301.2	19.2 / 319.9	26.5 / 7,150.3
	4: STRONGLY DISAGREE	17.3 / 259.9	10.2 / 155.0	7.9 / 115.3	9.1 / 88.7	7.4 / 74.1	7.2 / 67.5	6.1 / 61.1	6.4 / 68.2	4.7 / 90.9	7.7 / 185.2	7.0 / 129.3	8.9 / 164.8	10.3 / 92.0	7.1 / 63.7	5.8 / 114.4	5.4 / 72.3	5.1 / 73.3	5.2 / 67.2	4.4 / 72.8	7.5 / 2,015.8
	COL TOTAL	100.0 / 1,504.9	100.0 / 1,525.2	100.0 / 1,458.4	100.0 / 973.9	100.0 / 1,003.1	100.0 / 937.3	100.0 / 999.5	100.0 / 1,068.7	100.0 / 1,936.5	100.0 / 2,414.5	100.0 / 1,855.8	100.0 / 1,846.4	100.0 / 895.8	100.0 / 892.6	100.0 / 1,974.0	100.0 / 1,330.2	100.0 / 1,427.4	100.0 / 1,304.8	100.0 / 1,663.0	100.0 / 27,012.2

By viewing FEPRES, we can see that respondents were asked:

> If your party nominated a woman for President, would you vote for her if she were qualified for the job?

By viewing the variable YEAR, we can see that this variable corresponds to the survey year.

Step 3. Determine which time period the data are from. Remember that when you view a variable, you are seeing the combined data across all survey years in which the survey question was included. In some cases, this is more than 40 years of data.

The easiest way to determine the years in which the variable was included is to create a cross-tab of the variables in your analysis by the variable YEAR (the variable that corresponds to the survey year). Begin constructing your cross-tabs by entering FEFAM in the "Row" field and YEAR in the "Column" field. Be sure that the default weight, COMPWT, is selected before running the table. Running the table will produce the cross-tab shown in Figure 3.3.

After creating a bivariate table for FEFAM by YEAR, create another bivariate table for FECHLD by YEAR. Here again, the dependent variable FECHLD should go in the "Row" field, YEAR should remain in the "Column" field, and COMPWT should also be selected. Running the table should produce the cross-tab shown in Figure 3.4.

Finally, create a bivariate table for FEPRES and YEAR by entering FEPRES in the "Row" field and YEAR in the "Column" field. Running the table should produce the cross-tab shown in Figure 3.5.

Step 4. The fourth step is to conduct your analysis, but in this case, by making the cross-tabs you created in Step 3, you have actually already completed this step! By making the cross-tabs of FEFAM, FECHILD, and FEPRES by YEAR, we can easily see how the responses to these survey questions have changed over time.

Step 5. Interpret your results. There are five basic steps to interpreting a cross-tab.

1. Remind your audience of the basics.

When presenting your analyses to an audience, it is important to:

    a. *Restate your research question.* In this case, the research question is "How have beliefs about gender roles changed over the past four decades in the US?"

    b. *Remind your audience of the data source and the specific variables you used to answer the question.* In this example, the data analyzed come from the 1972–2014 General Social Surveys. More

Figure 3.5

Cells contain:
- Column percent
- Weighted N

Frequency Distribution

FEPRES		YEAR																			ROW TOTAL
		1972	1974	1975	1977	1978	1982	1983	1985	1986	1988	1989	1990	1991	1993	1994	1996	1998	2008	2010	
1: YES	%	74.0	79.9	80.0	80.3	82.2	86.2	85.7	83.0	86.5	88.4	86.5	90.6	91.4	90.4	92.5	93.3	93.7	94.0	96.2	87.1
	N	1,134.7	1,148.7	1,158.5	1,186.2	1,230.7	1,555.1	1,336.7	1,241.9	1,234.3	845.4	832.5	825.7	882.6	935.5	1,772.6	1,783.3	1,704.5	1,238.4	1,360.2	23,406.6
2: NO	%	26.0	20.1	19.8	19.7	17.8	13.8	14.3	17.0	13.5	11.6	13.5	9.4	8.6	9.6	7.5	6.7	6.3	6.0	3.8	12.9
	N	398.4	289.4	286.1	291.0	266.1	248.1	223.0	254.1	192.4	110.5	130.2	86.1	83.4	99.9	144.0	128.2	113.9	79.6	53.3	3,477.6
5: WOULDNT VOTE	%	.0	.0	.2	.0	.0	.0	.0	.0	.0	.0	.0	.0	.0	.0	.0	.0	.0	.0	.0	.0
	N	.0	.0	2.8	.0	.0	.0	.6	.0	.0	.0	.0	.0	.0	.0	.0	.0	.0	.0	.0	3.4
COL TOTAL	%	100.0	100.0	100.0	100.0	100.0	100.0	100.0	100.0	100.0	100.0	100.0	100.0	100.0	100.0	100.0	100.0	100.0	100.0	100.0	100.0
	N	1,533.1	1,438.2	1,447.4	1,477.3	1,496.8	1,803.2	1,559.4	1,496.0	1,426.7	955.9	962.7	911.8	966.0	1,035.4	1,916.5	1,911.5	1,818.4	1,317.9	1,413.5	26,887.7

specifically, the analysis focuses on three attitudinal questions: (1) "Please tell me whether you strongly agree, agree, disagree, or strongly disagree with it . . . It is much better for everyone involved if the man is the achiever outside the home and the woman takes care of the home and family." (2) "Please tell me whether you strongly agree, agree, disagree, or strongly disagree with it . . . A working mother can establish just as warm and secure a relationship with her children as a mother who does not work." (3) "If your party nominated a woman for President, would you vote for her if she were qualified for the job?" These attitudinal variables are analyzed over time using the variable YEAR, which corresponds to year in which the data were collected.

c. *Identify and describe the dependent and independent variables, clearly stating how each variable was coded.* Here one might say, "In this analysis, survey year is the independent variable and gender-related attitudes are the dependent variables. Beliefs about gender roles are coded into four categories: strongly agree (coded 1), agree, disagree, or strongly disagree (coded 4). Support for women presidential candidates is a dichotomous variable, where 1 represents respondents' willingness to vote for a woman and 2 represents respondents who would not vote for a qualified woman presidential candidate."

d. *Specify the number of cases included in each analysis.* The overall number of valid cases (N) included in each cross-tab is presented in the bottom right corner of each cross-tab. The number of cases in each analysis ranges from 26,712 to 27,012. In almost all survey years, the data include responses from more than 1,000 respondents.

2. Focus on specifics.

The first step in interpreting a bivariate table or cross-tab is to look carefully at the specific numbers in the tables and interpret them as specifically as you can. Focusing on the cell frequencies (the bottom number in each cell of the table) can be useful, but in most cases it is more helpful to examine the column percents—the top number in each cell.

For example, in the upper left corner of Figure 3.3, we see that, in the 1977 survey, 19% of respondents strongly agreed with the idea that "it is much better for everyone involved if the man is the achiever outside the home and the woman takes care of the home and family." Another 47% of respondents said they agreed (but not strongly) with this idea. Adding these two numbers together, we see that 66% of respondents—that is, about two thirds!—either agreed or strongly agreed with this idea.

If we compare the data from 1977 with the more recent data from 2014, we can see that things have changed pretty dramatically. When the same question was asked in 2014, only 6.3% of respondents said they "strongly agreed" that "it is much better for everyone involved if the man is the achiever outside the home and the woman takes care of the home and family." Another 24.7% agreed (but not strongly) with this idea. Adding these two numbers together, we see that only 31% of respondents agreed or strongly agreed with this idea in 2014. That's slightly less than one third of respondents surveyed.

In 1977, the modal category for FEFAM (that is, the category with the highest number of responses in it) was "agree," with 47% of respondents selecting this option. In 2014, the modal category for FEFAM was "disagree," with 48.1% of respondents selecting this option.

Looking at Figure 3.4, we can see that in 1977, only 15.4% of respondents "strongly agreed" that "a working mother can establish just as warm and secure a relationship with her children as a mother who does not work." In 2014, 30.1% of respondents strongly agreed with this idea and another 46.3% of respondents agreed.

Figure 3.5 provides insight into how beliefs about women in politics have changed over time. In 1972, slightly more than one fourth of respondents (26%) said they would not vote for a woman president who was qualified for the job. In 2010, the most recent year where there are data for this question, this number had decreased significantly to only 3.8% of respondents.

3. Consider the big picture.

After examining individual percentages within the tables, it is important to step back and take a larger view of the overall relationship presented in the tables. When examining each table individually, are there any patterns or trends that you can see with the column percentages, or do the percentages seem to go up and down at random? If you see clusters of dark blue or dark red cells in the table, then there is probably an identifiable pattern. If there are very few darkly colored cells or if they seem randomly scattered across the table, then there may not be an easily identifiable pattern. It's also important to think about how the individual analyses work together. Do they all point to the same overall conclusion, or are the results more mixed? If the individual analyses seem to point to different conclusions, how do you make sense of these results?

Look again at Figure 3.3 and focus on the row representing individuals who strongly agree that "it is much better for everyone involved if the man is the achiever outside the home and the woman takes care of the home and family." In general, moving from 1977 to 2014 (that is, left to right across the top row of the table), the numbers tend to get smaller. There are of course some exceptions—for instance, from 1998 to 2000, there is an increase in the percentage of people who strongly agree—but in general the percentage of people who strongly agree has dropped over time. Similarly, the percentage of people who strongly disagree with the idea that "it is much better for everyone involved if the man is the achiever outside the home and the woman takes care of the home and family" has increased significantly over time. Whereas in 1977, only 5.9% of respondents strongly disagreed with this idea, by 2014 this percentage had more than tripled to 20.9% of respondents. In general, this table suggests that in the past 37 years, a greater proportion of adults in the US have come to see alternatives to the husband as breadwinner/wife as homemaker ideal.

Figure 3.4 reveals a very similar trend. The proportion of respondents who strongly believe that working moms can establish warm and secure relationships with their children just as much as moms who aren't working has increased significantly. Here again we see respondents increasingly likely to reject the inherent superiority of the breadwinner/homemaker ideal. Finally, Figure 3.5 shows that an increasingly large proportion of adults in the United States are not opposed to the idea of women being political leaders. While about 4% of adults surveyed in 2010 said they would not vote for a qualified woman for president, this percentage has been dropping steadily over the past 40 years. As in the previous two analyses, Figure 3.5 shows that survey respondents are becoming more and more likely to support women in nondomestic roles. There is increasing support for women's participation in the paid labor force as well as in political leadership. These attitudinal trends are likely related to the successes of the women's movement, increases in the percentages of women who are going to college and earning advanced degrees, and changes in the broader economy. Many families depend on women's incomes to make ends meet.

4. Consider limitations.

An important part of all scientific research is to be clear about the limitations of the research. Should the above analyses be understood as the unquestioned "final word" on how gender-related attitudes have changed over time? Of course not! Every research project has limitations, some more than others, and it is important to make these clear when interpreting the results.

When considering the limitations of any survey research project, it is important to consider the issues of survey design, possible sample biases, and generalizability. For example, the results here apply only to adults in the US who are aged 18 and older. For the majority of survey years (that is, from 1972 to 2004), the results included only those respondents who were able to speak English.

Finally, while it is crucial to explain what the analyses reveal about the larger research question ("How have beliefs about gender roles changed over the past four decades?"), it is often useful to clarify what the analyses do *not* tell us about the research question. Anticipate possible misinterpretations. Clarify what the findings suggest and what they don't suggest. For example, while the above analyses indicate that individuals are increasingly supportive of women's participation in the workforce and in politics, the analyses do *not* tell us about individuals' actual behavior. Figures 3.3 and 3.4 tell us about individuals' beliefs about working mothers—not about individuals' actual family arrangements. Similarly, Figure 3.5 reflects what individuals report about their willingness to vote for a qualified woman presidential candidate, not their actual voting behavior. In addition, some individuals' responses may be influenced by social desirability—some respondents may fear that, if they were to admit they wouldn't vote for a woman presidential candidate, it would make them look sexist (as indeed it would!). Because respondents know that a "Yes" response here is the socially desirable response, the responses may be biased in favor of this option. Finally, the analyses here focus on a very narrow range of gender inequality, and it would be a mistake to conclude, from these limited findings, that gender inequality is necessarily on the way out. These findings don't tell us anything about gendered and sexualized violence, representations of women and men in the media, gender segregation across occupations, or gender inequality in educational attainment or earnings. All that said, the findings do suggest that in the US, societal ideas about women's roles in the family, at work, and in politics have changed dramatically over the past four decades.

5. Summarize your conclusions.

Interpreting these results within a social justice framework requires thinking through issues of power and inequality, socially constructed differences, links between the micro and macro levels of society, and the importance of intersecting inequalities. Taken together, these analyses suggest that gender ideology, and in particular beliefs about how men and women should arrange their work and family lives, have changed significantly over the past four decades. In this way, the analyses speak to the social construction of gender. Far from being stable, our societal ideas about gender clearly change over time. To more fully understand these attitudinal changes, it would be useful to connect the changes we see in Figures 3.3 through 3.5 to the macro-level social, political, and economic changes that have occurred during the past four decades. Further analysis of the GSS data could also provide valuable information concerning how gender ideology differs for men and women, younger and older people, heterosexual and LGBTQ people, and other social groups.

EXERCISES

The following exercises use data from the General Social Survey to explore issues related to work–family balance. Some of the GSS questions focus on how respondents currently deal with the demands of work and family, which can often conflict with one another. Other questions focus on respondents' beliefs about policies, such as paid family leave, which is meant to help individuals balance their obligations as employees and family members.

Use the GSS and the SDA website to answer these questions.

1. What is the precise wording of the survey question that corresponds to the variable PAIDLV?

   a. Do you think there should be paid leave available and, if so, for how long?

   b. Do you currently have access to paid leave at work?

   c. Does your spouse currently have access to paid leave at work?

   d. To the best of your knowledge, does the Family and Medical Leave Act provide families with paid leave for childcare and elder care?

2. A score of 8 on the variable PAIDLV represents a response of:

   a. eight weeks of paid leave

   b. eight months of paid leave

   c. "Don't know"

   d. "No answer"

3. If we assume that gender influences individuals' beliefs about family leave, then in this model, we are assuming that gender is the _____ variable and beliefs about family leave are the _____ variable.

   a. dependent; independent

   b. independent; dependent

   c. Both are dependent variables.

   d. Both are independent variables.

4. Use the SDA to make a cross-tab that analyzes the relationship between the survey year (YEAR) and the variable PAIDLV. This cross-tab shows that the variable PAIDLV was included in the GSS in which survey years?

   a. 1972–2014

   b. 2002, 2008, and 2014

   c. 2010 and 2012

   d. only 2012

5. Use the SDA to make a crosstab that analyzes the relationship between respondents' gender (SEX) and the variable PAIDLV. Enter the variable SEX in the "Column" field and the variable PAIDLV in the "Row" field. Which of the following statements is true based on the cross-tab you constructed?

   a. For men, the modal category on the variable PAIDLV is 2.

   b. For women, the modal category on the variable PAIDLV is 2.

   c. The percentage of women who answered "Yes" is higher than the percentage of men who answered "Yes."

   d. 85.9% of those who answered "Yes" were women.

6. What is the precise wording of the survey question that corresponds to the variable CAREPROV?

   a. People have different views on childcare for children under school age. Who do you think should primarily provide childcare?

   b. Who is the primary care-taker for your children?

   c. Who was the primary care-taker for you when you were growing up?

   d. Do you agree or disagree with the following? "A working mother can establish just as warm and secure a relationship with her children as a mother who does not work."

7. Use the SDA to make a cross-tab that analyzes the relationship between respondents' gender (SEX) and the variable CAREPROV. Enter the variable SEX in the "Column" field and the variable CAREPROV in the "Row" field. What is the total (approximate) number of people represented in this cross-tab?

   a. 313

   b. 519

   c. 623

   d. 1121

8. Which of the following statements is true based on the cross-tab you constructed in the above question?

   a. The majority of men who provided valid answers to the question believed that family members should provide child care for children under school age.

   b. Women were more likely than men to report believing that family members should provide child care for children under school age.

   c. The modal response for women was that government agencies should provide child care for children under school age.

d. Women were more likely than men to have been personally raised by family members.

9. The variable ELDHELP corresponds with the survey question "Thinking about elderly people who need some help in their everyday lives, such as help with grocery shopping, cleaning the house, doing the laundry, etc., who do you think should primarily provide this help?" Figure 3.6 shows a cross-tab of this variable by respondents' gender. What is the correct interpretation of the "67.6" in the first row of this figure?

a. Approximately 68 women believed that family members should be the primary providers of help for elderly people.

b. 67.6 percent of women who provided valid responses to the survey question responded that family members should be the primary providers of help for elderly people.

c. Of those who believed that family members should be the primary providers of help for elderly people, 67.6% were women.

d. Compared with men, women were 67.6 times as likely to believe that family members should be the primary providers of help for elderly people.

10. Which of the following statements is true, according to Figure 3.6?

a. Women were more likely to believe that family members should be the primary providers of help for elderly people.

b. 69.7 percent of men who responded believed that family members should be the primary providers of help for elderly people.

c. Of those who believed that family members should be the primary providers of help for elderly people, 67.5% were men.

d. The number of men who have valid responses on the variable ELDHELP is larger than the number of women who have valid responses for this variable.

Figure 3.6

Frequency Distribution				
		SEX		
Cells contain: -**Column percent** -Weighted N		1 MALE	2 FEMALE	**ROW TOTAL**
ELDHELP	1: Family members	**69.7** 384.8	**67.6** 415.8	**68.6** 800.6
	2: Government agencies	**14.5** 80.3	**16.4** 101.1	**15.5** 181.4
	3: Non-profit organizations (e.g., charitable organizations, churches/religious organizations)	**9.1** 50.3	**6.0** 36.8	**7.5** 87.1
	4: Private providers of this kind of help	**6.7** 37.0	**10.0** 61.4	**8.4** 98.4
	COL TOTAL	**100.0** 552.4	**100.0** 615.1	**100.0** 1,167.6

ANALYSES & ESSAYS

1. *What sociodemographic characteristics are related to respondents' attitudes about abortion?* Identify one variable that you think plays a role in determining abortion-related attitudes. Identify three questions that assess respondents' attitudes about abortion. Construct three separate cross-tabs that examine how the sociodemographic characteristic you have chosen relates to these three abortion-related variables. Interpret your results, being sure to identify and describe the dependent and independent variables in each analysis.

2. *To what extent do men and women feel differently about the social and career consequences of having children?* Create three different cross-tab analyses, where SEX is the independent variable in each one and KIDSOCST, KIDJOB, and KIDFINBU are the different dependent variables. Interpret your results, giving particular attention to how your findings relate to gender as a social institution.

3. *To what extent do people of different class statuses feel differently about the social and career consequences of having children?* Create three different cross-tab analyses, where DEGREE is the independent

variable in each one and KIDSOCST, KIDJOB, and KIDFINBU are the different dependent variables. Interpret your results, giving particular attention to the intersections of social class, gender, and family.

4. *To what extent do men and women feel differently about guns and gun control?* Create three different cross-tab analyses, where SEX is the independent variable in each one and GUNSALES, GUNSDRNK, and GUNS911 are the different dependent variables. Interpret your results, giving particular attention to how and to what extent these analyses illustrate cultural ideas about femininity and masculinity.

5. *To what extent do men and women report different feelings about altruistic love?* In 2004, the GSS included a special module focusing on altruistic love. Create four different cross-tab analyses, where SEX is the independent variable in each one and AGAPE1, AGAPE2, AGAPE3, and AGAPE4 are the different dependent variables. Interpret your results, giving particular attention to how and to what extent these analyses illustrate cultural ideas about femininity and masculinity. You might also think about the issue of social desirability.

NOTES

1. Lorber, Judith. 1994. *Paradoxes of Gender.* New Haven, CT: Yale University Press; West, Candace, and Don H. Zimmerman. 1987. "Doing Gender." *Gender & Society* 1(2):125–51.
2. Lorber, *Paradoxes of Gender.*
3. Risman, Barbara J. 2004. "Gender as a Social Structure: Theory Wrestling with Activism." *Gender & Society* 18(4):429–50.
4. Lorber, *Paradoxes of Gender*, p. 1.
5. King, Helen. 1993. "Once Upon a Text: Hysteria from Hippocrates." Pp. 3–90 in *Hysteria Beyond Freud*, edited by S. L. Gilman, H. King, R. Porter, G. S. Rousseau, and E. Showalter. Berkeley: University of California Press.
6. See, for example, Halberstam, Judith. 1998. *Female Masculinity*. Durham, NC: Duke University Press; Kessler, Suzanne J. 1998. *Lessons from the Intersexed*. New Brunswick, NJ: Rutgers University

Press; Pascoe, C. J. 2005. "'Dude, You're a Fag': Adolescent Masculinity and the Fag Discourse." *Sexualities* 8:329–46; Risman, Barbara J. 1999. *Gender Vertigo: American Families in Transition*. New Haven, CT: Yale University Press.
7. For a more extended discussion of how gender binaries are reproduced in survey design and analysis, see Harnois, Catherine E. 2013. *Feminist Measures in Survey Research*. Thousand Oaks, CA: SAGE; Westbrook, Laurel, and Aliya Saperstein. 2015. "New Categories Are Not Enough: Rethinking the Measurement of Sex and Gender in Social Surveys." *Gender & Society* 29(4):534–60.
8. For more information on weighting options, see Chapter 2.
9. For more information, see http://www.icpsr .umich.edu/icpsrweb/content/SAMHDA/help/ helpan.htm#Tcolor.

CHAPTER 4

ANALYZING RACE AND ETHNICITY WITH THE GSS

INTRODUCTION: KEY CONCEPTS IN RACE AND ETHNICITY

One of the most important arguments in the sociology of race and ethnicity is that race is a social construct. While differences in skin color, hair texture, eye shape, and eye color certainly exist, society plays an important role in determining which differences we consider important (e.g., skin color or eye shape) and which we tend to overlook (e.g., shoe size or the presence or absence of freckles). The meanings that we attach (or fail to attach) to these differences are also deeply intertwined with our cultural beliefs and historical traditions as well as our religious, political, educational, and economic institutions. Indeed, many of the racial and ethnic differences that may appear natural, universal, or obvious are actually the result of these very institutions. Differences in phenotype may exist apart from society, but "racial groups," "racial identities," "racial ideologies," and "racial inequality" do not. When analyzing inequalities related to race and ethnicity, it is always important to remember that, rather than a biological and stable property of individuals, race and ethnicity are created and maintained through social processes.

There is an ongoing debate in the social sciences about how to best collect and analyze the data needed to document racial/ethnic inequalities without simultaneously essentializing racial difference.[1] One perspective argues that, by asking respondents about their racial identities, surveys reproduce and strengthen racial categories and ultimately perpetuate racial inequalities.[2] When an official survey asks people, "What race do you consider yourself to be?" it can make it seem as if racial groups are straightforward,

Learning Objectives

By the end of this chapter, you should be able to:

1. Identify variables related to race, ethnicity, and citizenship.

2. Produce a bivariate table, also called a *cross-tab*.

3. Use control variables to examine how the relationship between two variables may be influenced by a third.

4. Interpret these analyses within a social justice framework.

self-evident, and natural. It can make race seem like an essential, natural, and obvious characteristic of individuals rather than a socially constructed idea. Another perspective, the perspective advanced here, insists that asking respondents about their racial/ethnic identities in the context of surveys is important because if we stop collecting data about race—if social surveys no longer ask respondents how they identify with respect to racial and ethnic categories—then we lose much of our ability to track racial/ethnic inequalities. Without information about respondents' racial/ethnic identities, we would risk losing our collective ability to document wage inequality, inequality in graduation rates and other educational outcomes, and inequalities in incarceration and crime victimization, just to name a few. As the American Sociological Association (ASA) stated in its 2003 "Statement on the Importance of Collecting Data and Doing Social Scientific Research on Race,"

> sociological scholarship on "race" provides scientific evidence in the current scientific and civic debate over the social consequences of the existing categorizations and perceptions of race; allows scholars to document how race shapes social ranking, access to resources, and life experiences; and advances understanding of this important dimension of social life, which in turn advances social justice. *Refusing to acknowledge the fact of racial classification, feelings, and actions, and refusing to measure their consequences will not eliminate racial inequalities. At best, it will preserve the status quo.*[3]

In short, collecting survey data about racial/ethnic identities, attitudes, and inequalities can provide valuable tools for fighting for social justice—if the surveys are designed well and if the results are interpreted appropriately.

Fortunately for us, the GSS includes a large number of carefully crafted questions concerning race and ethnicity, and many of these questions can and have been used to document and challenge racial and ethnic inequalities. The GSS includes multiple indicators of respondents' racial identity and ethnic identity as well as questions concerning their ancestry. A number of other questions focus on attitudes and beliefs about racial inequality. There are also questions concerning the racial composition of respondents' friendship networks, the racial/ethnic composition of respondents' neighborhoods, experiences of racial/ethnic discrimination, and citizenship status.

This chapter provides an introduction to analyzing race and ethnicity in the General Social Survey, with a focus on the dimensions of race and ethnicity described above.

IDENTIFYING VARIABLES RELATED TO RACE AND ETHNICITY

The GSS has included numerous questions related to race and ethnicity since its beginning in 1972. Just as our national conversations about race, ethnicity, and citizenship have changed over the past four decades, so too have the questions included in the survey. Some questions concerning respondents' racial identity and ethnic background have been asked regularly since the survey's beginning, but new questions have been added regularly in response to political, social, and cultural events as well as the changing sociodemographic composition of US society.[4]

Chapter 2 presented an overview of how to search for variables using the SDA website. When using the GSS to analyze issues related to race and ethnicity, three key aspects of the survey design must be taken into consideration. First is that racial and ethnic identities are too complex to be assessed with a single survey question. As a result, the GSS has some questions that focus on race, others that focus on ethnicity, and a handful of questions that combine the two. The variable RACE, for example, indicates respondents' racial status but makes no distinction between white respondents who identify as ethnically Mexican and those who identify as Irish American.

The variable ETHNIC asks respondents, "From what countries or part of the world did your ancestors come?" and includes response categories like "Germany," "Africa," "French Canada," "Other Canada," "China," "Czechoslovakia," "England," and "Wales." While this variable includes more detailed response categories, it is nonetheless limited in some important ways. The variable ETHNIC tells us nothing about how central these ethnic identities are to the respondent's sense of self, nor does it give us a clear picture of when the respondent's family came to the US. A further limitation to the variable ETHNIC is that it lumps together people of "African" descent while providing a much greater level of nuance for people with European ancestry. In response to these limitations, researchers often use information from multiple variables to construct new variables with greater levels of nuance.

A second key point to remember is that the variables concerning racial and ethnic identities have changed significantly over time. As explained on the GSS homepage, "until 2000, the GSS measured race mostly by interviewer observation" using the variable RACE, which is coded into three broad categories: "White," "Black," and "Other." Interviewers who were "in doubt" about a respondent's race were instructed to ask the respondent, "What race do you consider yourself?"[5] This approach to asking about race has some very clear limitations. First, this design strategy rests on the assumption that interviewers can, in most cases, accurately determine someone's racial identity simply by looking at them. This approach seems to rest upon, and to perpetuate, the idea that race is an essential, stable, and obvious characteristic of individuals rather than a socially constructed system of inequality. A second limitation concerns the response categories of "White," "Black," and "Other." Obviously, the "Other" category includes a very wide range of individuals: people who describe themselves as Chinese American, Latinos and Latinas, Native Americans, and biracial and multiracial people, to name a few. Combining these diverse groups into a single category, "Other," makes it difficult to examine the differences among these groups. Moreover, the clear focus on Black and White racial groups seems to marginalize non-Black minorities, which is particularly problematic, given the increasing percentage of the US population who identify as Latino/a, as Asian American, or with multiple racial/ethnic groups.

To address some of these limitations, beginning in 2002, the GSS included a new procedure for measuring race and ethnicity, following the procedures used in the US Census of 2000.[6] From this point forward, the survey asked all respondents, "What is your race? Indicate one or more races that you consider yourself to be." The GSS records up to three racial/ethnic groups mentioned by the respondent, and these groups are recorded in the variables RACECEN1, RACECEN2, and RACECEN3. For surveys from 2002 and later, the value of the variable RACE has been imputed based on how respondents answered RACCEN1 and other information.

A third key feature of the survey design, noted in Chapter 2, is that the GSS was administered to both English- and Spanish-speaking respondents beginning in 2006. This change is important because it significantly increased the percentage of respondents who identified as Hispanic and/or Latino/a. While between 2000 and 2004, approximately 9% of respondents identified as Hispanic, Latino, or Latina, this number increased to approximately 15% in 2006 and the following years. By allowing non-English-speaking Spanish speakers to participate in the GSS, the surveys from 2006 onward more fully represent the diverse experiences of Latinos and Latinas in the United States.

In addition to the three key design issues noted above, several other features of the survey are worth noting here. First, it is important to remember that the GSS is a survey that includes both US citizens and non-US citizens living in the United States. The variable CITIZEN asks respondents about whether they are citizens of America, though this variable is asked only to a subsample of respondents and was included only in years 1996, 2004, and 2014.[7] Second, as discussed in Chapter 2, the survey design includes a deliberate oversample of African American respondents in years 1982 and 1987. For these years in particular, the percentage of survey respondents who identified as Black or African American was higher than the percentage of people who identified with these groups in the general population. And finally, as also discussed in Chapter 2, it is important to remember that the GSS is administered only to individuals who are not currently living in institutions. To the extent that racial/ethnic minority groups are overrepresented in institutions such as prisons, jails, and homeless shelters, the survey likely gives us a more positive representation of racial/ethnic minorities' experiences than exists in the general population.

Despite the limitations mentioned above, the GSS remains a valuable tool for analyzing inequalities related to race and ethnicity. Given the number of questions pertaining to issues of race and ethnicity and the additional questions being developed for each new survey, the opportunities for analyzing racial and ethnic inequalities with the GSS are virtually limitless. As is the case with all research projects, however, it is important to communicate the limitations of your data and analysis along with your results.

Searching for Variables Related to Race and Ethnicity

The first step in identifying variables related to race, ethnicity, and multiculturalism is to brainstorm possible key words. *Race* and *ethnicity* are good starting points, but consider some others: *white, Hispanic, Black, color, African American, Asian, racial, ethnic, citizen, immigrant, immigration, language, minorities, country, family origin.*

WHOSE RACE AND ETHNICITY?

As you search for variables using the key word *race* or *ethnicity*, you will come across variables that ask about the respondents' racial/ethnic identities. Make note, however, that there are also variables that ask about the respondents' spouses' racial/ethnic identity as well as the racial/ethnic identities of respondents' friends, neighbors, and coworkers. The variables INTRACE1 ("What is your race?

Indicate one or more races that you consider yourself to be") and INTETHN ("*race of the interviewer*") do not correspond to the race or ethnicity of the respondent! These variables pertain to the interviewer, not the interviewee. Be careful not to mix them up. And always "view" a variable before analyzing it to make sure that you know exactly what the variable represents.

Browsing for Variables Related to Race and Ethnicity

Another approach for identifying variables related to race and ethnicity is to "browse" for variables using the online codebook. There are several headings that deal specifically with race, ethnicity, and multiculturalism, but several of the other sections include relevant variables as well.

If you are interested in browsing for variables related to race and ethnicity, you may find the following subject headings and subheadings to be particularly useful:

- Respondent Background Variables
    - Age, Gender, Race, and Ethnicity

- Personal Concerns
    - Race Issues

- Controversial Social Issues
    - Race Part Two
    - Social Issues Scales

- Obligations and Responsibilities
    - Government Responsibility

In addition, a number of special modules have been included that focus on issues of race, ethnicity, and multiculturalism. While the variables topics below are included in only a handful of survey years, analyses of these variables can provide a particularly nuanced analysis of attitudes and beliefs about race, ethnicity, and multiculturalism.

- 1985: Social Networks
- 1987: Social and Political Participation
- 1990: Inter-group Relations
- 1994: Multiculturalism
- 2000: Multi-ethnic United States
- 2002: Prejudice
- 2004: Immigration
- 2004: National Identity
- 2004: Citizenship
- 2012: Jewish Identity
- 2012: Skin Tone
- 2014: National Identity III
- 2014: Citizenship

Remember that there are many variables related to race and ethnicity that occur outside the subject headings mentioned above. By browsing through the codebook and searching for terms related to race and ethnicity, you should be able to find hundreds of survey questions directly related to race and ethnicity.

COMBINING RACE AND HISPANIC ETHNICITY

The variable RACEHISP, which is included from the 2000 survey onward, combines information from the variables RACE and HISPANIC to create a variable about respondents' racial/ethnic identity with four response categories: "White," "Black," "Hispanic," and "Other." In this variable, the category "White" does not include those who said they were Hispanic, and the category "Hispanic" does not include those who said they were Black. When viewing the variable in SDA, the response categories appear to be "White," "Black," "Hispanic," and "Other." When analyzing this variable and writing up your results, be sure to specify that "White" refers to "non-Hispanic whites," "Hispanic" refers to "non-Black Hispanics," and "Black" refers to "Blacks and African Americans, both Hispanic and non-Hispanic."

Viewing a Variable

Once you have identified potential variables to analyze, the next step is to "view" the variable so that you can determine exactly what survey question the variable represents. Viewing a variable in SDA is easy and is discussed in detail in Chapter 2. From the GSS SDA homepage, simply type the variable name into the "Variable Selection" field (this is in the upper left corner) and then click "View." A new window will open, in which you will find (in almost all cases) the exact wording of the question as well as the frequency distribution of the responses. Remember that when you view a variable in this way, the resulting frequency distribution shows the combined responses from *all* survey years in which the question was asked.

For example, Figure 4.1 shows the frequency distribution for the variable that results from viewing the variable IMMIMP. By viewing this variable, we can see that it assesses respondents' beliefs about immigration. In particular, the survey asks respondents, "How much do you agree or disagree with each of the following statements? a. Immigrants improve American society by bringing in new ideas and cultures."

Figure 4.1

IMMIMP   IMMIGRANTS IMPROVE AMERICAN SOCIETY

Description of the Variable

1461. There are different opinions about immigrants from other countries living in America. (By "immigrants" we mean people who come to settle in America.) How much do you agree or disagree with each of the following statements? a. Immigrants improve American society by bringing in new ideas and cultures

Percent	N	Value	Label
10.0	119	1	AGREE STRONGLY
47.2	563	2	AGREE
24.7	294	3	NEITHER AGREE NOR DISAGREE
14.8	176	4	DISAGREE
3.4	40	5	DISAGREE STRONGLY
	58,383	0	IAP
	23	8	CANT CHOOSE
	1	9	NA
100.0	**59,599**		**Total**

From this frequency distribution, we can see that 10% of respondents strongly agreed with the idea that immigrants improve American society, and another 47.2% agreed with this idea. Nearly a quarter of respondents neither agreed nor disagreed, and less than 20% disagreed. (For more information on how to interpret a frequency distribution, please review Chapter 2.)

An important limitation of viewing the variable in this way is that it does not provide information about *when* this variable was included in the GSS. The data could potentially have been collected anywhere between 1972 and 2014, or at multiple years within this time frame. To determine when the data were collected, it is necessary to construct a bivariate table. Bivariate tables, also called cross-tabulations or "cross-tabs" for short, will also allow us to assess the characteristics associated with beliefs about the effect of immigration on American society.

PRODUCING AND INTERPRETING A BIVARIATE TABLE OR "CROSS-TAB"

Background

Knowing how to produce and critically interpret a meaningful bivariate table is one of the most important tools of data analysis. Bivariate simply means "two variables," and bivariate tables are used to explore the relationship between two variables. If we were interested in knowing whether white, Black, and Hispanic adults report similar levels of home ownership, for example, we could make a cross-tab using the variables DWELOWN—"(Do you/Does your family) own your (home/apartment), pay rent, or what?"—and RACEHISP to explore this relationship. We could also examine the racial/ethnic differences in beliefs about racial inequality by analyzing the variables RACEHISP and WRKWAYUP. WRKWAYUP corresponds to the survey question "Do you agree strongly, agree somewhat, neither agree nor disagree, disagree somewhat, or disagree strongly with the following statement? Irish, Italians, Jewish and many other minorities overcame prejudice and worked their way up. [Blacks should do the same without special favors.]"[8]

Before creating a bivariate table, it is useful to consider whether you believe the relationship you are investigating is a causal relationship or if the relationship would be better understood as a correlation. (See Chapter 1 for a more in-depth discussion of causation and correlation.) In a causal relationship, the variable doing the causing is termed the independent variable and the variable that is affected is the dependent variable. In other words, the dependent variable is thought to depend on the independent variable.

In an analysis of racial/ethnic differences in home ownership, for example, respondents' racial/ethnic status would be the independent variable and home ownership would be the dependent variable. To the extent that a relationship between these two variables exists, it is racial/ethnic status that influences home ownership and not the other way around. Similarly, in an analysis of what whites, Blacks, Hispanics, and other racial/ethnic groups believe about the extent of racial inequality in the US, racial/ethnic status would be the independent variable and beliefs about racial inequality would be the dependent variable.

When testing for racial/ethnic differences in experiences, beliefs, attitudes, identities, and other social phenomena, racial/ethnic status will generally be the independent variable. The experiences, beliefs, attitudes, and identities that you believe will differ for people who hold different racial/ethnic identities will be dependent variables.

Creating a Cross-Tab in SDA

To produce a bivariate table in SDA, first make sure that you are on the "Analysis" section of the SDA website. In the upper left corner of the SDA page, click on the "Analysis" button.

The screen should look like Figure 4.2.

The left-hand side of the screen shows the codebook, and the right side is used to conduct the analysis. In cases where you believe there is a causal relationship, enter the name of your dependent variable in the "Row" field and the name of the independent variable in the "Column" field.

Let's use the example of racial/ethnic differences in home ownership as an example. Whether respondents own or rent their homes can be assessed with the variable DWELOWN: "(Do you/Does your family) own your (home/apartment), pay rent, or what?" This is a nominal-level variable and has been included regularly in the GSS,

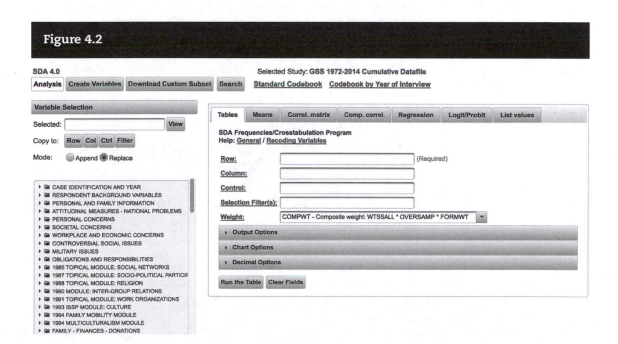

Figure 4.2

beginning in 1985. If we are interested in knowing whether homeownership differs across racial/ethnic groups, DWELOWN is the dependent variable and RACEHISP is the independent variable.

In the "Weight" field, you will see that the default setting for weights is "COMPWT - Composite weight WTSSALL *Oversamp* FORMWT." To replicate the analyses as presented in this chapter, keep this selection as is.[9]

Enter the dependent variable, DWELOWN, in the "Row" field and your independent variable, RACEHISP, in the "Column" field, and then click the "Run the Table" button. A new window will appear that presents the cross-tab. Figure 4.3 shows the resulting cross-tab.

Figure 4.3

	Variables					
Role	**Name**	**Label**	**Range**	**MD**	**Dataset**
Row	**DWELOWN**	DOES R OWN OR RENT HOME?	1-3	0,8,9	1
Column	**RACEHISP**	Race with Hispanic (2000 and later)	1-4	9	1
Weight	**COMPWT**	Composite weight = WTSSALL * OVERSAMP * FORMWT	.1913-11.1261		1

	Frequency Distribution					
Cells contain: **-Column percent** -Weighted N		**RACEHISP**				
		1 White	2 Black	3 Hispanic	4 Other	**ROW TOTAL**
DWELOWN	1: OWN OR IS BUYING	**74.3** 5,847.2	**46.8** 730.4	**48.4** 657.8	**56.1** 297.1	**66.5** 7,532.5
	2: PAYS RENT	**24.0** 1,886.9	**51.7** 806.8	**49.8** 677.0	**42.1** 222.9	**31.7** 3,593.6
	3: OTHER	**1.8** 139.0	**1.4** 22.6	**1.8** 23.8	**1.8** 9.8	**1.7** 195.1
	COL TOTAL	100.0 7,873.1	100.0 1,559.7	100.0 1,358.5	100.0 529.8	**100.0** 11,321.2

Color coding:	<-2.0	<-1.0	<0.0	>0.0	>1.0	>2.0	**Z**
N in each cell:	Smaller than expected			Larger than expected			

Interpreting a Cross-Tab

The window that appears contains three main parts. First is a description of the variables used in the analysis (labeled "Variables"), followed by the cross-tab (labeled "Frequency Distribution"). Below the cross-tab is a chart that gives a visual representation of the information presented in the cross-tab.

The "Variables" section, at the top, presents a summary of the analyses that follow, including variable names and short variable descriptions (variable labels). The "Variables" section also includes the range of valid response categories ("Range") and the response categories that correspond to nonvalid values ("MD" or "Missing Data").

The "Frequency Distribution" section shows your bivariate table. In the upper left corner of the frequency distribution chart, we see that the cells contain "column percents" and the number of cases (N) in each cell. Let's first look at those cells that are red or blue. The dark red cell in the upper left corner contains two numbers: 74.3 and 5,847.2. The N of 5,847.2 indicates that about 5,847 respondents in the GSS self-identified as non-Hispanic whites and also either owned their home outright or were in the process of paying off their home mortgage.

INTERPRETING THE "N" IN A CROSS-TAB THAT USES WEIGHTS

Recall that N stands for "number of respondents." While the number of respondents would typically be a whole number, the use of survey weights makes a slight adjustment to these numbers to make the results better reflect the US adult population. See Chapter 2 for a more detailed discussion of survey weights.

To the immediate right, we see a dark blue cell that contains the numbers 46.8 and 730.4. This tells us that about 730 respondents in the GSS identified as African American or Black and indicates that they too were in the process of paying off their mortgage or owned their home outright. Comparing the two Ns, we can see that far more white respondents owned their homes than did Black or African American respondents. These numbers can be misleading, however, because the number of non-Hispanic white people included in this analysis (7,873) was much greater than the number of Black or African American people included (1,560).

In addition to the number of cases in each cell (N), the cross-tab provides the column percents for each cell. Column percents are calculated by dividing the number of cases in a given cell by the total number of cases in each column and then multiplying the resulting proportion by 100. So, in the upper left corner, the column percent of 74.3 is calculated in the following way:

$$(5847.2 / 7873.1) * 100 = 74.3\%$$

The column percent tells us the percentage of individuals in each category of the column variable who fall into each category of the row variable. In this case, of the approximately 7,873 non-Hispanic white respondents, 74.3% reported that they were homeowners. The cell to the right indicates that about 46.8% of African American respondents indicated that they were homeowners. This number is calculated by dividing the total number of African Americans who answered the question by the number of African Americans who said they were homeowners:

$$(730.4 / 1559.7) * 100 = 46.8\%$$

The table also shows us that 48.4% of non-Black Hispanic respondents were in the process of paying off their mortgage or already owned their home outright. Of those respondents who identified with an "Other" racial/ethnic group, 56.1% owned their home or were in the process of paying off their mortgage.

The row totals at the far right-hand side of the table tell us the overall distribution of the row variable (DWELOWN). Taken on the whole, including people of all racial/ethnic groups, about 7,532 respondents indicated that they owned, or were in the process of buying, their homes, and this number corresponds to 66.5% of the total number of respondents:

$$(7532.5 / 11321.2) * 100 = 66.5\%$$

The column totals in the bottom row of the table tell us the overall distribution of the variable in the column (RACEHISP). Reading across the bottom row of the table, we see that approximately 7,873 respondents were non-Hispanic whites, about 1,560 were Black or African American, 1,358 were non-Black Hispanics, and about 530 were people who identified with other racial/ethnic groups.

The bottom right corner of the table shows a percentage of 100 and an N of approximately 11,321. This number corresponds to the total number of respondents included in the table. *Because we have not specified any specific time period for this analysis, the resulting bivariate table is drawing from all available data, anywhere from 1972 to 2014.* If we wanted to focus on a specific time period, we could use the "Filter" option in SDA, which is described below.

When we look at the percentages in the cross-tab, some big differences can be seen. For instance, 24% of whites indicate that they are currently renting their homes, but the percentages of Blacks and Hispanics who are renting are 51.7 and 49.8, respectively. In other words, compared to non-Hispanic whites, Blacks and Hispanics are more than twice as likely to be renters.

WHAT DO THE COLORS IN A BIVARIATE TABLE MEAN?

When you produce a cross-tab, you will notice that the cells are different shades of blue and red. These colors are meant to help analysts to identify patterns in the data and provide an indication of whether the relationship between two variables is statistically significant. The color of each cell reflects the Z-statistic, which shows whether the frequencies in a cell are greater or fewer than we would expect if there were no relationship between the variables in the general population.[10]

Again, because we have not yet limited the analysis to a particular time period, the analysis of racial/ethnic differences in homeownership (shown in Figure 4.3) combines information from every year in which data for the variables RACEHISP and DWELOWN are available. But let's imagine that we are interested in what's been happening more recently.

Applying a Filter

To limit the analysis so that it includes data from only recent years, add a **filter** by typing the following into the "Selection Filter" field:

YEAR (2010-2014)

To make a cross-tab of the variables DWELOWN and RACEHISP that focuses on data from 2010 to 2014, now type the variable DWELOWN into the row field and RACEHISP into the column field. Remember to keep the default of COMPWT in the "Weight" field. The resulting cross-tab is shown below in Figure 4.4. Notice that the table now includes a row for "Filter," which reminds us that the analysis includes only data from the 2010 to 2014 surveys. In this particular case, the results from our original analysis (Figure 4.3) are very similar to our results that use the filter. This is not always the case!

Filters can be used to limit the analysis to data from a particular time period (as shown above), but they can also be used to limit the analysis to particular social groups, to people within a specific age range, to those who identify with particular political parties, or to people who reside in particular types of communities.

When presented with the above analysis, a critical researcher might say something like, "The discrepancy between homeownership isn't so much about racial/ethnic

Figure 4.4

		Variables			
Role	**Name**	**Label**	**Range**	**MD**	**Dataset**
Row	**DWELOWN**	DOES R OWN OR RENT HOME?	1-3	0,8,9	1
Column	**RACEHISP**	Race with Hispanic (2000 and later)	1-4	9	1
Weight	**COMPWT**	Composite weight = WTSSALL * OVERSAMP * FORMWT	.1913-11.1261		1
Filter	**YEAR(2010-2014)**	GSS YEAR FOR THIS RESPONDENT	1972-2014		1

Frequency Distribution						
Cells contain: -**Column percent** -Weighted N		**RACEHISP**				
		1 White	2 Black	3 Hispanic	4 Other	**ROW TOTAL**
DWELOWN	1: OWN OR IS BUYING	**73.4** 2,122.9	**45.3** 295.7	**46.3** 295.8	**56.0** 120.8	**64.4** 2,835.3
	2: PAYS RENT	**25.2** 728.0	**53.8** 350.7	**51.4** 328.3	**41.8** 90.3	**34.0** 1,497.3
	3: OTHER	**1.5** 41.9	**.9** 6.0	**2.2** 14.3	**2.2** 4.7	**1.5** 66.9
	COL TOTAL	**100.0** 2,892.9	**100.0** 652.4	**100.0** 638.3	**100.0** 215.9	**100.0** 4,399.5

Color coding:	<-2.0	<-1.0	<0.0	>0.0	>1.0	>2.0	**Z**
N in each cell:	Smaller than expected			Larger than expected			

inequality but rather a reflection of the fact that racial/ethnic minorities are more likely than whites to reside in large cities, and in urban areas, people tend to rent more frequently." This critical researcher makes a reasonable point. Would the inequality we see in homeownership in Figure 4.4 remain if we were to examine only those living in large cities or only those living in small towns? Using a second filter can help us to answer this question.

By viewing the variable XNORCSIZ, we can see that this variable corresponds to the size of the town or city in which the respondent lives and that the value of "1" for this variable represents a city with a population of greater than 250,000 people. To examine whether racial/ethnic differences in homeownership persist when only those respondents who live in big cities are included, begin by entering DWELOWN in the "Row" field and the variable RACEHISP in the "Column" field. In the "Selection Filter" field, type:

YEAR (2010-2014) XNORCSIZ (1)

This filter will restrict the analysis to data collected between 2010 and 2014 and will now include only those respondents who lived in cities with populations greater than 250,000 people.

Figure 4.5 shows the resulting analysis. Notice that there are now two rows for filters and that the total number of cases in the table has been significantly reduced. In Figure 4.4, approximately 4,400 people were included in the analysis. Because we include only people living in large cities in Figure 4.5, the analysis is now restricted to approximately 790 people.

Figure 4.5 shows that, even when the analysis is focused only on those living in cities of more than 250,000 people, racial/ethnic differences in homeownership persist. Among non-Hispanic white respondents, the majority (61.4%) either own their home outright or are in the process of paying off their mortgage. Among Black and Hispanic respondents, the rate of homeownership is much lower (36.8% and 33.4%, respectively). For those respondents who live in big cities and who identify with other racial/ethnic groups, the rate of home ownership (61.1%) is similar to that of non-Hispanic whites.

For many people, the cross-tab above raises more questions than it answers. For example:

1. What factors in addition to respondents' racial/ethnic status might be influencing homeownership?

2. How might rates of homeownership differ for men and women of diverse racial/ethnic groups?

3. Does the unequal access to homeownership that we see here remain when we control for differences in education?

The first of these questions can be answered by constructing additional cross-tabs using DWELOWN as the dependent variable and including independent variables like DEGREE (highest degree earned), MARITAL (respondent's marital status), and SEX (respondent's gender). The second and third questions above can be assessed with control variables, which are discussed below.

Figure 4.5

Variables					
Role	**Name**	**Label**	**Range**	**MD**	**Dataset**
Row	**DWELOWN**	DOES R OWN OR RENT HOME?	1-3	0,8,9	1
Column	**RACEHISP**	Race with Hispanic (2000 and later)	1-4	9	1
Weight	**COMPWT**	Composite weight = WTSSALL * OVERSAMP * FORMWT	.1913-11.1261		1
Filter	**YEAR(2010-2014)**	GSS YEAR FOR THIS RESPONDENT	1972-2014		1
Filter	**XNORCSIZ(1)**	EXPANDED N.O.R.C. SIZE CODE(=CITY GT 250000)	1-10	0	1

Frequency Distribution						
Cells contain: -**Column percent** -Weighted N		**RACEHISP**				**ROW TOTAL**
		1 White	2 Black	3 Hispanic	4 Other	
DWELOWN	1: OWN OR IS BUYING	61.4 201.3	36.8 71.0	33.4 69.7	61.1 36.8	**48.0** 378.7
	2: PAYS RENT	37.5 122.8	62.1 119.9	64.4 134.4	38.1 23.0	**50.7** 400.1
	3: OTHER	1.1 3.6	1.1 2.1	2.3 4.7	.8 .5	**1.4** 10.9
	COL TOTAL	**100.0** 327.7	**100.0** 192.9	**100.0** 208.9	**100.0** 60.2	**100.0** 789.7

Applying Control Variables

A **control variable** is an independent variable that is included in the analysis in order to determine whether a relationship between two variable holds true when variation in a third variable (that is, the control variable) is held constant.

In the above example, we first examined the relationship between respondents' racial/ethnic group and their status as homeowners (Figure 4.4). We saw vast differences in homeownership across racial/ethnic groups and concluded that non-Hispanic whites were significantly more likely than African Americans, Hispanics, or other racial/ethnic minorities to own homes. In Figure 4.5, we then examined whether this relationship held true when only those respondents who were living in large cities were included in the analysis. But what about people living in medium-sized cities and small towns? We could rerun the analyses of RACEHISP and DWELOWN several times, each time using a different value for the filter value. We could start with the filter "XNORCSIZ (1)," and then replace that filter with "XNORCSIZ (2)," and then replace that filter with "XNORCSIZ (3)," and so forth.

A more efficient strategy is to use XNORCSIZ as a control variable rather than as a filter. To do this, simply enter DWELOWN in the "Row" field and RACEHISP in the "Column" field. Enter the variable XNORCSIZ in the "Control" field. In the "Selection Filter" field, keep the filter for YEAR (2010–2014). Run the table, and in the window that opens, you will see 11 bivariate tables, each followed by a bar chart. Each table examines the relationship between the main independent variable (RACEHISP) and the dependent variable (DWELOWN), but these tables show the relationship between these two variables, *holding community size (XNORCSIZ) constant*. The first table you see should be identical to that shown in Figure 4.5. Below that, the second table shows the racial/ethnic differences in homeownership in medium-sized cities (with populations of 50,000 to 250,000), as shown in Figure 4.6. The third shows this relationship for people living in the suburbs of large cities (Figure 4.7), and so forth. Scrolling all the way down, the last table will show a summary table with a cross-tab identical to that shown in Figure 4.4.

As you make your way through these tables, you may notice that the number of respondents in each table varies. This is because more people live in big cities and in

Figure 4.6

Statistics for XNORCSIZ = 2(CITY,50-250000)						
Cells contain: **-Column percent** -Weighted N		**RACEHISP**				
		1 White	2 Black	3 Hispanic	4 Other	*ROW TOTAL*
DWELOWN	1: OWN OR IS BUYING	**62.8** 252.9	**38.6** 48.3	**58.5** 68.4	**42.0** 13.4	*56.6* *383.0*
	2: PAYS RENT	**35.2** 141.7	**60.8** 76.1	**40.0** 46.8	**58.0** 18.5	*41.8* *283.0*
	3: OTHER	**2.0** 8.0	**.7** .8	**1.5** 1.8	**.0** .0	*1.6* *10.6*
	COL TOTAL	*100.0* 402.5	*100.0* 125.2	*100.0* 117.0	*100.0* 31.9	*100.0* 676.6

Figure 4.7

Statistics for XNORCSIZ = 3(SUBURB, LRG CITY)						
Cells contain: -**Column percent** -Weighted N		**RACEHISP**				
		1 White	2 Black	3 Hispanic	4 Other	**ROW TOTAL**
DWELOWN	1: OWN OR IS BUYING	**72.8** 428.4	**47.1** 60.8	**49.9** 85.6	**62.5** 35.5	**64.5** 610.4
	2: PAYS RENT	**26.5** 156.1	**51.8** 66.9	**48.5** 83.3	**37.5** 21.3	**34.6** 327.6
	3: OTHER	**.6** 3.6	**1.1** 1.4	**1.6** 2.8	**.0** .0	**.8** 7.8
	COL TOTAL	**100.0** 588.2	**100.0** 129.1	**100.0** 171.7	**100.0** 56.8	**100.0** 945.8

the suburbs of big cities than in small towns. Notice also that the pattern of racial/ethnic inequality in homeownership remains similar throughout each of these tables. The percentages of whites, African Americans, Hispanics, and other minorities who own their homes vary a little depending on the size of town or city considered. In almost all cases, however, non-Hispanic whites show significantly higher rates of homeownership than Hispanics, Blacks, and other racial/ethnic minorities. In other words, racial/ethnic disparities in home ownership persist, even when controlling for differences in community size.

APPLICATION: IS EDUCATION ASSOCIATED WITH BELIEFS ABOUT RACIAL INEQUALITY?

This application uses a series of cross-tabs to examine the relationship between respondents' educational attainment and their beliefs about racial inequality. While respondents' educational attainment and beliefs about racial/ethnic inequality can both be assessed with multiple variables, here we focus on the variables DEGREE and WRKWAYUP.

Step 1. Restate the research question and identify the independent and dependent variables.

The research question is "How and to what extent is educational attainment related to beliefs about racial inequality?" The dependent variable, beliefs about racial inequality, is measured with the variable WRKWAYUP. The independent variable is DEGREE—respondents' highest educational degree.

Step 2. View each variable to make sure it means what you think it means. By viewing the variable, you can see the precise wording of the survey question that corresponds to the variable.

By viewing the variable WRKWAYUP, we can see that this is an ordinal-level variable corresponding to the following survey question:

> Do you agree strongly, agree somewhat, neither agree nor disagree, disagree somewhat, or disagree strongly with the following statement? Irish, Italian, Jewish and many other minorities overcame prejudice and worked their way up. [Blacks should do the same without special favors.]

The variable DEGREE is a special case where viewing the variable does not reveal the exact survey question because the variable values were based on respondents' answers to multiple other questions.[11] DEGREE is an ordinal-level variable with five categories ranging from 0, which represents less than a high school degree, to 4, which represents a graduate degree.

Step 3. Determine which time period the data is from and choose a selection filter based on the time frame you wish to analyze. Remember that when you view a variable, you are viewing the combined data across all survey years for which there are data. If the question was asked regularly since 1972, this is four decades of data. If the question was asked only once—say, in 1985—then we could still analyze the data, but we would want to specify that the data are more than 30 years old. It is thus always crucial to determine the survey years in which the variable you are analyzing was included.

The easiest way to do this is by creating a quick cross-tab of the variables in your analysis by the variable YEAR (the variable that corresponds to the survey year). Producing a cross-tab with WRKWAYUP in the "Row" field and YEAR in the "Column" field (with COMPWT selected in the "Weight" field) will result in Figure 4.8.

As shown in Figure 4.8, the variable WRKWAYUP has been included in the GSS regularly since 1994. Unless we limit our analysis to recent data using the "Filter" command, the resulting cross-tabs will be drawing from all of this data.

DEGREE is also a core variable in the GSS and is included with every survey year. To double-check, simply produce a cross-tab of the variable DEGREE by the variable YEAR.

For this exercise, let's limit the analysis to very recent years: 2012 and 2014.

Step 4. Conduct the relevant analysis. Create a cross-tab of the variable WRKWAYUP by the variable DEGREE with a selection filter for YEAR (2012-2014). When examining how respondents' beliefs about racial inequality are shaped by respondents' educational attainment, we are assuming that beliefs about racial

Figure 4.8

Frequency Distribution (WRKWAYUP)

Cells contain:
- **Column percent**
- Weighted N

	YEAR											ROW TOTAL
	1994	1996	1998	2000	2002	2004	2006	2008	2010	2012	2014	
1: AGREE STRONGLY	**44.7** / 638.1	**44.7** / 866.4	**42.4** / 777.7	**44.3** / 808.4	**47.7** / 425.0	**41.0** / 365.3	**44.6** / 873.7	**44.4** / 586.3	**41.1** / 582.9	**41.7** / 535.1	**39.4** / 651.0	**43.3** / 7,110.1
2: AGREE SOMEWHAT	**30.1** / 429.2	**28.9** / 560.6	**30.7** / 563.8	**28.5** / 519.6	**26.5** / 235.9	**27.7** / 246.7	**29.0** / 568.9	**30.2** / 399.1	**30.7** / 436.1	**29.1** / 373.4	**29.0** / 478.5	**29.3** / 4,811.8
3: NEITHER AGREE NOR DISAGREE	**10.1** / 144.5	**11.7** / 227.1	**12.8** / 234.9	**11.0** / 200.5	**12.7** / 113.2	**15.5** / 138.2	**13.0** / 253.7	**12.6** / 166.5	**13.1** / 186.4	**14.5** / 185.9	**14.9** / 246.8	**12.8** / 2,097.7
4: DISAGREE SOMEWHAT	**9.7** / 138.0	**9.2** / 178.7	**8.4** / 153.5	**9.4** / 170.7	**7.5** / 66.4	**10.6** / 94.7	**8.4** / 164.4	**7.9** / 104.7	**8.6** / 121.3	**9.1** / 117.0	**10.0** / 165.7	**9.0** / 1,475.2
5: DISAGREE STRONGLY	**5.4** / 76.3	**5.4** / 104.3	**5.8** / 106.2	**6.9** / 126.3	**5.6** / 49.6	**5.1** / 45.7	**5.0** / 98.6	**4.8** / 63.5	**6.5** / 92.4	**5.5** / 70.6	**6.7** / 110.7	**5.7** / 944.2
COL TOTAL	**100.0** / 1,426.2	**100.0** / 1,937.0	**100.0** / 1,836.0	**100.0** / 1,825.6	**100.0** / 890.2	**100.0** / 890.7	**100.0** / 1,959.3	**100.0** / 1,320.2	**100.0** / 1,419.2	**100.0** / 1,282	**100.0** / 1,652.7	**100.0** / 16,439

Figure 4.9

Frequency Distribution							
		DEGREE					
Cells contain: **-Column percent** -Weighted N		0 LT HIGH SCHOOL	1 HIGH SCHOOL	2 JUNIOR COLLEGE	3 BACHELOR	4 GRADUATE	*ROW TOTAL*
WRKWAYUP	1: AGREE STRONGLY	**40.8** 153.9	**46.2** 689.7	**49.2** 113.4	**28.7** 155.1	**25.3** 74.1	*40.4* *1,186.2*
	2: AGREE SOMEWHAT	**33.6** 126.8	**29.1** 435.4	**25.7** 59.3	**29.8** 160.8	**23.7** 69.6	*29.0* *851.9*
	3: NEITHER AGREE NOR DISAGREE	**14.0** 52.9	**13.1** 195.0	**15.1** 34.8	**19.1** 103.1	**16.0** 46.9	*14.7* *432.6*
	4: DISAGREE SOMEWHAT	**7.3** 27.6	**7.2** 108.2	**4.9** 11.3	**13.4** 72.6	**21.5** 63.1	*9.6* *282.7*
	5: DISAGREE STRONGLY	**4.2** 15.8	**4.4** 65.7	**5.1** 11.8	**9.0** 48.4	**13.5** 39.6	*6.2* *181.3*
	COL TOTAL	*100.0* *377.1*	*100.0* *1,493.9*	*100.0* *230.6*	*100.0* *539.9*	*100.0* *293.2*	*100.0* *2,934.7*

inequality are the dependent variable and education level is the independent variable.

Begin constructing your cross-tabs by entering WRKWAYUP in the "Row" field (since it is the dependent variable) and DEGREE in the "Column" field (since it is the independent variable).

Use the Selection Filter field to restrict the analysis to very recent data by typing:

YEAR (2012-2014)

Figure 4.9 shows the resulting cross-tab.

Step 5. Interpret your results. There are five basic step to interpreting a cross-tab.

1. Remind your audience of the basics.

When presenting your analyses to an audience, it is important to:

a. *Restate your research question.* In this case, the research question is "Among adults in the contemporary US, is there a relationship between educational attainment and beliefs about racial inequality?"

b. *Remind your audience of the data source and the specific variables that you used to answer this question.* In this case, the data source is the 2012–2014 General Social Surveys. Respondents were asked, "Do you agree strongly, agree somewhat, neither agree nor disagree, disagree somewhat, or disagree strongly with the following statement? Irish, Italian, Jewish and many other minorities overcame prejudice and worked their way up. [Blacks should do the same without special favors.]" Respondents were also asked about the highest degree they earned.

c. *Identify and describe the dependent and independent variables, clearly stating the level of measurement for each variable and how each variable was coded.* In this case, beliefs about racial inequality are the dependent variable and are assessed with a five-category ordinal-level variable, where higher values indicate stronger disagreement. DEGREE is the independent variable, which is also an ordinal-level variable with five categories, but here values range from 0 to 4.

d. *Specify the number of cases included in the analysis.* The overall number of valid cases (N) included in the cross-tab is presented in the bottom right corner of each cross-tab. In Figure 4.9, the weighted number of cases in the analysis consists of about 2,935 respondents.

2. Focus on specifics.

The first step in interpreting a cross-tab is to look carefully at the numbers in the tables and interpret them as specifically as you can. Focusing on the cell frequencies (the bottom number in each cell of the table) can be useful, but in most cases it is more helpful to examine the column percents—the top number in each cell.

For example, the numeric cell in the bottom left corner of Figure 4.9 contains the number 377.1, and this number is the column frequency. This number tells us that there were approximately 377 individuals with less than a high school education who provided information about their highest degree and their beliefs about racial ideology. The top row of Figure 4.9 corresponds with a response of "strongly agree." In the upper left corner of Figure 4.9, we see that approximately 154 people with less than a high school education responded that they "strongly agreed" with this statement. The 40.8 in this cell is the column percent and shows us the percentage of people with less than a high school degree who strongly agreed with this statement.

$$(153.9 / 377.1) * 100 = 40.8\%$$

In the top right cell, we see that 25.3% of respondents who had a graduate degree strongly agreed with the idea that Blacks should overcome prejudice and work their way up without special favors.

Looking at the row that corresponds with "strongly disagree," we can see that 4.2% of respondents with less than a high school degree strongly disagreed with this idea. This increased to 13.5% for respondents with a graduate degree.

The modal category (the category containing the highest number of cases) is "strongly agree" or "agree" for all levels of education.

3. Consider the big picture.

After examining individual percentages within the table, it is important to step back and take a larger view of the overall relationship presented in the tables. When examining each table individually, can you see any patterns or trends in the column percentages, or do the percentages seem to go up and down at random? If you see clusters of dark blue or dark red cells in the table, then there is probably an identifiable pattern. If there are very few darkly colored cells or if they seem randomly scattered across the table, then there may not be an easily identifiable pattern. It's also important to think about how the individual analyses work together. In situations where you are analyzing multiple bivariate tables, do they all point to the same overall conclusion, or are the results more mixed? If the individual analyses seem to point to different conclusions, how do you make sense of these results?

Look again at Figure 4.9 and focus on the row representing individuals who strongly agree that Blacks should "work their way up without special favors." Moving from the least educated to the most educated groups (that is, left to right across the table), the percentages tend to get smaller. The percentage of respondents who strongly agree decreases as education increases. Looking at the percentages of people who somewhat disagree or strongly disagree, we can see that those with a college or graduate degree are more likely to disagree than are those with lower levels of education.

4. Consider limitations.

An important part of all scientific research is to be clear about the limitations of the research. The analyses described above should not be understood as the unquestioned "final word" on the relationship between education and racial ideology. Every research project has limitations, some more than others, and it is important to make these clear when interpreting the results.

When considering the limitations of any survey research project, it is important to consider issues of survey design, possible sample biases, and generalizability. For example, the results here apply only to adults in the US who are aged 18 and older. Since the analyses are restricted to the years 2012 through 2014, respondents include

English- and Spanish-speaking adults, but adults in the US who are not able to speak either language are not included in the analysis. Nor are those living in institutions such as prisons or mental institutions included in this analysis.

It is also important to consider potential **confounding variables**, variables that are not included in the analyses but might be affecting the relationship between the independent and dependent variables. For example, how might differences in respondents' racial/ethnic statuses shape the relationship between education and racial ideology? This question is addressed further in the Exercises, which "control" for respondents' racial/ethnic status when examining the relationship between education and racial ideology.

Finally, while it is crucial to explain what the analyses reveal about the larger research question ("Is education associated with beliefs about racial inequality?"), it is often useful to clarify what the analyses do *not* tell us about the research question. Anticipate possible misinterpretations. Clarify what the findings suggest and what they don't suggest. For example, while respondents with greater levels of education are less likely to believe that Blacks should "work their way up without special favors," almost half of respondents with a graduate degree either agree or strongly agree with this idea (25.3% + 23.7% = 49%). While there does appear to be a relationship between education and racial ideology as it is measured here, it is also important to note that individuals' beliefs about racial issues are complicated and sometimes contradictory. A single indicator of racial ideology likely does not capture the full complexity of how people think about racial issues.

5. Summarize your conclusions.

Interpreting these results within a social justice framework requires thinking through issues of power and inequality, socially constructed differences, links between the micro and macro levels of society, and the importance of intersecting inequalities. We might first ask, why would individuals with lower levels of education be more likely to believe that Blacks should "work their way up without special favors" compared to individuals with higher levels of education? The analyses presented in Figures 4.8 and 4.9 do not take racial/ethnic differences into account. How would the patterns we see in these beliefs change if we were to examine the intersections of race and class? Among every level of education considered, the modal category for WRKWAYUP was either agree strongly or agree somewhat, likely speaking to a broader ideology of the American Dream—the idea that through hard work, persistence, and creative problem-solving, individuals can work their way up in society. Analyzing these results within a social justice framework, we might ask, to what extent are ideals about the American Dream connected to respondents' reluctance to extend "special favors" to disadvantaged social groups racialized? These questions can be answered by combining further analyses of GSS data with research that is qualitative, historical, comparative, and theoretical.

EXERCISES

To what extent does the relationship between education and racial ideology differ for respondents of different racial/ethnic groups? Figure 4.10, which spans multiple pages, examines the relationship between educational attainment and racial ideology, controlling for respondents' racial/ethnic group. As discussed above, RACEHISP is a nominal-level variable that indicates respondents' self-identification as non-Hispanic white, Black or African American, non-Black Hispanic, or another racial/ethnic minority group.

The top portion of the figure shows the variables used to construct the analysis and indicates that RACEHISP was used as a control variable and YEAR was used as a filter.

1. What is the dependent variable in this analysis?
   a. YEAR
   b. RACEHISP
   c. WRKWAYUP
   d. DEGREE

2. Of the racial/ethnic groups analyzed in this figure, which group has the highest number of respondents?
   a. non-Hispanic whites
   b. Blacks
   c. non-Black Hispanics
   d. other racial/ethnic groups

3. The analysis presented in Figure 4.10 uses a filter that:
   a. restricts the analysis to survey years 2012 through 2014.
   b. restricts the analysis to survey years 2000 through 2014.
   c. restricts the analysis to people who describe themselves as white.
   d. restricts the analysis to people who describe themselves as non-white.

4. Of the racial/ethnic groups analyzed in this figure, which group has the smallest number of respondents?
   a. non-Hispanic whites
   b. Blacks
   c. non-Black Hispanics
   d. other racial/ethnic groups

5. Looking at the first cross-tab in Figure 4.10, the 53.5 in the upper left corner tells us that:
   a. 53.5% of non-Hispanic white respondents strongly agreed that "Blacks should work their way up without special favors."
   b. 53.5% of non-Hispanic whites responded that they had not earned a high school diploma.
   c. Of the people who strongly agreed that "Blacks should work their way up without special favors," 53.5% had less than a high school diploma.
   d. Among non-Hispanic white respondents, 53.5% of those with less than a high school diploma strongly agreed that "Blacks should work their way up without special favors."

6. Approximately how many non-Black Hispanic respondents reported that they had a bachelor's degree but not a graduate degree?
   a. 409
   b. 46
   c. 36
   d. 170

7. Looking at the first cross-tab in Figure 4.10, the 44.2 in the upper right corner tells us that:
   a. 44.2% of all respondents strongly agreed that "Blacks should work their way up without special favors."
   b. 44.2% of non-Hispanic white respondents strongly agreed that "Blacks should work their way up without special favors."
   c. 44.2% of non-Hispanic whites responded that they had earned a graduate degree.
   d. 44.2% of respondents surveyed identified as non-Hispanic whites.

8. Comparing the first and second cross-tabs in Figure 4.10 (pgs 91–92), which of the following statements is correct?
   a. Across all education levels, the percentage of non-Hispanic white respondents who strongly agreed that "Blacks should work their way up without special favors" is higher than the percentage of Black respondents who strongly agreed with this statement.

b. Across all education levels, the percentage of non-Hispanic white respondents who strongly agreed that "Blacks should work their way up without special favors" is lower than the percentage of Black respondents who strongly agreed with this statement.

c. In terms of who is represented in the table, the number of Black respondents with less than a high school degree is larger than the number of white respondents with less than a high school degree.

d. In terms of who is represented in the table, the number of Black respondents with a graduate degree is larger than the number of white respondents with less than a high school degree.

9. Which of the following statements best describes the relationship between educational attainment and racial ideology among non-Black Hispanic respondents? (Hint: See page 93.)

a. Non-Black Hispanic respondents who have less than a high school education are more likely to "strongly agree" than are non-Black Hispanic respondents with a higher level of education.

b. For all education levels, the modal category for the dependent variable WRKWAYUP is "agree strongly."

c. Non-Black Hispanic respondents with a bachelor's degree or higher are significantly more likely to disagree (strongly or somewhat) with the idea that "Blacks should work their way up without special favors" than are non-Black Hispanic respondents with lower levels of education.

d. The percentage of non-Black Hispanic respondents who "strongly disagree" with the idea that "Blacks should work their way up without special favors" is higher than the percentage of Black respondents who "strongly disagree" with this idea.

10. What limitations are worth noting when interpreting this table?

a. The analysis does not represent individuals who are currently residing in institutions.

b. Individuals who are unable to speak either English or Spanish are not represented in the GSS.

c. Beliefs about whether Blacks should be able to "work their way up without special favors" is only one aspect of racial ideology and likely does not capture the full complexity of how people think about racial issues.

d. All of the above are important limitations for interpreting this table.

Figure 4.10					

Variables					
Role	Name	Label	Range	MD	Dataset
Row	**WRKWAYUP**	BLACKS OVERCOME PREJUDICE WITHOUT FAVORS	1-5	0,8,9	1
Column	**DEGREE**	RS HIGHEST DEGREE	0-4	7,8,9	1
Control	**RACEHISP**	Race with Hispanic (2000 and later)	1-4	9	1
Weight	**COMPWT**	Composite weight = WTSSALL * OVERSAMP * FORMWT	.1913-11.1261		1
Filter	**YEAR(2012-2014)**	GSS YEAR FOR THIS RESPONDENT	1972-2014		1

Statistics for RACEHISP = 1(White)						
		DEGREE				
Cells contain: -**Column percent** -Weighted N		0 LT HIGH SCHOOL	1 HIGH SCHOOL	2 JUNIOR COLLEGE	3 BACHELOR	4 GRADUATE	*ROW TOTAL*
WRKWAYUP	1: AGREE STRONGLY	**53.5** 81.5	**51.2** 506.0	**54.3** 82.7	**28.9** 118.1	**27.2** 57.5	*44.2* *845.8*
	2: AGREE SOMEWHAT	**30.7** 46.8	**28.7** 283.8	**26.4** 40.1	**30.8** 126.0	**22.4** 47.3	*28.4* *544.0*
	3: NEITHER AGREE NOR DISAGREE	**8.9** 13.5	**11.7** 115.8	**12.8** 19.5	**20.8** 85.1	**18.0** 38.0	*14.2* *271.9*
	4: DISAGREE SOMEWHAT	**3.9** 6.0	**5.7** 56.8	**5.4** 8.1	**12.7** 51.9	**21.2** 44.6	*8.8* *167.5*
	5: DISAGREE STRONGLY	**3.0** 4.6	**2.7** 26.8	**1.1** 1.6	**6.9** 28.1	**11.2** 23.6	*4.4* *84.8*
	COL TOTAL	*100.0* *152.5*	*100.0* *989.3*	*100.0* *152.1*	*100.0* *409.2*	*100.0* *211.0*	*100.0* *1,914.0*

Color coding:	<-2.0	<-1.0	<0.0	>0.0	>1.0	>2.0	Z
N in each cell:	Smaller than expected			Larger than expected			

Statistics for RACEHISP = 2(Black)						
		DEGREE				
Cells contain: -**Column percent** -Weighted N		0 LT HIGH SCHOOL	1 HIGH SCHOOL	2 JUNIOR COLLEGE	3 BACHELOR	4 GRADUATE	*ROW TOTAL*
WRKWAYUP	1: AGREE STRONGLY	**35.6** 27.5	**29.9** 69.2	**39.6** 14.9	**22.6** 11.0	**5.4** 1.8	*29.0* *124.3*
	2: AGREE SOMEWHAT	**16.5** 12.7	**24.7** 57.2	**13.2** 5.0	**22.0** 10.7	**26.5** 8.9	*22.0* *94.5*
	3: NEITHER AGREE NOR DISAGREE	**18.6** 14.4	**17.3** 40.1	**21.7** 8.2	**7.9** 3.9	**7.9** 2.6	*16.1* *69.2*
	4: DISAGREE SOMEWHAT	**17.8** 13.7	**14.2** 32.9	**3.6** 1.3	**24.8** 12.1	**27.5** 9.2	*16.1* *69.2*
	5: DISAGREE STRONGLY	**11.6** 9.0	**14.0** 32.3	**21.9** 8.3	**22.6** 11.0	**32.8** 11.0	*16.7* *71.5*
	COL TOTAL	*100.0* *77.3*	*100.0* *231.6*	*100.0* *37.7*	*100.0* *48.6*	*100.0* *33.5*	*100.0* *428.7*

Color coding:	<-2.0	<-1.0	<0.0	>0.0	>1.0	>2.0	**Z**
N in each cell:	Smaller than expected			Larger than expected			

Statistics for RACEHISP = 3(Hispanic)						
	DEGREE					
Cells contain: **-Column percent** -Weighted N	0 LT HIGH SCHOOL	1 HIGH SCHOOL	2 JUNIOR COLLEGE	3 BACHELOR	4 GRADUATE	*ROW TOTAL*
WRKWAYUP 1: AGREE STRONGLY	**28.2** 38.0	**44.9** 98.5	**48.0** 10.3	**30.8** 14.2	**36.0** 8.7	*38.1* *169.7*
2: AGREE SOMEWHAT	**48.2** 64.8	**33.4** 73.2	**12.0** 2.6	**28.7** 13.2	**14.3** 3.5	*35.3* *157.3*
3: NEITHER AGREE NOR DISAGREE	**17.6** 23.6	**14.1** 31.0	**28.7** 6.2	**13.0** 6.0	**8.1** 2.0	*15.4* *68.8*
4: DISAGREE SOMEWHAT	**4.7** 6.3	**5.8** 12.7	**4.2** .9	**15.9** 7.3	**21.3** 5.2	*7.3* *32.4*
5: DISAGREE STRONGLY	**1.3** 1.8	**1.8** 3.9	**7.1** 1.5	**11.6** 5.3	**20.4** 5.0	*3.9* *17.5*
COL TOTAL	*100.0* *134.6*	*100.0* *219.3*	*100.0* *21.5*	*100.0* *46.0*	*100.0* *24.3*	*100.0* *445.7*

Color coding:	<-2.0	<-1.0	<0.0	>0.0	>1.0	>2.0	**Z**
N in each cell:	Smaller than expected			Larger than expected			

Statistics for RACEHISP = 4(Other)						
		DEGREE				
Cells contain: -**Column percent** -Weighted N		0 LT HIGH SCHOOL	1 HIGH SCHOOL	2 JUNIOR COLLEGE	3 BACHELOR	4 GRADUATE	*ROW TOTAL*
WRKWAYUP	1: AGREE STRONGLY	**54.3** 7.0	**29.8** 16.0	**28.5** 5.5	**32.8** 11.8	**24.8** 6.1	*31.7* *46.3*
	2: AGREE SOMEWHAT	**19.4** 2.5	**39.5** 21.2	**60.1** 11.6	**30.1** 10.9	**40.9** 10.0	*38.4* *56.2*
	3: NEITHER AGREE NOR DISAGREE	**10.5** 1.3	**15.1** 8.1	**4.6** .9	**22.3** 8.1	**17.8** 4.3	*15.5* *22.7*
	4: DISAGREE SOMEWHAT	**12.4** 1.6	**10.7** 5.7	**4.6** .9	**3.7** 1.3	**16.6** 4.0	*9.3* *13.6*
	5: DISAGREE STRONGLY	**3.5** .4	**4.9** 2.6	**2.1** .4	**11.0** 4.0	**.0** .0	*5.1* *7.5*
	COL TOTAL	*100.0* *12.8*	*100.0* *53.6*	*100.0* *19.4*	*100.0* *36.1*	*100.0* *24.4*	*100.0* *146.3*

Color coding:	<-2.0	<-1.0	<0.0	>0.0	>1.0	>2.0	**Z**
N in each cell:	Smaller than expected			Larger than expected			

Statistics for all valid cases						
		DEGREE				
Cells contain: -**Column percent** -Weighted N		0 LT HIGH SCHOOL	1 HIGH SCHOOL	2 JUNIOR COLLEGE	3 BACHELOR	4 GRADUATE	*ROW TOTAL*
WRKWAYUP	1: AGREE STRONGLY	**40.8** 153.9	**46.2** 689.7	**49.2** 113.4	**28.7** 155.1	**25.3** 74.1	*40.4* *1,186.2*
	2: AGREE SOMEWHAT	**33.6** 126.8	**29.1** 435.4	**25.7** 59.3	**29.8** 160.8	**23.7** 69.6	*29.0* *851.9*
	3: NEITHER AGREE NOR DISAGREE	**14.0** 52.9	**13.1** 195.0	**15.1** 34.8	**19.1** 103.1	**16.0** 46.9	*14.7* *432.6*
	4: DISAGREE SOMEWHAT	**7.3** 27.6	**7.2** 108.2	**4.9** 11.3	**13.4** 72.6	**21.5** 63.1	*9.6* *282.7*
	5: DISAGREE STRONGLY	**4.2** 15.8	**4.4** 65.7	**5.1** 11.8	**9.0** 48.4	**13.5** 39.6	*6.2* *181.3*
	COL TOTAL	*100.0* *377.1*	*100.0* *1,493.9*	*100.0* *230.6*	*100.0* *539.9*	*100.0* *293.2*	*100.0* *2,934.7*

Color coding:	<-2.0	<-1.0	<0.0	>0.0	>1.0	>2.0	**Z**
N in each cell:	Smaller than expected			Larger than expected			

ANALYSES & ESSAYS

1. *What sociodemographic characteristics are related to respondents' beliefs about racial or ethnic inequality?* Identify one variable that you think plays a role in determining beliefs about racial inequality. Identify three questions that assess respondents' beliefs about racial/ethnic inequality. Construct three separate cross-tabs that examine how the sociodemographic characteristic you have chosen relates to these beliefs about racial/ethnic inequality. Interpret your results.

2. *To what extent do people of different racial/ethnic groups have different ideas about citizenship and patriotism?* Create three different cross-tab analyses in which RACEHISP is the independent variable in each one and NTCITVTE, CRIMLOSE, SHORTCOM are the different dependent variables. Interpret your results.

3. *To what extent do people of different racial/ethnic groups differ in their confidence in social institutions?* Create three different cross-tab analyses in which RACEHISP is the independent variable in each one and CONEDUC, CONPRESS, and CONFINAN are the different dependent variables. Use a filter to restrict your analysis to data from the years 2010 through 2014. Interpret your results, giving particular attention to how your findings highlight the connections between the micro and macro levels of society.

4. *To what extent are contemporary marriage and family arrangements structured by race, ethnicity, and gender?* Create a cross-tab where MARITAL is the dependent variable, SEX is the independent variable, and RACEHISP is the control variable. Use a filter to restrict your analysis to data from the years 2010 through 2014. Interpret your results, giving particular attention to the intersections of gender and racial/ethnic inequality.

5. *To what extent do people of different racial/ethnic groups have different experiences at work?* Create three different cross-tab analyses in which RACEHISP is the independent variable in each one and WKRACISM, RESPECT, and SATJOB1 are the different dependent variables. Use a filter to restrict your analysis to data from the years 2010 through 2014. Interpret your results, giving particular attention to how your findings highlight the connections between the micro and macro levels of society.

NOTES

1. See, for example, Zuberi, Tukufu, and Eduardo Bonilla-Silva, eds. 2008. *White Logic, White Methods: Racism and Methodology.* Lanham, MD: Rowman & Littlefield.

2. This perspective is dominant in contemporary France, for example, and as a result there are relatively little governmental data available for documenting racial inequality.

3. American Sociological Association. 2003. *The Importance of Collecting Data and Doing Social Scientific Research on Race.* Washington, DC: American Sociological Association. (Emphasis added.)

4. Describing the value of the GSS for analyzing racial/ethnic relations in US society, Tom W. Smith (2002:7) writes that the GSS includes "359 different items a total of 836 times, from 1972 to 2000 . . ." Smith reports that there are at least 69 questions related to intergroup relations that have been asked regularly over time, and there are a number of special modules focusing on intergroup relations. Smith, Tom W. 2002. "GSS Methodological Report No. 96 Measuring Racial and Ethnic Discrimination." National Opinion Research Center University of Chicago. Retrieved September 18, 2016 (http://gss.norc.org/Documents/reports/methodological-reports/MR096.pdf).

5. See "FAQ #12: What Happened to Information on Race After 2000?" (http://www3.norc.org/GSS+Website/FAQs/).

6. Ibid.

7. The variable USCITZN also asks about citizenship but uses slightly different wording and was asked to an even smaller subset of cases in these years.

8. There are a handful of instances where viewing the variable in SDA does not produce the precise wording of the survey question. The variable WRKWAYUP is one such example. As shown on the GSS Data Explorer, the full question reads, "Do you agree strongly, agree somewhat, neither agree nor disagree, disagree somewhat, or disagree strongly with the following statement? (HAND CARD TO RESPONDENT) Irish, Italians, Jewish and many other minorities overcame prejudice and worked their way up. Blacks should do the same without special favors" (https://gssdataexplorer.norc.org/variables/424/vshow).

9. For more information on weighting options, see Chapter 2.

10. For more information, see http://www.icpsr.umich.edu/icpsrweb/content/SAMHDA/help/helpan.htm#Tcolor.

11. Appendix D of the GSS Cumulative Codebook (2015) provides the precise questions that respondents were asked. To generate the value of degree, for example, respondents were asked, "What is the highest grade in elementary school or high school that you finished and got credit for? Did you ever get a high school diploma or a GED certificate? Did you ever complete one or more years of college for credit—not including schooling such as business college, technical or vocational school? If yes, how many years did you complete? Do you have any college degrees? If yes, what degree or degrees?"

CHAPTER 5

ANALYZING CLASS WITH THE GSS

INTRODUCTION: KEY CONCEPTS IN CLASS

Class is one of the key concepts in social science research. In formal terms, class refers to "a grouping of individuals with similar positions and similar political and economic interests within the stratification system."[1] More informally, social class is a shorthand way to describe how the wealth, social status, and political power of an individual, along with that of her or his family, structures privilege and opportunity. Financial resources are deeply connected to class, but class is not reducible to money alone.

Educational attainment and occupational prestige are important dimensions of class, as are more intangible resources, such as social capital and cultural capital. Social capital, as described by sociologist Pierre Bourdieu, refers to the "resources that one gains from being part of a network of social relationships, including group membership."[2] Individuals with high levels of social capital have social networks that include people with economic resources, political resources, and/or cultural know-how. Compared with people with low levels of social capital, those who have a high level of social capital are often given extra opportunities (consider a college student whose aunt is a CEO and creates a paid internship for him despite his being a lazy person and a mediocre student). People with a high level of social capital are also privileged in that they are often able to draw from their social networks in times of trouble (consider the same lazy and mediocre student who regularly doesn't show up for his internship—rather than being fired, he might be given positive evaluations, because, after all, his aunt is the CEO!).

Learning Objectives

By the end of this chapter, you should be able to:

1. Identify GSS variables related to class and socioeconomic status.

2. Construct new categories for variables (recoding).

3. Conduct comparisons of means for ordinal- and interval-ratio-level variables.

4. Conduct bivariate analyses related to class and interpret these within a social justice framework.

Cultural capital includes "non-economic resources that enable social mobility," including resources such as knowledge, skills, and education.[3] The more familiar and comfortable a person is with middle- and upper-class culture, the more likely it is that he or she is going to be able to take advantage of middle- and upper-class opportunities. People who have at least one parent who has graduated from college, for example, have an easier time navigating the college admissions process and are more likely to succeed in college than people who are the first in their family to attend college. Part of the reason for this is that parents who have themselves been to college are more likely to be familiar with how to prepare for the ACT and SAT exams, how to write a "good" college essay, and how and when to apply for financial aid and scholarships. In this way, and in others, parents with high levels of cultural capital are able to pass along their cultural know-how to their children.

In addition to the "objective" indicators of class position described above, social scientists recognize the importance of class-based identities. While in some cases a person's identity corresponds to the more objective indicators of her or his class, in other cases there is a mismatch between the two. Consider, for example, the millionaire, college-educated corporate lawyer who insists that, despite her high level of education, income, wealth, multiple homes, and prestigious career, she "really is middle class!"

In addition to analyzing class-based statuses and identities, a key area of social science research examines class-based ideologies: attitudes and beliefs about class-based inequalities. How do individuals make sense of persistent, and indeed growing, socioeconomic inequality? To what extent do we, as a culture, view individuals as responsible for their own financial successes or failures? To what extent do we view poverty as an important social problem? How do views about poverty and economic inequality vary across racial/ethnic, gender, and socioeconomic groups?

The General Social Survey includes dozens of survey questions about class. A good number of these questions are included in every survey year, and by analyzing these questions, we are able to investigate how class-based issues have changed over time. This chapter provides an introduction to analyzing socioeconomic class in the General Social Survey, with a focus on the dimensions of class described above.

IDENTIFYING VARIABLES RELATED TO SOCIOECONOMIC CLASS

Searching for Variables Related to Class

When analyzing data related to social class, it is important to keep in mind the multiple dimensions of class discussed above and think carefully about which of these dimensions are of most interest to you. Are you, for example, interested in the concrete indicators of socioeconomic class, such as income, wealth, and educational attainment? Are you more interested in individuals' sense of themselves as working, middle, or upper class? Or are you more interested in how people understand class as a system of inequality—the extent of class-based inequality and why it persists? Further information on each of these is discussed below.

Income, Education, and Occupational Prestige

Income

The GSS includes questions concerning the respondents' *personal income* (e.g., RINCOM06, REALRINC) and also includes questions about respondents' *total family income* (e.g., INCOME06, REALINC). When analyzing income, it's always important to clarify which kind of income you are using in your analysis!

An additional thing to keep in mind when analyzing income data in the GSS is that the survey regularly introduces new variables for income so that the categories keep up with inflation. The variable INCOME, for example, measures family income on a scale of 1 to 12, where 1 represents total annual family incomes of less than $1,000 and 12 represents family incomes of $25,000 or more. This variable was first included in the 1973 GSS, when the median family income of households in the US was $10,500 and a family income of $25,000 indicated that a family was doing very well financially.[4] Four decades later, in 2013, the median family income was $52,250, and a family with total earnings of $25,000 per year was just above the federal poverty line.[5,6] To account for inflation, the GSS regularly adds new income variables, with new income categories. For family income, for example, the GSS has the variables INCOME72, INCOME77, INCOME82, INCOME86, INCOME91, INCOME98, and INCOME06. The corresponding variables for respondents' personal income include RINCOME, RINCOM77, RINCOM82, RINCOM86, RINCOM91, RINCOM98, and RINCOM06. For each of these variables, the number at the end of the variable name corresponds to the first year in which the variable was included. The variables RINCOM98 and INCOME98, for example were introduced in the 1998 survey, and information for these variables is available for every subsequent survey year. In general, when analyzing data from recent survey years, it is best to use data from the most recent income variable (i.e., RINCOM06 or INCOME06).

Education

Just as the GSS includes a number of different variables about income, it also includes a number of questions about educational attainment. The most basic are EDUC, which corresponds to the number of years of formal education the respondent has had, and DEGREE, which corresponds to the respondent's highest degree earned (e.g., a high school diploma, a bachelor's degree, or a master's degree). In addition to these questions, the GSS includes information about the respondent's father's educational attainment (PAEDUC and PADEG), the respondent's mother's educational attainment (MAEDUC and MADEG), and the educational attainment of the respondent's spouse if she or he is married (SPEDUC).

"VIEWING" VARIABLES RELATED TO EDUCATIONAL ATTAINMENT

In general, "viewing" a variable in the SDA is a quick and easy way to determine the precise wording of the survey question. Variables related to educational attainment, including the respondent's educational attainment (DEGREE and EDUC), the respondent's mother's educational attainment (MADEG), the respondent's father's educational attainment (PADEG), and for married respondents, their spouse's educational attainment (SPEDUC), are important exceptions.

In the survey, respondents are asked a number of questions about their educational attainment, including:

- What is the highest grade in elementary school or high school that you finished and got credit for?

- Did you ever get a high school diploma or a GED certificate?

- Was that a diploma awarded by your high school at graduation at the end of 12th grade, a GED awarded after you took a test, or something else?

- Did you ever complete one or more years of college for credit—not including schooling such as business college, technical or vocational school?

- Do you have any college degrees?

- What degree or degrees?

A similar series of questions are included when asking about the educational attainment of respondents' parents and (if respondents are married) spouses. Viewing the variables related to educational attainment shows only one of these questions (e.g., "What is the highest grade in elementary school or high school that you finished and got credit for?"), but in fact the variables reflect educational attainment more generally.

Occupation and Occupational Prestige

Occupational prestige scores are indicators of the status or prestige that we, as a society, attach to various occupations. In the GSS, the variable PRESTG80 indicates the respondent's occupational prestige, and the variable SPPRES80 indicates the occupational prestige of the respondent's spouse (in cases where the respondent is married). Occupational *prestige* scores are interval-ratio-level variables, with higher levels indicating jobs with higher levels of prestige. Both variables, PRESTG80 and SPRES80, range from 17 to 86, with higher scores representing higher levels of prestige. Physicians, for example, have the occupational prestige score of 86, and social workers have an occupational prestige score of 52. Sales workers in the apparel industry have a relatively low occupational prestige score of 30, news vendors have an occupational prestige of 19, and "miscellaneous food preparation occupations" have a score of 17.[7] The variables PRESTG80 and SPPRES80 are included in survey years 1988 through 2010, and updated measures of occupational prestige are in the process of being created. At the time of this writing, survey years 2012 and 2014 do not currently have occupational prestige scores.

In addition to occupational prestige, the GSS includes variables that provide information about respondents' actual occupation. The variables OCC10 (respondent's occupation category), SPOCC10 (respondent's spouse's occupation category), MAOCC10 (respondent's mother's occupation category), and PAOCC10 (respondent's father's occupation category) are all presently available for survey years 2012 and 2014. Occupation categories are nominal-level variables and have no intrinsic order. A score of 10 on the variable OCC10, for example, indicates chief executives, a score of 4140 corresponds to dishwashers, and 9140 corresponds to taxi drivers and chauffeurs.[8]

Social and Cultural Capital

As explained above, social scientists recognize that, in addition to financial resources, social and cultural resources play an important role in shaping individuals' opportunities. Though the GSS does not contain a subset of variables specifically focusing on social or cultural capital, a number of its variables can be used to assess cultural and social resources. Most notably, respondents' educational attainment (DEGREE, EDUC) and parents' level of education (MAEDUC, PAEDUC) are all good measures of cultural capital. The GSS has also recently asked questions about how often the respondent has visited an art museum in the past year (VISART), how often the respondent has visited a science museum in the past year (VISSCI), and the respondent's musical tastes (RAP, FOLK, CLASSICL, GOSPEL, OLDIES).

Class-Based Identity

In addition to the more objective indicators of class statuses described above, it is sometimes useful to assess how people view themselves within the class structure. The variable CLASS indicates respondents' subjective class status—that is, their sense of themselves as part of the lower class, the working class, the middle class, or the upper class. This variable is included in every survey year of the GSS, and in every year, the vast majority of respondents (approximately 90%) describe themselves as either working or middle class.

Class-Based Ideology

As is the case with race, gender, and sexuality, the GSS contains many questions focusing on beliefs and attitudes about class-based inequality. Some of these questions assess perceptions of inequality, opportunity, and social mobility in a general way. Some questions are specific to beliefs about people in poverty, and some focus more on the relationship between rich and poor people in society. The variable

EQUALIZE, for example, asks respondents, "On the whole, do you think it should or should not be the government's responsibility to reduce income differences between the rich and poor?" and was included in multiple survey years between 1985 and 2006. The variable HELPPOOR is included over an even greater range of time, 1975 through 2014, and asks, "Some people think that the government in Washington should do everything possible to improve the standard of living of all poor Americans; they are at point 1 on this card. Other people think it is not the government's responsibility, and that each person should take care of himself; they are at point 5. Where would you place yourself on this scale, or haven't you made up your mind on this?"

Browsing for Variables Related to Class

The codebook on the left-hand side of the SDA website allows users to easily identify clusters of variables about specific topics, such as class. If you are interested in browsing for variables related to class, you may find the following subject headings and subheadings to be particularly useful:

- Respondent Background Variables
  - Education
  - Socio-economic and Status Indicators

- Personal and Family Information
  - Respondent's Employment
  - Spouse's Employment
  - Mother's Employment
  - Father's Employment
  - Respondent's Background and Childhood
  - Income

- Workplace and Economic Concerns

- Controversial and Social Issues

- Personal Concerns
  - Alienation Measures

- 2002 Topical Module: Quality of Working Life

- 2002 Topical Module: Employee Compensation

- 2004 Topical Module: Work Environment

- 2012 Topical Module: Workplace Violence

- 2014 Topical Module: The Quality of Working Life

- 2014 Topical Module: Employee Compensation

- 1987 ISSP Module: Social Inequality

RECODING VARIABLES

Motivations for Recoding Variables

When designing social surveys, researchers think carefully about the number of possible response categories for each variable. Some variables have only two categories, "Yes" and "No" (recall that these are called dummy variables). Attitudinal variables often have four or five categories (strongly agree, agree, neither agree nor disagree, disagree, strongly disagree). Other variables, such as income, years of education, or age, can have 20 categories or more! In cases where variables have a relatively high number of categories, it is often useful to recode the variable so that there are fewer categories. Reducing the number of categories in a variable can be a way to design categories that are more useful for your particular research question and can also produce a cross-tab that is easier to read.

To get us started, let's imagine that we're interested in looking at class-based differences in health and well-being. In what follows, family income is used as the independent variable and days of poor mental health is used as the dependent variable. In identifying mental health as the dependent variable, this framework suggests that class-based inequalities shape respondents' mental health (though mental health can certainly affect one's class position as well).

Viewing the variable INCOME06, we see that this variable corresponds to the survey question "In which of these groups did your total family income, from all sources, fall last year before taxes, that is." Figure 5.1 below shows us the frequency distribution produced by viewing this variable.

Figure 5.1 aggregates the responses from every year in which the question was asked—from 2006 to 2014. Note that this variable has 25 valid response categories (values ranging from 1 to 25) and that the values 0, 26, and 98 represent nonvalid responses. A value of 0 on this variable indicates a response of IAP (short for "Inapplicable") and indicates that 46,510 people were not asked this question. The reason that so many people were not asked this question is that INCOME06 is a measure of income that was included only in survey years 2006 and later. All respondents who participated in the GSS in years 1972 through 2004 have a response of IAP on this variable.

By viewing the variable MNTLHLTH, we can see that this variable corresponds to the survey question "Now thinking about your mental health, which includes stress, depression, and problems with emotions, for how many days during the past 30 days was your mental health not good?" The variable ranges from 0 to 30, with higher values indicating greater frequency of poor mental health. A cross-tab of the variable MNTLHLTH with the variable YEAR shows us that this variable was included in the GSS from 2002 to 2014.

In order to see firsthand the usefulness of recoding a variable, make a cross-tab (also called a "bivariate table") of the variables MNTLHLTH and INCOME06. Cross-tabs are discussed at greater length in Chapters 3 and 4. To make a cross-tab, first

Figure 5.1

INCOME06			TOTAL FAMILY INCOME
	Description of the Variable		

In which of these groups did your total family income, from all sources, fall last year before taxes, that is.

Percent	N	Value	Label
1.4	167	**1**	UNDER $1 000
1.2	141	**2**	$1 000 TO 2 999
0.9	107	**3**	$3 000 TO 3 999
0.6	66	**4**	$4 000 TO 4 999
0.9	105	**5**	$5 000 TO 5 999
1.1	123	**6**	$6 000 TO 6 999
1.2	144	**7**	$7 000 TO 7 999
2.1	243	**8**	$8 000 TO 9 999
3.9	446	**9**	$10000 TO 12499
3.3	381	**10**	$12500 TO 14999
3.2	374	**11**	$15000 TO 17499
2.4	281	**12**	$17500 TO 19999
3.6	417	**13**	$20000 TO 22499
3.6	419	**14**	$22500 TO 24999
5.2	604	**15**	$25000 TO 29999
5.7	659	**16**	$30000 TO 34999
5.2	597	**17**	$35000 TO 39999
8.8	1,009	**18**	$40000 TO 49999
8.2	942	**19**	$50000 TO 59999
9.7	1,118	**20**	$60000 TO 74999
7.5	865	**21**	$75000 TO $89999
6.3	731	**22**	$90000 TO $109999

4.1	473	**23**	$110000 TO $129999
2.7	310	**24**	$130000 TO $149999
7.0	802	**25**	$150000 OR OVER
	46,510	**0**	IAP
	986	**26**	REFUSED
	579	**98**	DK
100.0	**59,599**		**Total**

Properties	
Data type:	numeric
Missing-data codes:	0,26-99
Mean:	16.72
Std Dev:	5.75
Record/columns:	1/247-248

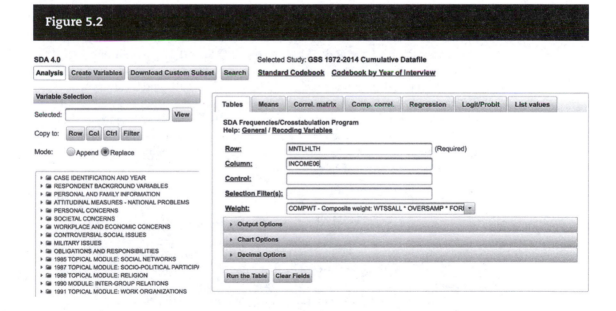

Figure 5.2

SDA 4.0   Selected Study: **GSS 1972-2014 Cumulative Datafile**

Analysis   Create Variables   Download Custom Subset   Search   **Standard Codebook** / **Codebook by Year of Interview**

Variable Selection

Selected: _____ View

Copy to: Row Col Ctrl Filter

Mode: ○ Append ● Replace

- ▸ CASE IDENTIFICATION AND YEAR
- ▸ RESPONDENT BACKGROUND VARIABLES
- ▸ PERSONAL AND FAMILY INFORMATION
- ▸ ATTITUDINAL MEASURES - NATIONAL PROBLEMS
- ▸ PERSONAL CONCERNS
- ▸ SOCIETAL CONCERNS
- ▸ WORKPLACE AND ECONOMIC CONCERNS
- ▸ CONTROVERSIAL SOCIAL ISSUES
- ▸ MILITARY ISSUES
- ▸ OBLIGATIONS AND RESPONSIBILITIES
- ▸ 1985 TOPICAL MODULE: SOCIAL NETWORKS
- ▸ 1987 TOPICAL MODULE: SOCIO-POLITICAL PARTICIPA
- ▸ 1988 TOPICAL MODULE: RELIGION
- ▸ 1990 MODULE: INTER-GROUP RELATIONS
- ▸ 1991 TOPICAL MODULE: WORK ORGANIZATIONS

Tables | Means | Correl. matrix | Comp. correl. | Regression | Logit/Probit | List values

SDA Frequencies/Crosstabulation Program
Help: **General** / **Recoding Variables**

Row: MNTLHLTH (Required)

Column: INCOME06

Control:

Selection Filter(s):

Weight: COMPWT - Composite weight: WTSSALL * OVERSAMP * FORI ▾

▸ Output Options

▸ Chart Options

▸ Decimal Options

Run the Table | Clear Fields

make sure you are on the "Tables" section of the "Analysis" screen, shown in Figure 5.2. In the "Row" field, type in the variable MNTLHLTH, and in the "Column" field, type in the variable INCOME06. Click "Run the Table," and be prepared to see a gigantic table that is very difficult to make sense of!

A small portion of the resulting table is shown in Figure 5.3. Because both of the variables have so many categories, it is difficult to view the analysis on a single screen and even more difficult to make sense of it. The top row of the table indicates that there were a large number of people who reported having had no days of poor mental health in the past 30 days, but in each of the subsequent rows, there are very few people represented. Many of the cells are completely empty. Even though there is a lot of detail in this table, it is difficult to determine if there is or is not a relationship between family income and respondents' mental health.

In cases such as these, where variables have a relatively high number of categories, it is often useful to recode the variable so that the data are organized in a more meaningful way.

How to Recode Variables in SDA

To recode the variable, INCOME06, in this way, simply modify what you typed in the "Column" box to the following:

INCOME06 (r: 1-12; 13-17; 18-19; 20-21; 22; 23; 24; 25)

Here "r:" stands for "recode into the following categories." Categories are separated by a semicolon (;). The first category includes values 1 through 12, which includes family income levels from under $1,000 through $19,999. The second category includes values from 13 to 17, which corresponds to family income levels of $20,000 to $39,999. The third category includes values of 18 and 19, which corresponds to family incomes of $40,000 to $59,999. The fourth category includes values of 20 and 21, which corresponds to family incomes of $60,000 to $89,999, and the fifth category includes only values from 22 on the original variable, corresponding to family incomes of $90,000 to $109,999. The sixth category includes values from 23, the seventh from 24, and the eighth from 25.

Similarly, now modify the "Row" field to read as follows:

MNTLHLTH (r: 0; 1; 2; 3-10; 11-30)

By recoding the variable MNTLHLTH in this way, we have created an ordinal-level variable with five categories. The first category represents respondents who reported having no days of poor mental health in the past 30 days, the second category includes those who had just one day of poor mental health, and the third includes those who reported having two days of poor mental health. The fourth category includes respondents who reported having between 3 and 10 days of poor

Figure 5.3

Frequency Distribution

Cells contain: **Column percent** Weighted N		1 UNDER $1 000	2 $1 000 TO 2999	3 $3 000 TO 3999	4 $4 000 TO 4999	5 $5 000 TO 5999	6 $6 000 TO 6999	7 $7 000 TO 7999	8 $8 000 TO 9999	9 $10000 TO 12499	10 $12500 TO 14999	11 $15000 TO 17499
MNTLHLTH	0	**51.6** 12.8	**53.6** 14.3	**45.1** 15.1	**73.2** 8.1	**60.8** 13.5	**60.2** 14.1	**49.9** 10.8	**57.9** 26.6	**44.7** 43.1	**54.3** 44.7	**48.6** 51.9
	1	**3.3** .8	**.0** .0	**.0** .0	**.0** .0	**5.8** 1.3	**5.5** 1.3	**5.7** 1.2	**4.0** 1.8	**.0** .0	**5.0** 4.1	**3.4** 3.6
	2	**.0** .0	**6.2** 1.6	**8.0** 2.7	**4.0** .4	**.0** .0	**11.6** 2.7	**9.6** 2.1	**4.7** 2.1	**7.3** 7.0	**5.5** 4.5	**12.5** 13.3

mental health in the past 30 days, and the fifth category includes those who had 11 or more days of poor mental health in the past 30 days. By running the table with these recoded variables, the cross-tab in Figure 5.4 will result.

The data used to create Figure 5.4 are the same as the data used to create Figure 5.3, but with the recoded categories, the table is both easier to read and easier to interpret. In Figure 5.4, we can see clearly that respondents with higher family incomes are more likely than respondents with low family incomes to report having had no days of poor mental health in the past 30 days. The left-most column shows that among the poorest respondents in the sample (those with families earning below $20,000 per year), 50.1% of respondents reported having had no days of poor mental health in the past 30 days. The right-most column shows us that among the wealthiest respondents (those with family incomes of $150,000 per year or more), 65% reported having had no days of poor mental health in the past 30 days. Among all income groups, the most common response (that is, the modal category) is no days of poor mental health, but respondents with high family incomes are nonetheless more likely to have no days of poor mental health than respondents with low family incomes. Similarly, the bottom row of the table shows us that respondents with low incomes are more likely than those with high incomes to report having 11 or more days of poor mental health in the past 30 days. Among

Figure 5.4

Frequency Distribution										
Cells contain: **-Column percent** -Weighted N		**INCOME06**								**ROW TOTAL**
		1 1-12	2 13-17	3 18-19	4 20-21	5 22	6 23	7 24	8 25	
MNTLHLTH	1: 0	50.1 286.0	56.9 558.5	55.9 510.2	59.0 599.4	59.4 264.7	64.4 175.5	61.5 119.6	65.0 331.5	58.0 2,845.4
	2: 1	3.4 19.2	4.5 44.5	4.5 41.3	7.0 70.7	5.2 23.4	5.6 15.3	9.9 19.3	5.9 30.0	5.4 263.6
	3: 2	7.4 42.1	6.7 65.4	9.8 89.7	8.5 86.1	8.4 37.6	4.2 11.5	7.0 13.5	5.5 28.0	7.6 374.0
	4: 3-10	22.1 126.4	18.5 181.3	19.9 181.9	18.9 192.0	19.2 85.6	19.2 52.3	16.9 32.8	17.3 88.4	19.2 940.7
	5: 11-30	17.0 97.1	13.5 132.4	9.8 89.7	6.7 68.1	7.6 34.0	6.5 17.8	4.7 9.2	6.2 31.8	9.8 480.3
	COL TOTAL	100.0 570.9	100.0 982.1	100.0 912.9	100.0 1,016.4	100.0 445.3	100.0 272.4	100.0 194.4	100.0 509.7	100.0 4,904.0

respondents with family incomes of $20,000 or less, 17% reported having had 11 or more days of poor mental health in the past 30 days. Among respondents with family incomes of $150,000 or more, only 6.2% reported having had 11 days or more of poor mental health.

COMPARING THE MEAN RESPONSE FOR DIFFERENT GROUPS

In cases where the dependent variable is measured at the ordinal or interval-ratio level, it is often useful to compare how the mean value of a variable differs for various groups. We might ask, for example, "On average, how many days of poor mental health are reported by low-income respondents, and how does this compare to middle- and high-income respondents?" On a different topic, we might ask, "What is the average occupational prestige score for non-Hispanic white, non-Hispanic Black, and Hispanic/Latino/a respondents?" Or we might ask, "On average, do respondents who describe themselves as upper class visit art museums more than respondents who describe themselves as middle class?" All of these questions (and many more!) can be answered easily by a "Comparison of Means" in SDA.

COMPARISONS OF MEANS AND LEVELS OF MEASUREMENT

When comparing the mean response for different groups, it is vital that the *dependent* variable is either an ordinal-level or interval-ratio-level variable. Recall that nominal-level variables (also called "categorical-level" variables) do not have an inherent order to them. The order of the categories is meaningless, and, as a result, it is not possible to calculate a meaningful average or mean.

If you ask for it, the SDA program will provide you with a mean for any variable, including nominal-level variables. In these situations,

you must remember that the mean has no real meaning!

While the *dependent* variable must be either an ordinal-level or interval-ratio-level variable, the *independent* variable (the variable that corresponds to the groups being compared) can be nominal, ordinal, or even interval-ratio. For our purposes, it's best to compare the means across a relatively small number of groups so that the resulting analysis is easy to read and each category of the grouping variable has a sufficient number of people.

To illustrate the value of a comparison of means, let's continue to explore the relationship between class and mental health. More specifically, we can ask the following research question: "On average, how many days of poor mental health are reported by low-income respondents, and how does this compare to middle- and high-income respondents?"

Figure 5.5

SDA 4.0   Selected Study: **GSS 1972-2014 Cumulative Datafile**

| Analysis | Create Variables | Download Custom Subset | Search | **Standard Codebook**   **Codebook by Year of Interview**

Variable Selection

Selected: [   ] [View]

Copy to: [Dep] [Row] [Col] [Ctrl] [Filter]

Mode: ○ Append ● Replace

| Tables | **Means** | Correl. matrix | Comp. correl. | Regression | Logit/Probit | List values |

SDA Comparison of Means Program
Help: **General** / **Recoding Variables**

Dependent: [MNTLHLTH] (Required)

Row: [INCOME06 (r: 1-12; 13-17; 18-19; 20-21; 22;23;24;2] (Required)

Column: [   ]

Control: [   ]

Selection Filter(s): [   ]

Weight: [COMPWT - Composite weight: WTSSALL * OVERSAMP * FORI ▾]

Main statistic to display: [Means ▾]

Optional transformation of the dependent variable: [(None) ▾]

▸ Output Options

▸ Chart Options

▸ Decimal Options

[Run the Table] [Clear Fields]

- ▸ ▣ CASE IDENTIFICATION AND YEAR
- ▸ ▣ RESPONDENT BACKGROUND VARIABLES
- ▸ ▣ PERSONAL AND FAMILY INFORMATION
- ▸ ▣ ATTITUDINAL MEASURES - NATIONAL PROBLEMS
- ▸ ▣ PERSONAL CONCERNS
- ▸ ▣ SOCIETAL CONCERNS
- ▸ ▣ WORKPLACE AND ECONOMIC CONCERNS
- ▸ ▣ CONTROVERSIAL SOCIAL ISSUES
- ▸ ▣ MILITARY ISSUES
- ▸ ▣ OBLIGATIONS AND RESPONSIBILITIES
- ▸ ▣ 1985 TOPICAL MODULE: SOCIAL NETWORKS
- ▸ ▣ 1987 TOPICAL MODULE: SOCIO-POLITICAL PARTICIP/
- ▸ ▣ 1988 TOPICAL MODULE: RELIGION
- ▸ ▣ 1990 MODULE: INTER-GROUP RELATIONS
- ▸ ▣ 1991 TOPICAL MODULE: WORK ORGANIZATIONS
- ▸ ▣ 1993 ISSP MODULE: CULTURE
- ▸ ▣ 1994 FAMILY MOBILITY MODULE
- ▸ ▣ 1994 MULTICULTURALISM MODULE
- ▸ ▣ FAMILY - FINANCES - DONATIONS
- ▸ ▣ HOW WILLING VIGNETTE
- ▸ ▣ ATTITUDES TOWARDS MENTAL HEALTH

To analyze how the mean response varies for different social groups, begin on the "Analysis" tab of SDA. The "Analysis" tab is in the upper left corner. Once you are there, select the "Means" tab, which is located more toward the middle of the screen. (See Figure 5.5.)

In the "Dependent" field, type the name of the dependent variable, MNTLHLTH. In the "Row" field, type the variable that contains the groups that you would like to analyze. In this case, I have entered the variable INCOME06 along with the recoding language described above:

INCOME06 (r: 1-12; 13-17; 18-19; 20-21; 22; 23; 24; 25)

Were I to just type INCOME06 in the row field without the recoding language, the analysis would produce the mean income levels for each of the 25 income values.

Make sure that your "Weight" field is set to COMPWT, and then click "Run the Table." The analysis shown in Figures 5.6 and 5.7 should result.

Figure 5.6 shows the mean, or average, days of poor mental health reported by respondents at various income levels. The top number in each cell corresponds to the mean. So, in the top cell, we see that on average, respondents whose total family income was below $20,000 reported having had 5.11 days of poor mental health in

Figure 5.6

Main Statistics		
Cells contain: -**Mean** -Complex Std Errs -Weighted N		
INCOME06	1: 1-12	**5.11** .444 570.9
	2: 13-17	**4.19** .279 982.1
	3: 18-19	**3.49** .260 912.9
	4: 20-21	**2.73** .214 1,016.4
	5: 22	**2.85** .313 445.3
	6: 23	**2.33** .435 272.4
	7: 24	**2.12** .400 194.4
	8: 25	**2.32** .263 509.7
	COL TOTAL	**3.36** .111 4,904.0

the past 30 days. Respondents whose total family income was $130,000 to $149,999 are represented in category 7 (We know this because 7 represents a score of 24 on the original, unrecoded variable INCOME06), and on average, these respondents reported having had only 2.12 days of poor mental health in the past 30 days.

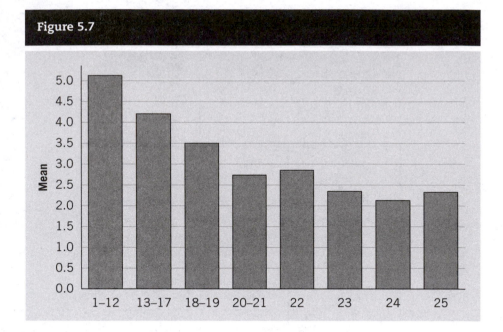

Figure 5.7

Figure 5.7 shows the same information provided in Figure 5.6, but in a graph. The vertical axis shows the mean number of days of poor mental health, and each bar represents a different income group. The left-most bar represents respondents with the lowest family incomes, and the right-most bar represents individuals with the highest family incomes. Here it is easy to see that, as you move from left to right (that is, from low to high income levels), the average number of poor mental health days generally gets smaller.

APPLICATION: MOTHERS' EDUCATIONAL ATTAINMENT AND THE SOCIAL CLASS OF THEIR ADULT CHILDREN

As explained previously, the General Social Survey is an excellent resource for analyzing issues related to class and socioeconomic status. In this application, the focus is on how class is transmitted across generations. The guiding question is "How does mothers' educational attainment relate to adult children's financial, cultural, and social capital?" More specifically, this analysis will look at three different groups of respondents: (1) those whose mothers had less than a high school education, (2) those whose mothers had a high school education but not a bachelor's degree, and (3) those whose mothers had a bachelor's degree or higher. It will assess how these groups compare to one another in terms of their average scores on three measures of social class.

Step 1. Restate the research question, and identify the independent and dependent variables.

The research question here is "How does mothers' educational attainment relate to adult children's financial, cultural, and social capital?" Mothers' educational attainment (MADEG) is the independent variable, and there are three dependent variables: respondents' family income (INCOME06), respondents' years of formal education (EDUC), and the number of lawyers known by respondents (ACQLAWS).

Step 2. View each variable to make sure that you understand what it measures. Viewing the variable shows the precise wording of the survey question that corresponds to the variable and also shows how responses are coded. When viewing the variable, make note of the level of measurement: Is it nominal, ordinal, or interval-ratio?

By viewing INCOME06, we can see that it corresponds to the following survey question:

> In which of these groups did your total family income, from all sources, fall last year before taxes, that is.

As discussed above, INCOME06 is an ordinal-level variable, with responses ranging from 1 (which indicates family incomes below $1,000) to 25 (which indicates family incomes of $150,000 or more).

By viewing the variable ACQLAWS, we can see that it is also an ordinal-level variable, corresponding to the following survey question:

> I'm going to ask you some questions about all the people that you are acquainted with, meaning that you know their name and would stop and talk at least for a moment if you ran into the person on the street or in a shopping mall. Some of these questions may seem unusual but they are an important way to help us understand more about social networks in America. Please answer the questions as best you can. 1103b. How many are lawyers?

When viewing ACQLAWS, it is also important to note that responses range from 1 to 5, where a response of 1 indicates that the respondent knows no lawyers, a response of 2 indicates that the respondent knows one lawyer, a response of 3 indicates that the respondent knows between two and five lawyers, a response of 4 indicates that the respondent knows six to ten lawyers, and a response of 5 indicates that the respondent knows more than ten lawyers.

As discussed above in the box on "viewing" variables related to educational attainment, viewing the variables for respondents' educational attainment and mother's highest degree shows only a partial description of the survey question. When describing the meanings of these variables, it is sufficient to say that EDUC is an interval-ratio-level variable corresponding to the highest year of school that the respondent completed and MADEG is a five-category, ordinal-level variable corresponding to the highest degree earned by the respondent's mother.

Step 3. Determine which time period the data is from and specify which years you would like to analyze. Remember that when you view a variable, you are viewing the combined data across all survey years. You may want to restrict your analysis to a particular time frame, perhaps using only the most recent years of survey data. You can do this easily by setting a filter (see more on filters in Chapters 4 and 6). Whether you use a filter or not, always be sure to be clear about which survey years are included in your analysis when describing your data and interpreting your results.

The easiest way to determine when particular variables were included in the GSS is by creating a cross-tab for each of the variables in your analysis by the variable YEAR (the variable that corresponds to the survey year). To do this, make sure you are on the "Analysis" page of the SDA website and on the tab that corresponds to "Tables." Producing a cross-tab of ACQLAWS in the "Row" field and YEAR in the "Column" field will result in Figure 5.8, which shows us that this variable was included only in the 2006 survey. As mentioned previously, INCOME06 has been included in every survey year since 2006. Respondent's educational attainment (EDUC) has been asked in every survey year, as has respondent's mother's highest degree (MADEG).

Figure 5.8

Frequency Distribution			
Cells contain:		**YEAR**	
-Column percent			**ROW**
-Weighted N		2006	**TOTAL**
	1: 0	**42.3** 284.7	**42.3** 284.7
	2: 1	**16.9** 113.7	**16.9** 113.7
	3: 2-5	**32.7** 220.0	**32.7** 220.0
ACQLAWS	4: 6-10	**4.7** 31.6	**4.7** 31.6
	5: More than 10	**3.3** 22.2	**3.3** 22.2
	COL TOTAL	**100.0** 672.2	**100.0** 672.2

When analyzing respondents' educational attainment and income, we can restrict our analysis to recent survey years by typing the following into the "Filter" field:

YEAR (2010-2014)

Step 4. Conduct the analysis. To conduct a comparison of means, begin by specifying the groups within the independent variable whose means you'd like to compare. In this example, we are assessing the relationship between respondents' mothers' education (measured in terms of mother's highest educational degree) and respondents' social class. Mother's highest degree (MADEG) is the independent variable, which is originally coded into five categories, where 0 equals less than high school, 1 equals a high school diploma, 2 equals a junior college degree, 3 equals a bachelor's degree, and 4 equals a graduate degree.

We could conduct this comparison of means using the five educational categories described above. Instead, let's recode the variable into three broader categories: (1) respondents whose mothers had less than a high school diploma, (2) respondents whose mothers had a high school diploma or a junior college degree but not a bachelor's degree, and (3) respondents whose mothers had a bachelor's degree or higher. To do this, we will need to recode the variable MADEG as follows:

MADEG (r: 0; 1-2; 3-4)

Now run a comparison of means between the independent variable (MADEG) and each of the dependent variables.

Begin by making sure you are on the "Analysis" page of the SDA website (as opposed to the "Search" page, for example), and then make sure you have the tab for "Means" selected (as opposed to the tab for "Tables").

Construct your comparison of means by entering one of the dependent variables in the "Dependent" field and then entering the independent variable in the "Row" field. In this example, we have one independent variable (MADEG) and three dependent variables (INCOME06, EDUC, and ACQLAWS). Let's start with the first of these, INCOME06.

Enter INCOME06 in the "Dependent" field, and in the "Row" field enter the independent variable MADEG, followed by the recoding instructions:

MADEG (r: 0; 1-2; 3-4)

Before running the table, be sure that you have the default, COMPWT, selected in the "Weight" field. Make sure that you restrict your analysis to the most recent surveys by entering the following into the "Filter" field:

YEAR (2010-2014)

The resulting analysis, which includes a summary table, a table of means, and a bar graph, is shown in Figures 5.9 and 5.10.

Next, run a comparison of means using the same independent variable (MADEG) but the second dependent variable, EDUC, which corresponds to respondents'

Figure 5.9

		Variables			
Role	**Name**	**Label**	**Range**	**MD**	**Dataset**
Dependent	**INCOME06**	TOTAL FAMILY INCOME	1-25	0,26-99	1
Row	**MADEG(Recoded)**	MOTHERS HIGHEST DEGREE	1-3		1
Weight	**COMPWT**	Composite weight = WTSSALL * OVERSAMP * FORMWT	.1913-11.1261		1
Filter	**YEAR(2010-2014)**	GSS YEAR FOR THIS RESPONDENT	1972-2014		1

Main Statistics	
Cells contain: **-Mean** -Complex Std Errs -Weighted N	
MADEG	1: 0
	2: 1-2
	3: 3-4
	COL TOTAL

1: 0	**15.75** .280 1,609.0
2: 1-2	**18.14** .187 2,971.8
3: 3-4	**19.30** .285 836.0
COL TOTAL	**17.61** .200 5,416.8

highest year of formal education. In the "Independent" field, keep the recoded variable corresponding to mother's highest degree:

MADEG (r: 0;1-2; 3-4)

In the "Dependent" field, now enter the new dependent variable, EDUC. Make sure COMPWT is selected in the "Weight" field. Check to make sure that the filter is restricting your analysis to recent data with the command "YEAR (2010-2014)." Running the table should produce the results shown in Figures 5.11 and 5.12.

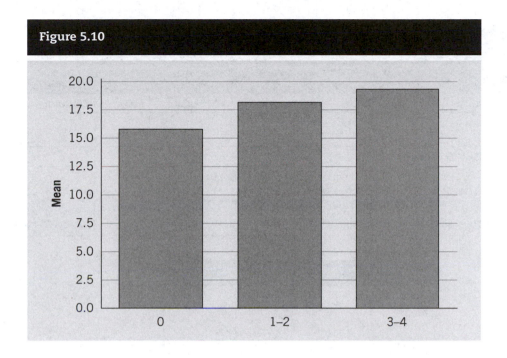

Figure 5.10

Finally, run a comparison of means using the same independent variable (MADEG) but the third indicator of respondents' social class, ACQLAWS, which corresponds to the number of lawyers the respondent is acquainted with—an indication of the respondent's social capital. In the "Independent" variable field, keep the recoded variable corresponding to mother's highest degree:

MADEG (r: 0; 1-2; 3-4)

In the "Dependent" field, now enter the new dependent variable, ACQLAWS. Make sure COMPWT is selected in the "Weight" field. Recall that, unlike the variables for income and education, the variable ACQLAWS is included only in the 2006 GSS. If you run your analysis using the "Filter" described above, YEAR (2010-2014), you will receive an error message; there are no data for the variable ACQLAWS during this time period. Instead, you can run the analysis with no filter; since the variable ACQLAWS is included only in 2006, only data from 2006 will be included in your analysis. Alternatively, you can run the analysis by including a filter of YEAR (2006). Both approaches will produce identical results.

Running the table should produce the results shown in Figures 5.13 and 5.14.

Step 5. Interpret your results. There are five basic steps for interpreting a comparison of means.

Figure 5.11

		Variables			
Role	**Name**	**Label**	**Range**	**MD**	**Dataset**
Dependent	**EDUC**	HIGHEST YEAR OF SCHOOL COMPLETED	0-20	97,98,99	1
Row	**MADEG(Recoded)**	MOTHERS HIGHEST DEGREE	1-3		1
Weight	**COMPWT**	Composite weight = WTSSALL * OVERSAMP * FORMWT	.1913-11.1261		1
Filter	**YEAR(2010-2014)**	GSS YEAR FOR THIS RESPONDENT	1972-2014		1

Main Statistics	
Cells contain: -**Mean** -Complex Std Errs -Weighted N	
MADEG 1: 0	**11.99** .146 1,840.9
2: 1-2	**14.04** .076 3,308.4
3: 3-4	**15.63** .098 940.7
COL TOTAL	*13.67* *.096* *6,090.0*

1. Remind your audience of the basics.

When presenting your analyses to an audience, it is important to:

    a. *Restate your research question.* In this case, the research question is "How does mothers' educational attainment relate to adult children's financial, cultural, and social capital?"

    b. *Remind your audience of the data source and the specific variables that you used to answer this question.* In this case, the data source

Figure 5.12

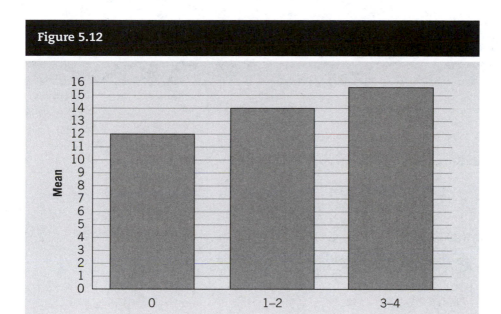

is the 2006 survey (for the analysis of lawyers known to the respondent) and the 2010–2014 surveys (for the remaining analyses). Respondents were asked about the highest educational degree their mothers had received as well as about their own educational attainment, their total family income, and the number of lawyers they personally knew.

c. *Identify and describe the dependent and independent variables, clearly stating how each variable was coded. If you recoded variables in your analysis, be sure to discuss the new categories that you created and what each means.* In this case, the independent variable, mother's education, was measured in terms of her highest degree: less than a high school diploma, a high school diploma or junior college degree, or a bachelor's degree or higher. There are three dependent variables: Respondents' educational attainment was measured in terms of the number of years of formal education they had; respondents' family income was assessed with an ordinal-level variable, with responses ranging from 1 (which indicates family incomes below $1,000) to 25 (which indicates family incomes of $150,000 or more); and the number of lawyers that the respondent was acquainted with is an ordinal-level variable with five categories, where 1 represents knowing no lawyers, 2 represents knowing one lawyer, 3 represents knowing between two and five lawyers, 4 represents knowing between six and ten lawyers, and 5 represents knowing more than ten lawyers.

Figure 5.13

Variables					
Role	**Name**	**Label**	**Range**	**MD**	**Dataset**
Dependent	**ACQLAWS**	NUMBER OF LAWYER R IS ACQUAINTED WITH	1-5	0,8,9	1
Row	**MADEG(Recoded)**	MOTHERS HIGHEST DEGREE	1-3		1
Weight	**COMPWT**	Composite weight = WTSSALL * OVERSAMP * FORMWT	.1913-11.1261		1
Filter	**YEAR(2006)**	GSS YEAR FOR THIS RESPONDENT	1972-2014		1

Main Statistics		
Cells contain: -**Mean** -Complex Std Errs -Weighted N		
MADEG	1: 0	**1.93** .083 165.3
	2: 1-2	**2.09** .067 348.7
	3: 3-4	**2.55** .129 91.6
	COL TOTAL	*2.12* *.052* *605.5*

> d. *Specify the number of cases included in each analysis.* The overall number of valid cases (N) included in each analysis is presented in the bottom right corner of the "Main Statistics" table. In the analysis of how mothers' education influences respondents' family income (Figures 5.9 and 5.10), the weighted number of cases is approximately 5,417. In the analysis of how mothers' education influences respondents' education (Figures 5.11 and 5.12), the weighted number of cases is 6,090 people, and in the analysis of how mothers' education influences respondents' social networks (Figures 5.13 and 5.14), the weighted number of cases is approximately 606.

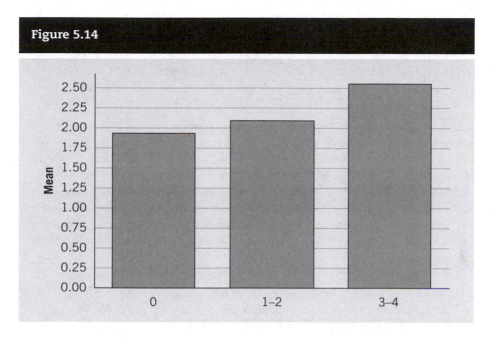

Figure 5.14

2. Focus on specifics.

The first step in interpreting a comparison of means is to look carefully at the specific numbers in the tables and interpret them as specifically as you can. The "Main Statistics" table within each of the three analyses presents the mean, or average score, for the dependent variable for each group within the independent variable. So, for example, the "Main Statistics" table within Figure 5.9 shows that, among respondents whose mothers had less than a high school education, the mean family income score was 15.75. But how do we determine what this 15.75 actually means? By viewing the variable INCOME06 (results are shown in Figure 5.1), we can see that a score of 15 on this variable represents a total family income of $25,000 to $29,999 and a 16 represents a family income of $30,000 to $34,999. A score of 15.75, then, is somewhere between $25,000 and $35,000.

Looking back at Figure 5.9, which shows the mean family incomes for respondents whose mothers had low, middle, and high levels of formal education, we can see that the mean income score for respondents whose mothers had a high school diploma or junior college degree was 18.14, and respondents whose mothers had at least a bachelor's degree had a mean family income score of 19.3. As shown in Figure 5.1, the value of 18 on this variable corresponds to a family income of $40,000 to 49,999 and 19 corresponds to a value of $50,000 to $59,999. Taking all of this together, we can see that compared with respondents whose mothers had low levels of education, respondents whose mothers had a high level of education tended to have higher family incomes.

Figures 5.11 and 5.12 show the relationship between mothers' education and children's education. Here we see that among respondents whose mothers had low levels of education (less than a high school diploma), the average educational attainment was 12 years (11.99). For respondents whose mothers had a moderate level of education, the average educational attainment was 14 years, and for respondents whose mothers had obtained a bachelor's degree or more (category 3), the average educational attainment was 15.6 years. In general, as with financial capital, respondents whose mothers had higher educational attainment are shown here to have also had higher levels of cultural capital.

Finally, Figures 5.13 and 5.14 show the relationship between mothers' educational attainment and the number of lawyers respondents are acquainted with. The same general pattern is shown here. Respondents whose mothers had high levels of education have a higher mean for the variable ACQLAWS, showing that these respondents were more likely than respondents whose mothers had low levels of education to be acquainted with a high number of lawyers. More generally, respondents whose mothers had a high level of cultural capital (measured in terms of education) were themselves more likely to personally know more lawyers and thus more likely to have a high level of social capital.

3. Consider the big picture.

After examining individual values within each table, it is important to step back and take a larger view of the overall relationship presented in the tables. When examining each table individually, are there any patterns or trends that you can see with the means, or do the percentages seem to go up and down at random? The bar charts that SDA produces can also be of great help here. Think also about how the individual analyses work together. Do they all point to the same overall conclusion, or are the results more mixed? If the individual analyses seem to point to different conclusions, how do you make sense of these results?

In the analyses of mothers' education and respondents' financial, cultural, and social capital, all of the individual analyses point to the same general conclusion: Respondents whose mothers had high levels of education were more likely to have high levels of financial capital (measured in terms of family income), cultural capital (measured in terms of education), and social capital (measured in terms of the number of lawyers one is acquainted with).

4. Consider limitations.

An important part of all scientific research is to be clear about the limitations of the research. The above analyses should be understood as a starting point and not the unquestioned "final word" on the relationship between mothers' educational attainment and children's social class. Every research project has limitations, some more than others, and it is important to make these clear when interpreting the results.

When considering the limitations of any survey research project, it is important to consider issues of survey design, possible sample biases, and generalizability. For example, the results here apply only to adults in the US who are aged 18 and older. Respondents include English- and Spanish-speaking adults, but adults in the US who are not able to speak either language are not included in the analysis. Nor are those living in institutions such as prisons or mental institutions included in this analysis.

It is also important to consider potential confounding variables—variables that are not included in the analyses but might be affecting the relationship between the independent and dependent variables. For example, how might differences in fathers' educational attainment affect children's social, financial, and cultural capital? Respondents' age, gender, race, and ethnicity likely play an important role as well. In more complex analyses, we could "control for" these additional factors to help answer this question. For our purposes here, however, it is sufficient to point out potential confounding variables and other limitations.

Finally, while it is crucial to explain what the analyses reveal about the larger research question, it is often useful to specify what the analyses do *not* tell us about the research question. Anticipate possible misinterpretations. Clarify what the findings suggest and also what they don't suggest. For example, the above analyses indicate that respondents whose mothers had college degrees are more likely to have high levels of education compared to respondents whose mothers had lower levels of education. At the same time, among respondents whose mothers had high levels of education, the mean educational attainment was still *less* than 16 years.

5. Summarize your conclusions.

Interpreting your results within a social justice framework requires thinking through issues of power and inequality, socially constructed differences, and links between the micro and macro levels of society as well as the importance of intersecting inequalities. What do the above analyses reveal about the multiple dimensions of social class, the ways in which it is passed down through generations, and the ways in which class-based inequalities are maintained and reproduced? Are class-based privileges passed down to LGBT children to the same extent they are transmitted to heterosexuals? How might the findings presented here differ if, in addition to class-based differences, we examined racial/ethnic differences as well? What social policies could be enacted to help people overcome the disadvantages associated with having parents who themselves had low levels of education? These questions can be answered by combining further analyses of GSS data with research that is qualitative, historical, comparative, and theoretical.

EXERCISES

Use the SDA website to answer the following questions:

1. What does the variable VISART represent?

    a. the number of times the respondent visited an art museum last year

    b. the number of visual artists the respondent is acquainted with

    c. the respondent's support for government funding for the arts

    d. the number of times the respondent purchased art in the past 12 months

2. The variable VISART is best described as:

    a. nominal level.

    b. ordinal level.

    c. interval-ratio level.

3. In what year(s) was the variable VISART included in the General Social Survey?

(Hint: to determine the answer, make a cross-tab of the variables VISART and YEAR. Make sure you are on the "Tables" tab within the "Analysis" page of the SDA.)

a. 1972–2014

b. 2006 only

c. 2008 and 2012

d. 2008, 2010, and 2012

4. Conduct a comparison of means by entering DEGREE in the "Row" field and VISART in the "Dependent" field, using no filter for survey year. (Hint: Make sure you are on the "Means" tab within the "Analysis" page of the SDA.) Based on the resulting table, which of the following statements best describes the relationship between DEGREE and VISART?

a. 32% of those who scored a 0 on degree also scored a 1 on VISART.

b. Respondents who scored a 4 on degree were 250 times more likely than other respondents to report a high score on the variable VISART.

c. Compared with respondents who had low levels of education, respondents with higher levels of education reported, on average, lower values on the variable VISART.

d. Compared with respondents who had low levels of education, respondents with higher levels of education reported, on average, higher values on the variable VISART.

For the following questions, it is useful to note that the variable PADEG is an ordinal-level variable corresponding to the respondent's father's highest educational degree. The variable PRESTG80 is an interval-ratio-level variable corresponding to the respondent's occupational prestige.

5. Excluding the nonvalid response categories (IAP, NA, DK), the variable PADEG has _____ valid response categories.

a. 4

b. 5

c. 20

d. 25

6. Recoding the variable PADEG with the command "PADEG (r: 0; 1-2; 3-4)" transforms PADEG into a variable with _____ categories.

a. 2

b. 3

c. 4

d. 10

7. When the variable PADEG is recoded with the command "PADEG (r: 0; 1-2; 3-4)," a score of 3 on this new variable indicates that:

a. the respondent's father had a high school diploma but no degree higher than a high school diploma.

b. the respondent's father had a bachelor's degree but no degree higher than a bachelor's degree.

c. the respondent's father had at least a bachelor's degree.

d. the respondent's father had a graduate degree.

8. Conduct a comparison of means by entering "PADEG (r: 0; 1-2; 3-4)" into the "Row" field, PRESTG80 into the "Dependent" field, and "YEAR (2010-2014)" into the "Filter" field. (Hint: Make sure you are on the "Means" tab within the "Analysis" page of the SDA.) What is the best interpretation of the top number in the resulting table of "Main Statistics" (40.88)?

a. 40.88% of respondents had fathers with less than a high school diploma.

b. Among respondents whose fathers had less than a high school diploma, the average occupational prestige score was 40.88.

c. Of respondents whose fathers had less than a high school diploma, 40.88% had no occupational prestige.

9. More generally, the resulting analysis reveals that:

a. compared with respondents whose fathers had low levels of education, respondents with higher levels of education had, on average, a higher level of occupational prestige.

b. compared with respondents whose fathers had low levels of education, respondents with higher levels of education had, on average, a higher level of occupational prestige.

c. on average, respondents whose fathers had a high school diploma but no degree beyond a high school diploma had the highest occupational prestige scores.

10. In general, when conducting a comparison of means, the dependent variable can be ____ or ____ but should not be _____.

a. interval-ratio; ordinal; categorical

b. categorical; interval-ratio; ordinal

c. ordinal; categorical; interval-ratio

ANALYSES & ESSAYS

1. *What sociodemographic characteristics are related to respondents' beliefs about class-based inequality?* Identify one variable that you think plays a role in determining beliefs about class inequality. Identify three questions that assess respondents' beliefs about class inequality. Construct three separate cross-tabs that examine how the sociodemographic characteristic you have chosen relates to these beliefs about class inequality. If you use an ordinal- or interval-ratio-level variable such as AGE, recode it so that it has four categories or fewer. Interpret your results.

2. Sociologists use the term *job autonomy* to refer to the amount of control workers can exercise over their scheduling and work pace as well as the extent to which they are able to exercise creativity and independence on the job.[9] To what extent do people of different class statuses have different access to job autonomy? Create three different cross-tab analyses where DEGREE is the independent variable in each one and LOTOFSAY, MYSKILLS, and SETTHNGS are the different dependent variables. Interpret your results, giving particular attention to how your findings highlight the connections between the micro and macro levels of society.

3. *To what extent does class structure physical and mental health?* Conduct three comparisons of means by entering CLASS in the "Row" field and PHYSHLTH, MNTLHLTH, and HLTHDAYS (separately) in the "Dependent" field. Use a filter to restrict your analysis to data from the years 2010 through 2014. (Hint: Make sure you are on the "Means" tab within the "Analysis" page of the SDA.)

Interpret your results, giving particular attention to how your findings highlight the connections between the micro and macro levels of society.

4. Sociologists use the term *homophily* to refer to the fact that individuals tend to create and maintain relationships with people who are similar to themselves.[10] To what extent do those GSS respondents who are married end up marrying people with similar class backgrounds? To answer this question, first create a cross-tab of DEGREE and SPDEG using DEGREE as the independent variable and SPDEG as the dependent variable. Use a filter to restrict your analysis to data from the years 2010 to 2014. Then conduct a comparison of means using DEGREE as the "Row" variable and SPPRES80 as the "Dependent" variable. In this comparison of means, use a filter to restrict your analysis to data from the year 2010—the most recent year for which occupational prestige data exist. Interpret your results.

5. *To what extent do racial/ethnic and gender differences relate to differences in personal income?* Conduct two comparisons of means by entering RINCOM06 in the "Dependent" field and RACEHISP and then SEX in the "Row" field. Use a filter to restrict your analysis to data from the years 2010 through 2014. Interpret your results, remembering that you may have to view the variable RINCOM06 to understand what the mean values represent. In your interpretation, give particular attention to how your findings highlight the intersections of race/ethnicity and gender with class.

NOTES

1. Kerbo, Harold R. 2009. *Social Stratification and Inequality*. 7th ed. New York, NY: McGraw-Hill, p. 11.

2. Raskoff, Sally. 2014. "Social and Cultural Capital at School." *Everyday Sociology Blog*, November 14. Retrieved October 3, 2015 (http://www.everydaysociologyblog.com/2014/11/social-and-cultural-capital-at-school.html).

3. Ibid.

4. US Bureau of the Census. 1974. "Household Money Income in 1973 and Selected Social and Economic Characteristics of Households." Retrieved September 16, 2016 (http://www2.census.gov/prod2/popscan/p60-096.pdf).

5. Noss, Amanda. 2014. "Household Income: 2013." U.S. Bureau of the Census. Retrieved September 16, 2016 (https://www.census.gov/content/dam/Census/library/publications/2014/acs/acsbr13-02.pdf).

6. US Department of Health and Human Services, Office of the Assistant Secretary for Planning and Evaluation. 2013. "2013 Poverty Guidelines." Retrieved September 16, 2016 (http://aspe.hhs.gov/2013-poverty-guidelines).

7. For a list of occupations and their prestige scores, see https://gssdataexplorer.norc.org/documents/446/display.

8. See https://gssdataexplorer.norc.org/variables/16/vshow for a complete list of occupational codes for 2012 and 2014.

9. Adler, Marina A. 1993. "Gender Differences in Job Autonomy: The Consequences of Occupational Segregation and Authority Position." *Sociological Quarterly* 34(3):449–65.

10. See McPherson, Miller, Lynn Smith-Lovin, and James M. Cook. 2001. "Birds of a Feather: Homophily in Social Networks." *Annual Review of Sociology* 27:415–44.

CHAPTER 6

ANALYZING SEXUALITY WITH THE GSS

INTRODUCTION: KEY CONCEPTS IN SEXUALITY

In general, social scientists argue that sexuality is a social construct. What does this mean? It means, first, that social factors shape how, with whom, and when we engage in sexual behaviors.[1] As sociologist Steven Seidman explains, "Social factors determine which desires [and behaviors] are sexual, which serve as identities, which desires and identities are acceptable, and what forms of sexual intimacy are considered appropriate" in any particular time and place.[2] The very way we understand sexuality—what we consider to be "normal" sexual activity, what we consider to be "deviant" sexuality, and even what we consider to be sexual or not sexual—is deeply rooted in culture and society.

Conceptualizing sexuality as a social construct refutes the idea that sexuality is rooted entirely in nature and draws attention to sexuality as it operates as a socially created system of inequality.[3] As Plante (2006, xvi) argues, "the study of sexuality must include critical analysis of the things we often take for granted and an acknowledgement of how power, oppression, and inequalities are part of US [and global] culture."[4]

When people think of "sexuality," they often think of either sexual identities (such as lesbian, gay, bisexual, queer, or straight) or sexual acts (kissing, oral sex, other types of sexual activities). While social scientists do often study these aspects of sexuality, the social study of sexuality refers to a much broader range of social inquiry. Social scientists interested in sexuality often focus on how society influences people's beliefs and attitudes about sexuality (attitudes

Learning Objectives

By the end of this chapter, you should be able to:

1. Identify variables related to sexuality.

2. Construct new categories for variables (recoding).

3. Use filters to restrict the analysis to a particular time period or subgroup (selecting cases).

4. Conduct bivariate analyses related to sexuality and interpret these within a social justice framework.

toward premarital sex or beliefs about same-sex marriage), individuals' sexual practices (for example, how many sexual partners people have had in the past five years, or what percentage of people used a condom during their most recent sexual encounter), and sexual identities (whether people describe themselves as gay, lesbian, heterosexual, queer, or something else). In addition to studying sexuality at the level of the individual, social scientists seek to understand sexuality as a macro-level social institution—a system that "establishes patterns of expectations for individuals" and "orders the social processes of everyday life."[5] Sexuality, like class, race, and gender, operates as a system of inequality that structures opportunities and privilege.

For a century, survey research on sexuality has helped to draw attention to the diversity in the sexual desires, identities, and behaviors of adults in the US.[6] Moreover, survey research on sexuality has played an important role in documenting discrimination and oppression faced by sexual minorities.[7] As with race and gender, however, there are ongoing debates in the social sciences about how to best collect and analyze the data needed to document sexuality-based inequalities without simultaneously essentializing sexuality.[8]

Analyzing sexuality with a survey like the GSS is further complicated by the fact that individuals who identify as sexual minorities—that is, people who describe themselves as bisexual, queer, gay, homosexual, lesbian, asexual, pansexual, or other nonheterosexual or nonstraight identities—represent a relatively small proportion of the overall US population. A large-scale national survey conducted by the US Centers for Disease Control and Prevention in 2013 estimated that less than 3% of the US population identify themselves as gay, lesbian, or bisexual; 1.6% of adults surveyed self-identified as gay or lesbian, and 0.7% considered themselves to be bisexual.[9] Since 2008, the GSS has included a question asking respondents about their sexual identity, and in this survey too, approximately 95% of respondents describe themselves as heterosexual or straight. Because the GSS includes a very small number of respondents who identify as sexual minorities, it is difficult to draw meaningful conclusions about sexual minority respondents in this survey.

While only about 5% of adults surveyed in the GSS describe themselves as gay, lesbian, or bisexual, these sexual identities do not necessarily correspond to respondents' sexual behaviors. Social scientists and health researchers draw a distinction between identities (the words people use to describe themselves and the social groups to which they consider themselves to belong) and behaviors (the types of activities in which they engage). Not everyone who has sexual relations with people of the same sex describes herself or himself as gay, lesbian, or bisexual. Not everyone who describes herself or himself as gay, lesbian, bisexual, or queer is sexually active with a same-sex partner.[10] And, for that matter, many people who describe themselves as straight or heterosexual are not sexually active at all. The distinction between these two concepts—identity and behavior—is particularly important in sexuality research.

For the past four decades, the General Social Survey has asked a range of survey questions about sexuality. The majority of questions related to sexuality focus on individuals' sexual behaviors as well as their beliefs about sexuality. These include beliefs about premarital sex, same-sex marriage, and more recently beliefs about casual sex or "hooking up." This chapter provides an introduction to analyzing sexuality in the General Social Survey, with a focus on the dimensions of sexuality described above.

IDENTIFYING VARIABLES RELATED TO SEXUALITY

When analyzing and interpreting data related to sexuality in the GSS, it is important to remember how much our national and global conversations about sexuality have changed over the past four decades. At this time, issues of same-sex marriage; sexual assault; gay, lesbian, and bisexual people in the military; and the HPV vaccine are dominating the news headlines, but this has not always been the case. In the 1980s, debates about pornography (the "sex wars") were more pressing than they are now, and premarital sex (that is, sex before marriage) was much more controversial. Abortion has been an important issue for the past four decades—and indeed long before—but the conversations about abortion have changed considerably during this time.

The GSS questions related to sexuality reflect these cultural changes. While some of the survey questions in the GSS have been included regularly since the start of the survey (e.g., attitudes about abortion), others have emerged only recently (e.g., respondents' sexual orientation). Like questions about race and ethnicity, the survey questions about sexuality provide a window into how much our cultural conversations about sexuality have changed over the past four decades.

Searching for Variables Related to Sexuality

The first step in identifying variables related to sexuality is to brainstorm possible key words. *Sex* is an obvious choice, but remember that "sex" can also refer to someone's status as a male or female. And, as discussed in Chapter 3, in the GSS

SEARCH TIP

When searching for variables related to sexuality, remember that terminology about sexuality has changed a lot over the past several decades.

- Avoid abbreviations and acronyms (for example, don't search for *LGBTQ*).

- While people are more likely to use terms such as *gay*, *lesbian*, or *queer* in contemporary casual conversations, the GSS more often uses terms like *homosexual* and *homosexuality*.

the variable SEX, for example, actually represents the interviewer's assessment of the respondent's gender. Searching with the key word *sex* will yield a number of questions that focus on gender, not sexuality, and will leave you searching through more than 100 individual survey questions.

A more focused search is a better strategy. Depending on your interest, some key words and phrases to try include *sexual, sex education, homosexual, heterosexual, pornography, sex partners, love, abortion, birth control, rape, lesbian, gay,* and *bisexual*.

To get started with searching for variables, type SEX EDUCATION in the "Variable search term(s)" box, and then click the "Search" button. The results appear on the bottom portion of the screen and show us that our search produced three hits. Clicking on the "View" button for the variable SEXEDUC, we can see that the variable corresponds to the survey question "Would you be for or against sex education in the public schools?" Viewing the variable also produces a frequency table showing that the vast majority of respondents answered that they would indeed support sex education in the public schools. (Remember that the frequency table produced when "viewing" the variable in this way represents the combined responses across all survey years in which the question was asked.) By producing a cross-tab of the variables SEXEDUC and YEAR (see Chapter 2 for a review), we can see that this question has been asked regularly since 1974.

The other variables that include the phrase *sex education* are each included in only one survey year. The variable AIDSSXED corresponds to the survey question "Do you support or oppose the following measures to deal with AIDS? b. Require the teaching of safe sex practices, such as the use of condoms, in sex education courses

IDENTITIES, BEHAVIORS, AND BELIEFS

Remember that questions about individuals' sexuality can be about (1) identities, (2) behaviors, or (3) attitudes and beliefs.

For example, the variable SEXORNT focuses on identity and asks respondents, "Which of the following best describes you? Gay, Lesbian, or Homosexual; Bisexual; Heterosexual or Straight?" Same-sex sexual behaviors are better assessed with survey questions that focus on respondents' practices, experiences, or behaviors. For example, the variable SEXSEX5 asks respondents, "Have your sex partners in the last five years been exclusively

male, both male and female, or exclusively female?"

While for many individuals, their sexual identity might align well with their sexual behaviors, sociological and psychological research documents that this is not always the case. Many individuals who have sex with people of the same sex do not claim a gay, lesbian, bisexual, or queer identity. When analyzing and interpreting a survey question, it is important to remember which of these concepts you are dealing with and convey that information accurately.

in public schools." By making a quick cross-tab with the variable AIDSSXED and YEAR, we can see that AIDSSXED was asked only in 1988—when the HIV and AIDS epidemic was gaining visibility in the US. Similarly, the variable HSSEXED corresponds to the question "Here are some things that might be taught in school. How important is it that schools teach each of these to 15-year-olds? . . . Sex education." This question was included only once, in 1985.

Browsing for Variables Related to Sexuality

The codebook on the left-hand side of the SDA website allows users to easily identify clusters of variables about specific topics, such as sexuality. While there are some headings that deal specifically with sexuality (e.g., "Controversial Social Issues: Pornography"), many of the most interesting questions about sexual identity, beliefs about homosexuality, and support for the rights of sexual minorities are best found through searching rather than browsing.

If you are interested in browsing for variables related to sexuality, you may find the following subject headings and subheadings to be particularly useful:

- Controversial Social Issues
  - Abortion
  - Family Planning, Sex, and Contraception
    - ❖ Pornography
    - ❖ Abortion Part Two

- Family, Finances, Donations
  - Exchange of Human Organs, Babies, Sex

- 2008 Variables
  - Sex/Gay/Marital/Kids
  - Sexual Advances/Harassment/Clergy

This chapter focuses on analyzing inequalities related to sexuality, with an emphasis on using filters and recoding variables. To get us started, let's imagine that we're interested in looking at gender differences in the number of sexual partners reported by respondents. Viewing the variable PARTNERS reveals that this variable corresponds to the survey question "How many sex partners have you had in the last 12 months?" Figure 6.1 shows the frequency distribution produced by viewing this variable.

Note that this variable has 10 ten valid response categories. Values of –1, 98, and 99 represent nonvalid responses, that is, "missing data." PARTNERS is an ordinal-level variable, where 0 indicates that the respondent reported having had no sexual partners in the past year and 8 indicates that the respondent reported having had more than 100 partners in the past year. A value of 9 on this variable indicates that the respondent reported having had at least one sexual partner in the past year, but that she or he is uncertain about the exact number.

Figure 6.1

PARTNERS		HOW MANY SEX PARTNERS R HAD IN LAST YEAR	
Description of the Variable			
1541. How many sex partners have you had in the last 12 months?			
Percent	N	Value	Label
22.1	6,770	0	NO PARTNERS
64.2	19,665	1	1 PARTNER
6.5	1,990	2	2 PARTNERS
3.0	927	3	3 PARTNERS
1.7	513	4	4 PARTNERS
1.5	451	5	5-10 PARTNERS
0.3	107	6	11-20 PARTNERS
0.1	42	7	21-100 PARTNERS
0.0	11	8	MORE THAN 100 PARTNERS
0.5	150	9	1 OR MORE, # unknown
0.0	0	95	SEVERAL
	28,583	-1	IAP
	19	98	DK
	371	99	NA
100.0	59,599		**Total**

APPLYING A FILTER

Figure 6.1 combines the responses from every year in which the question was asked. But let's imagine that we are interested in what's been happening more recently and want to pay special attention to differences between men and women.

To explore gender differences in the number of sex partners reported by men and women respondents, make a cross-tab of the variables PARTNERS and SEX by typing PARTNERS into the "Row" field and SEX into the "Column" field. Add a filter by typing the following into the "Selection Filter" field:

YEAR (2008-2014)

Figure 6.2

Frequency Distribution				
		SEX		
Cells contain: -**Column percent** -Weighted N		1 MALE	2 FEMALE	*ROW* *TOTAL*
PARTNERS	0: NO PARTNERS	**15.6** 549.2	**21.7** 900.0	*18.9* *1,449.2*
	1: 1 PARTNER	**68.1** 2,392.9	**68.4** 2,838.3	*68.3* *5,231.2*
	2: 2 PARTNERS	**6.2** 218.1	**5.4** 225.7	*5.8* *443.8*
	3: 3 PARTNERS	**3.9** 136.7	**2.0** 81.0	*2.8* *217.7*
	4: 4 PARTNERS	**2.5** 88.2	**.8** 34.7	*1.6* *123.0*
	5: 5-10 PARTNERS	**2.1** 73.6	**.6** 24.9	*1.3* *98.5*
	6: 11-20 PARTNERS	**.6** 21.1	**.1** 3.9	*.3* *25.0*
	7: 21-100 PARTNERS	**.3** 9.7	**.0** 1.6	*.1* *11.3*
	8: MORE THAN 100 PARTNERS	**.0** 1.8	**.0** 1.4	*.0* *3.1*
	9: 1 OR MORE, # unknown	**.7** 23.2	**.9** 36.3	*.8* *59.5*
	COL TOTAL	*100.0* *3,514.5*	*100.0* *4,147.9*	*100.0* *7,662.4*

Color coding:	<-2.0	<-1.0	<0.0	>0.0	>1.0	>2.0	**Z**
N in each cell:	Smaller than expected			Larger than expected			

Filters are used to focus the analysis on a particular subset of data. The above filter restricts the analysis based on values of the variable YEAR and will limit the analysis to respondents from the 2008 through 2014 surveys. Remember also to keep the default of COMPWT in the "Weight" field. Run the table, and you should produce the cross-tab shown in Figure 6.2.

Figure 6.2 shows that 15.6% of men answered that they had had no sexual partners in the past 12 months, compared to 21.7% of women. Further down the table, we see that 2.1% of men surveyed and 0.6% of women surveyed indicated that they had had between 5 and 10 sexual partners in the past 12 months. (A more detailed explanation of cross-tabs is provided in Chapters 3 and 4, and you should refer to these chapters should you have any difficulty interpreting this table.)

THE NEED FOR CAUTION WHEN INTERPRETING SENSITIVE SURVEY QUESTIONS

Questions about sexuality—especially sexual behaviors and experiences—are very sensitive and can be influenced by issues of social desirability and gender norms. For example, in our current society, having "too many" sexual partners is generally looked down upon—particularly for women. So there may be social pressures for men and women who have had multiple sex partners to downplay the number of partners they've had. On the other hand, our cultural notions of masculinity sometimes reward men for having multiple sex partners. Some men respondents might exaggerate the number of sex partners they've had in efforts to appear more masculine.

Self-reports of past behaviors are always susceptible to these types of issues, but this is especially true for questions related to sensitive issues such as sexuality.

RECODING VARIABLES

Motivations for Recoding Variables

In addition to showing some interesting gender differences in the number of sex partners reported by men and women respondents, Figure 6.2 reveals that the variable PARTNERS has a highly **skewed** distribution. The vast majority of respondents indicated that they had had one sex partner, a substantial minority had had either no partners or two partners, and very few people—men or women— reported having had more than two partners.

Given that there are so few people who indicated having five or more partners, and consequently the tiny number of respondents in each cell in the bottom portion of the table, we might want to recode this variable into a smaller number of categories.

Reducing the number of categories in a variable can be a way to design categories that are more useful for your particular research question and can also produce a cross-tab that is easier to read. In this case, it might be easier to interpret this table if, for example, the categories were no partners, one partner, two partners, three partners, four partners, and five or more partners.

How to Recode Variables in SDA

To recode the variable PARTNERS in this way, simply modify what you typed in the "Row" box to the following:

PARTNERS (r: 0; 1; 2; 3; 4; 5-8)

Here the "r:" stands for "Recode into the following categories." Categories are separated by a semicolon (;), and the last category, "5-8," indicates that categories 5, 6, 7, and 8 should all be combined into one category. The last category in Figure 6.1 ("1 or more, # unknown") indicates that the respondent had at least one partner but didn't know the precise number. While interesting, this category is not particularly useful for the present research question, and so you may want to exclude it from the resulting analysis. If you did want to include this category, you could simply change the recode instructions to:

PARTNERS (r: 0; 1; 2; 3; 4; 5-8; 9)

Figure 6.3 shows the cross-tab for the recoded variable, where the categories have been recombined. Note that the sixth category (6: 5-8) combines the fifth, sixth, seventh, and eighth categories on the original variable, including respondents who had at least five and up to more than 100 sex partners. At first glance, it might look as if category 6 represents only those respondents who reported having had five to eight sex partners in the past 12 months, but this is not the case. The notation "5-8" refers to categories 5 through 8 on the original variable PARTNERS, before the recoding took place. With the newly recoded variable, category 6 includes people who reported having had five or more sexual partners.

The data used to create Figure 6.3 are basically the same as the data shown in Figure 6.2, except that those who answered "at least one partner, but I don't know how many" are now excluded. With the recoded categories, the table is both easier to read and easier to interpret. In Figure 6.3, we can see clearly that men are more likely than women to report having had three, four, five, or more sex partners in the past 12 months. Of the men respondents, 3.9% reported having had three sex partners in the past 12 months, compared to only 2.0% of women respondents. Men were also more likely than women to report having had five or more partners; of the men who provided valid answers to this question, 3.0% said they had had five or more partners, compared with less than 1.0% of women. Remember not to take these responses at face value, though. As discussed above, for a number of reasons, respondents' answers to questions about sexual behavior might not be entirely accurate.

Figure 6.3

		Variables			
Role	**Name**	**Label**	**Range**	**MD**	**Dataset**
Row	**PARTNERS (Recoded)**	HOW MANY SEX PARTNERS R HAD IN LAST YEAR	1-6		1
Column	**SEX**	RESPONDENTS SEX	1-2	0	1
Weight	**COMPWT**	Composite weight = WTSSALL * OVERSAMP * FORMWT	.1913-11.1261		1
Filter	**YEAR (2008-2014)**	GSS YEAR FOR THIS RESPONDENT	1972-2014		1

Frequency Distribution				
Cells contain: -**Column percent** -Weighted N		**SEX**		
		1 MALE	2 FEMALE	*ROW TOTAL*
PARTNERS	1: 0	**15.7** 549.2	**21.9** 900.0	*19.1* *1,449.2*
	2: 1	**68.5** 2,392.9	**69.0** 2,838.3	*68.8* *5,231.2*
	3: 2	**6.2** 218.1	**5.5** 225.7	*5.8* *443.8*
	4: 3	**3.9** 136.7	**2.0** 81.0	*2.9* *217.7*
	5: 4	**2.5** 88.2	**.8** 34.7	*1.6* *123.0*
	6: 5-8	**3.0** 106.2	**.8** 31.8	*1.8* *138.0*
	COL TOTAL	**100.0** 3,491.4	**100.0** 4,111.5	*100.0* *7,602.9*

APPLICATION: IS AGE ASSOCIATED WITH BELIEFS ABOUT HOMOSEXUALITY?

As explained previously, the GSS is an excellent resource for analyzing issues related to sexuality. There are many questions related to sexuality, some of which have been asked repeatedly over time and others of which reflect more contemporary social issues. In this application, the focus is on two variables that have been asked in recent survey years.

Step 1. Restate the research question and identify the independent and dependent variables.

In this case, the guiding research question is "Is respondents' age associated with beliefs about same-sex relations?" To answer this question, we can explore the relationship between the independent variable AGE with two dependent variables, HOMOSEX and MARHOMO.

Step 2. View each variable to make sure that it means what you think it means. Viewing the variable shows the precise wording of the survey question that corresponds to the variable as well as the variable's response categories.

By viewing HOMOSEX, we can see that this is an ordinal-level variable corresponding to the following survey question:

> What about sexual relations between two adults of the same sex?
> Would you say that they are: always wrong, almost always wrong,
> sometimes wrong, or not wrong at all?

By viewing MARHOMO, we can see that this is also an ordinal-level variable, where respondents were asked the following question:

> Do you agree or disagree? Homosexual couples should have the
> right to marry one another. (Strongly agree, agree, neither agree nor
> disagree, disagree, strongly disagree)

By viewing the variable AGE, we can see that this is an interval-ratio-level variable corresponding to the age of the survey respondent. Note that a score of 89 represents respondents aged 89 or above, and scores of 98 and 99 on the AGE variable indicate nonvalid responses of "Don't know" or "No answer."

Step 3. Determine which time period the data are from. Remember that when you view a variable, you are viewing the combined data across all survey years. If one particular question was asked regularly since 1972, then this is four decades of data. If another question was asked only once—say, in 1994—then you need to be very careful about comparing the responses for these two questions. It is thus always crucial to determine the survey years in which the variable you are analyzing was included.

The easiest way to do this is by creating a quick cross-tab of the variables in your analysis by the variable YEAR (the variable that corresponds to the survey year). Producing a cross-tab with HOMOSEX in the "Row" field and YEAR in the "Column" field (with the default, COMPWT, selected in the "Weight" field) will result in Figure 6.4.

As shown in Figure 6.4, the variable HOMOSEX has been asked regularly since 1973. Unless we limit our analysis to recent data using the "Filter" command, the resulting cross-tabs will be drawing from all of this data.

Producing a cross-tab of the variable MARHOMO with the variable YEAR will yield the table shown in Figure 6.5. As shown in this table, the variable MARHOMO was first asked in 1988, was not asked throughout the 1990s, but has been included regularly in more recent survey years.

AGE is a core variable in the GSS that has been asked in every year of the survey. If you want to double-check, produce a cross-tab of the variable AGE by the variable YEAR. But be warned—due to the number of categories in both variables, this will result in a very large table that is almost impossible to interpret.

Step 4. Conduct the analysis.

Begin constructing your cross-tabs by entering HOMOSEX in the "Row" field (since it is the dependent variable) and AGE in the "Column" field (since it is the independent variable). Before running the table, be sure that you have the default, COMPWT, selected in the "Weight" field. When you do this, you will see a very large table that is difficult to read, since the AGE variable has so many categories. To make a cross-tab that is more interpretable and meaningful, we can recode AGE into a smaller number of categories. Delete that large cross-tab and make a new one. Keep the variable HOMOSEX in the "Row" field, but now type the following into the "Column" box:

AGE (r: 18-29; 30-44; 45-59; 60-74; 75-89)

The above command is transforming the variable AGE into an ordinal-level variable that has only five categories. Note that the last category, "75-89," includes respondents who are aged 75 and older, since a score of 89 on the variable AGE included respondents aged 89 or older.

Since the two attitudinal variables we are interested in span a vast time period, and since attitudes about homosexuality have changed so much in the past four decades (see Figures 6.4 and 6.5), we might want to restrict our analysis to recent survey years. To restrict the analysis to data collected in the 2014 survey, in the "Filter" field type:

YEAR (2014)

Figure 6.4

Frequency Distribution

Cells contain:
- Column percent
- Weighted N

HOMOSEX	YEAR												
	1973	1974	1976	1977	1980	1982	1984	1985	1987	1988	1989	1990	1991
1: ALWAYS WRONG	**72.5** 1,048.5	**69.4** 981.0	**70.3** 1,005.9	**72.9** 1,062.3	**74.4** 1,044.0	**74.1** 1,315.2	**75.9** 1,074.6	**74.8** 1,121.6	**77.3** 1,364.5	**77.4** 731.7	**74.4** 732.9	**76.4** 662.6	**77.4** 718.5
2: ALMST ALWAYS WRG	**6.7** 96.9	**5.6** 78.8	**6.3** 90.3	**5.8** 85.0	**5.5** 77.8	**5.0** 88.9	**4.6** 64.4	**4.2** 62.7	**4.2** 74.5	**4.4** 42.0	**4.0** 39.3	**5.0** 43.0	**3.8** 35.1
3: SOMETIMES WRONG	**7.7** 110.7	**8.5** 120.7	**7.9** 113.6	**7.5** 109.7	**5.7** 80.6	**6.8** 120.6	**6.4** 90.8	**7.0** 104.9	**6.5** 115.1	**5.5** 51.5	**6.3** 62.3	**5.8** 49.9	**4.0** 37.2
4: NOT WRONG AT ALL	**11.2** 161.4	**12.9** 182.7	**15.5** 221.8	**13.7** 199.6	**14.4** 201.7	**14.1** 249.7	**13.1** 185.4	**14.0** 209.3	**12.0** 211.9	**12.7** 119.6	**15.3** 151.2	**12.9** 111.6	**14.9** 138.1
5: OTHER	**2.0** 28.3	**3.5** 49.9	**.0** .0	**.0** .0	**.0** .0	**.0** .0	**.0** .0	**.0** .0	**.0** .0	**.0** .0	**.0** .0	**.0** .0	**.0** .0
COL TOTAL	**100.0** 1,445.8	**100.0** 1,413.0	**100.0** 1,431.6	**100.0** 1,456.5	**100.0** 1,404.1	**100.0** 1,774.4	**100.0** 1,415.2	**100.0** 1,498.6	**100.0** 1,766.0	**100.0** 944.7	**100.0** 985.7	**100.0** 867.1	**100.0** 928.8

Frequency Distribution

Cells contain:
- Column percent
- Weighted N

HOMOSEX	YEAR												ROW TOTAL
	1993	1994	1996	1998	2000	2002	2004	2006	2008	2010	2012	2014	
1: ALWAYS WRONG	**66.1** 662.3	**67.6** 1,290.9	**61.0** 1,084.8	**58.5** 1,027.4	**58.7** 1,001.8	**55.8** 500.3	**58.2** 493.6	**56.2** 1,066.8	**52.4** 667.7	**45.7** 556.2	**45.7** 560.0	**40.1** 666.1	**65.0** 22,439.9
2: ALMST ALWAYS WRG	**4.2** 42.3	**3.7** 70.9	**5.1** 91.3	**5.9** 104.0	**4.4** 75.8	**5.2** 46.3	**4.8** 41.1	**4.9** 92.1	**3.1** 39.0	**3.7** 44.5	**2.9** 35.2	**3.4** 57.1	**4.7** 1,618.2
3: SOMETIMES WRONG	**7.8** 77.7	**5.9** 112.0	**6.0** 105.9	**7.3** 128.7	**8.1** 137.9	**7.3** 65.8	**6.9** 58.5	**6.7** 126.7	**6.7** 85.2	**7.9** 96.1	**7.7** 94.4	**7.2** 119.6	**6.9** 2,376.2
4: NOT WRONG AT ALL	**21.9** 219.9	**22.8** 434.6	**27.9** 495.9	**28.3** 496.2	**28.8** 491.6	**31.7** 284.5	**30.1** 255.3	**32.3** 612.9	**37.8** 481.5	**42.7** 518.9	**43.8** 536.8	**49.3** 819.1	**23.2** 7,991.1
5: OTHER	**.0** .0	**.0** .0	**.0** .0	**.0** .0	**.0** .0	**.0** .0	**.0** .0	**.0** .0	**.0** .0	**.0** .0	**.0** .0	**.0** .0	**.2** 78.2
COL TOTAL	**100.0** 1,002.1	**100.0** 1,908.4	**100.0** 1,777.9	**100.0** 1,756.2	**100.0** 1,707.0	**100.0** 896.9	**100.0** 848.6	**100.0** 1,897.5	**100.0** 1,273.4	**100.0** 1,215.7	**100.0** 1,226.3	**100.0** 1,661.9	**100.0** 34,503.6

Figure 6.5

		Frequency Distribution							
		YEAR							
Cells contain: -**Column percent** -Weighted N		1988	2004	2006	2008	2010	2012	2014	*ROW TOTAL*
MARHOMO	1: STRONGLY AGREE	**2.8** 36.1	**11.9** 140.9	**15.1** 299.4	**15.4** 206.5	**21.1** 265.8	**25.2** 322.8	**31.8** 539.7	*18.0* *1,811.0*
	2: AGREE	**8.9** 115.8	**18.9** 224.1	**20.2** 399.9	**23.9** 320.7	**25.4** 320.5	**23.7** 304.3	**24.9** 423.3	*21.0* *2,108.7*
	3: NEITHER AGREE NOR DISAGREE	**15.1** 197.1	**14.0** 165.3	**13.5** 266.4	**13.0** 175.1	**12.8** 161.5	**12.0** 153.9	**11.3** 191.1	*13.0* *1,310.4*
	4: DISAGREE	**26.1** 340.6	**20.4** 241.0	**15.8** 312.1	**15.6** 209.8	**15.6** 196.5	**14.2** 181.7	**13.0** 220.3	*16.9* *1,702.0*
	5: STRONGLY DISAGREE	**47.2** 617.4	**34.8** 412.2	**35.3** 698.5	**32.1** 432.1	**25.1** 316.6	**24.9** 319.8	**19.0** 322.6	*31.0* *3,119.2*
	COL TOTAL	*100.0* *1,307.1*	*100.0* *1,183.4*	*100.0* *1,976.3*	*100.0* *1,344.2*	*100.0* *1,260.9*	*100.0* *1,282.4*	*100.0* *1,697.0*	*100.0* *10,051.3*

Figure 6.6 shows the resulting cross-tab.

After creating a cross-tab for HOMOSEX by AGE, create another bivariate table for MARHOMO by AGE, using the same recoding instructions for AGE. Here again, the dependent variable MARHOMO should go in the "Row" field, AGE should remain in the "Column" field, and COMPWT should remain selected in the "Weight" field. Make sure that the filter is restricting your analysis to recent data with the command "YEAR (2014)." Running the table should produce the results shown in Figure 6.7.

Step 5. Interpret your results. There are five basic step to interpreting a cross-tab.

1. Remind your audience of the basics.

When presenting your analyses to an audience, it is important to:

  a. *Restate your research question.* In this case, the research question is "Among adults in the contemporary US, is there a relationship between age and views about homosexuality?"

Figure 6.6

Frequency Distribution							
Cells contain: **-Column percent** -Weighted N		**AGE**					***ROW*** ***TOTAL***
		1 18-29	2 30-44	3 45-59	4 60-74	5 75-89	
HOMOSEX	1: ALWAYS WRONG	**26.7** 86.0	**34.7** 155.6	**44.6** 202.7	**46.7** 147.6	**63.9** 72.4	*40.1* *664.3*
	2: ALMST ALWAYS WRG	**2.9** 9.4	**3.7** 16.8	**3.8** 17.3	**2.1** 6.8	**6.0** 6.8	*3.4* *57.1*
	3: SOMETIMES WRONG	**7.1** 22.8	**8.0** 36.1	**4.3** 19.5	**10.3** 32.5	**7.1** 8.0	*7.2* *118.9*
	4: NOT WRONG AT ALL	**63.3** 203.6	**53.6** 240.4	**47.3** 215.3	**40.9** 129.2	**23.1** 26.1	*49.2* *814.6*
	COL TOTAL	*100.0* *321.8*	*100.0* *448.9*	*100.0* *454.8*	*100.0* *316.1*	*100.0* *113.3*	*100.0* *1,654.8*

Color coding:	<-2.0	<-1.0	<0.0	>0.0	>1.0	>2.0	**Z**
N in each cell:	Smaller than expected			Larger than expected			

b. *Remind your audience of the data source and the specific variables that you used to answer this question.* In this case, the data source is the 2014 General Social Survey. Respondents were asked whether they believed that "sexual relations between two adults of the same sex" were always wrong, almost always wrong, sometimes wrong, or not wrong at all. Respondents were also asked the extent to which they believed that "homosexual couples should have the right to marry one another." Respondents were also asked their age.

c. *Identify and describe the dependent and independent variables, clearly stating how each variable was coded.* In this case, there are two dependent variables. Respondents' beliefs about sexual relations between two adults of the same sex were assessed on a scale of 1 to 4, with higher values indicating greater support for homosexual relations. Beliefs about same-sex marriage were assessed on a scale of 1 to 5, where lower values indicate greater support for same-sex marriage. Age, the independent variable,

Figure 6.7

Frequency Distribution							
Cells contain: -**Column percent** -Weighted N		**AGE**					
		1 18-29	2 30-44	3 45-59	4 60-74	5 75-89	**ROW** **TOTAL**
MARHOMO	1: STRONGLY AGREE	**48.8** 159.3	**35.1** 159.5	**28.3** 132.0	**22.6** 74.1	**12.5** 14.2	*31.9* *539.2*
	2: AGREE	**22.4** 73.0	**29.5** 133.9	**22.9** 107.1	**25.7** 84.2	**19.0** 21.7	*24.8* *419.9*
	3: NEITHER AGREE NOR DISAGREE	**10.5** 34.4	**11.1** 50.3	**12.1** 56.5	**10.4** 34.1	**13.8** 15.8	*11.3* *191.1*
	4: DISAGREE	**7.9** 25.9	**9.8** 44.7	**13.9** 65.0	**19.1** 62.8	**19.2** 21.9	*13.0* *220.3*
	5: STRONGLY DISAGREE	**10.4** 33.9	**14.5** 66.0	**22.7** 106.2	**22.2** 72.8	**35.5** 40.4	*18.9* *319.4*
	COL TOTAL	*100.0* *326.5*	*100.0* *454.4*	*100.0* *466.8*	*100.0* *328.1*	*100.0* *114.0*	*100.0* *1,689.9*

was recoded into five categories: 18–29, 30–44, 45–59, 60–74, and 75 and above.

d. *Specify the number of cases included in each analysis.* The overall number of valid cases (N) included in each cross-tab is presented in the bottom right corner of the cross-tab. In Figure 6.6, the weighted number of cases is approximately1,655; the weighted number of cases in Figure 6.7 is slightly higher at approximately 1,690.

2. Focus on specifics.

The first step in interpreting a bivariate table or cross-tab is to look carefully at the specific numbers in the tables and interpret them as precisely as you can. Focusing on the cell frequencies (the bottom number in each cell of the table) can be useful, though in most cases it is more useful to examine the column percents—the top number in each cell.

For example, focus on the top row of Figure 6.6—the line that corresponds with "always wrong." In the upper left corner, we see that 86 people between the ages of 18 and 29 responded that they thought homosexual relations were "always wrong."

The column total, located in the bottom row of the table, tells us that there were approximately 322 individuals aged 18 to 20 who answered this question. The "26.7" in the upper left corner of the table is the column percent and shows us that, of those aged 18 to 29, 26.7% believed that homosexual relations were "always wrong."

$$(86 / 322) * 100 = 26.7\%$$

In the top right cell, we see that 63.9% of respondents aged 75 to 89 believed that "sexual relations between two adults of the same sex" are always wrong.

Looking at the row that corresponds with "not wrong at all," we see that almost two thirds of younger respondents (aged 18 to 29) said they believed that "sexual relations between two adults of the same sex" are "not wrong at all." Among the oldest age group, only 23.1% (approximately 26 of the 113 people in this age group) supported same-sex relations to this extent.

Among the youngest three age groups, the modal category (the category containing the highest number of cases) for MARHOMO is "not wrong at all." Among the oldest two age groups, in contrast, the modal category for this variable is "always wrong."

Figure 6.7 examines the relationship between age and support for same-sex marriage, where a response of "strongly agree" represents being highly supportive of same-sex marriage. Here we see that among respondents aged 18 to 29, almost half (48.8%) "strongly agreed" that "homosexual couples should have the right to marry one another." Another 22.4% "agreed" with this idea. Among the oldest age group considered, there was considerably less support for same-sex marriage. More than a third (35.5%) of respondents aged 75 and older indicated that they "strongly disagreed" that homosexual couples should have the right to marry one another. Another 19.2% reported that they "disagreed" with this idea.

3. Consider the big picture.

After examining individual percentages within the table, it is important to step back and take a larger view of the overall relationship presented in the tables. When examining each table individually, can you see any patterns or trends in the column percentages, or do the percentages seem to go up and down at random? If you see clusters of dark blue or dark red cells in the table, then there is probably an identifiable pattern. If there are very few darkly colored cells or if they seem randomly scattered across the table, then there may not be an easily identifiable pattern. It's also important to think about how the individual analyses work together. Do they all point to the same overall conclusion, or are the results more mixed? If the individual analyses seem to point to different conclusions, how do you make sense of these results?

Look again at Figure 6.6 and focus on the row representing individuals who believed that "sexual relations between two adults of the same sex" are always wrong. Moving from the youngest to the oldest age groups (that is, left to right across the table), the percentages tend to get larger. The percentage of respondents who strongly agreed increases as age group increases. Figure 6.7 reveals a very similar pattern. Support for same-sex marriage is highest among the youngest group and decreases steadily as age increases. Taken together, both tables show a similar result.

4. Consider limitations.

An important part of all scientific research is to be clear about the limitations of the research. The above analyses are exploratory and should not be understood as the unquestioned "final word" on the relationship between age and attitudes about homosexuality. Every research project has limitations, some more than others, and it is important to make these clear when interpreting the results.

When considering the limitations of any survey research project, it is important to consider issues of survey design, possible biases, and generalizability. The results here, for example, apply only to adults in the US who are aged 18 and older and who are not living in institutions. Respondents include English- and Spanish-speaking adults, but adults in the US who are not able to speak either language are not included in the analysis.

It is also important to consider potential confounding variables, variables that are not included in the analyses but might be affecting the relationship between the independent and dependent variables. For example, how might differences in religious affiliation and political party affiliation affect views related to homosexuality? In more complex analyses, we could "control for" these additional factors to help answer this question. For our purposes here, however, it is sufficient to point out potential confounding variables and other limitations.

Finally, while it is crucial to explain what the analyses reveal about the larger research question ("Among adults in the contemporary US, is there a relationship between age and views about homosexuality?"), it is often useful to clarify what the analyses do *not* tell us about the research question. Anticipate possible misinterpretations. Clarify what the findings suggest and what they don't suggest. For example, while the above analyses indicate that younger individuals are more likely to support same-sex marriage and are more likely to be supportive of homosexual relationships, not all older people are unsupportive. Even among those respondents aged 75 and older, nearly a third (12.5% + 19% = 31.5%) agree or strongly agree that same-sex couples should be allowed to marry.

5. Summarize your conclusions.

Interpreting your results within a social justice framework requires thinking through issues of power and inequality, socially constructed differences, and links between the micro and macro levels of society as well as the importance of intersecting inequalities. The analyses reveal increasingly supportive attitudes towards same-sex relations, but it is important not to overstate these results. Support for same-sex relations and marriage rights are no doubt important components of social justice, but these questions stop short of assessing respondents' acceptance of queer sexuality more generally. In addition, the analyses do not address the extent to which respondents endorse a socially constructed or essentialistic ideas about sexual orientation and identities. The data in the above analysis come from 2014, the year before the US Supreme Court affirmed the right of same-sex couples to marry. In response to this decision and the national attention drawn to this issue, support for same-sex marriage will likely increase in the future. Further analyses of GSS data, along with research that is qualitative, historical, comparative, and theoretical, will help to assess these issues in the future.

EXERCISES

Figures 6.8 and 6.9 present two analyses that examine the relationship between political party affiliation and (1) beliefs about whether teenagers should have access to birth control and (2) beliefs about whether sex education should be taught in public schools. The top portion of each figure shows the variables used to construct the analysis and indicates that the variable PARTYID was recoded and that a filter based on the variable YEAR was used to restrict the analysis to a subsample of cases.

In Figures 6.8 and 6.9, the variable PARTYID was recoded so that values of 0 to 2 on the original variable are now scored 1, a value of 3 on the original variable is coded 2, and values of 4 to 6 on the original variable are coded 3. Values above 6 (7, 8, and 9) are excluded from the recoded variable and are not represented in Figures 6.8 and 6.9.

1. What is the precise wording of the survey question that is associated with the variable PILLOK?

    a. "Do you strongly agree, agree, or strongly disagree that all teenagers aged 14-16 should be given free access to birth control pills?"

    b. "Do you strongly agree, agree, or strongly disagree that methods of birth control should be available to teenagers between the ages of 14 and 16 if their parents do not approve?"

    c. "Do you strongly agree, agree, or strongly disagree that parents who provide birth control to their teenagers aged 14-16 are morally irresponsible?"

    d. "When you were between the ages of 14 and 16, did you have access to birth control pills?"

2. The analysis presented in Figure 6.9 uses a filter that:

    a. restricts the analysis to survey years between 1972 and 2014.

    b. restricts the analysis to survey years between 2010 and 2014.

    c. restricts the analysis to people who describe themselves as Democrats.

    d. recodes the variable PARTYID into different categories.

3. The overall approximate number of cases presented in Figure 6.9 is:

    a. 4,218.

    b. 1,604.

    c. 3,819.

    d. 100.

4. Before it was recoded, a score of 3 on the variable PARTYID represented:

    a. Republicans.

    b. Democrats.

    c. independents.

    d. an answer of "No answer."

    e. an answer of "Don't know."

Figure 6.8

Variables					
Role	**Name**	**Label**	**Range**	**MD**	**Dataset**
Row	**PILLOK**	BIRTH CONTROL TO TEENAGERS 14-16	1-4	0,8,9	1
Column	**PARTYID(Recoded)**	POLITICAL PARTY AFFILIATION	1-3		1
Weight	**COMPWT**	Composite weight = WTSSALL * OVERSAMP * FORMWT	.1913-11.1261		1
Filter	**YEAR(2010-2014)**	GSS YEAR FOR THIS RESPONDENT	1972-2014		1

Frequency Distribution					
Cells contain: -**Column percent** -Weighted N		**PARTYID**			
		1 0-2	2 3	3 4-6	***ROW TOTAL***
PILLOK	1: STRONGLY AGREE	**30.8** 609.0	**28.0** 231.4	**14.1** 197.3	**24.7** *1,037.8*
	2: AGREE	**35.5** 701.5	**33.9** 280.0	**30.9** 431.5	**33.7** *1,413.1*
	3: DISAGREE	**22.5** 444.5	**23.0** 190.1	**29.6** 413.3	**25.0** *1,047.9*
	4: STRONGLY DISAGREE	**11.2** 222.0	**15.0** 123.6	**25.4** 354.1	**16.7** *699.6*
	COL TOTAL	***100.0*** *1,976.9*	***100.0*** *825.1*	***100.0*** *1,396.3*	***100.0*** *4,198.3*

Color coding:	<-2.0	<-1.0	<0.0	>0.0	>1.0	>2.0	**Z**
N in each cell:	Smaller than expected			Larger than expected			

5. On the recoded variable PARTYID, a score of 3 represents:

   a. strong Republicans, not strong Republicans, and independents near Republicans.

   b. strong Democrats, not strong Democrats, and independents near Democrats.

   c. independents.

   d. other political parties.

Figure 6.9

		Variables			
Role	**Name**	**Label**	**Range**	**MD**	**Dataset**
Row	**SEXEDUC**	SEX EDUCATION IN PUBLIC SCHOOLS	1-3	0,8,9	1
Column	**PARTYID(Recoded)**	POLITICAL PARTY AFFILIATION	1-3		1
Weight	**COMPWT**	Composite weight = WTSSALL * OVERSAMP * FORMWT	.1913-11.1261		1
Filter	**YEAR(2010-2014)**	GSS YEAR FOR THIS RESPONDENT	1972-2014		1

		Frequency Distribution			
Cells contain: -**Column percenat** -Weighted N		**PARTYID**			
		1 0-2	2 3	3 4-6	**ROW TOTAL**
SEXEDUC	1: FAVOR	**95.0** 1,887.8	**89.2** 735.6	**85.0** 1,195.3	**90.5** 3,818.7
	2: OPPOSE	**5.0** 99.4	**10.8** 88.9	**15.0** 210.6	**9.5** 398.9
	COL TOTAL	**100.0** 1,987.2	**100.0** 824.6	**100.0** 1,405.9	**100.0** 4,217.6

6. On the recoded variable PARTYID, a score of 1 represents:

   a. strong Republicans, not strong Republicans, and independents near Republicans.

   b. strong Democrats, not strong Democrats, and independents near Democrats.

   c. independents.

   d. other political parties.

7. What is the precise wording of the survey question associated with the variable SEXEDUC?

   a. "Would you be for or against sex education in the public schools?"

   b. "Would you be for or against sex education in the public elementary schools?"

   c. "When you were growing up, did your parents favor or oppose sex education in public schools?"

   d. "Do you believe that most Democrats favor or oppose sex education in the public schools?"

   e. "Do you believe that most Republicans favor or oppose sex education in the public schools?"

8. Which of the following statements is the correct interpretation of the number 95.0 in the upper left corner of Figure 6.9?

a. 95.0% of Democrat-leaning respondents (including "strong Democrats," "not strong Democrats," and "independents who are near Democrats") favor teaching sex education in public schools.

b. 95.0% of Republican-leaning respondents (including "strong Republicans," "not strong Republicans," and "independents who are near Republicans") favor teaching sex education in public schools.

c. 95.0% of those who favor teaching sex education in public schools are Democrat-leaning respondents (including "strong Democrats," "not strong Democrats," and "independents who are near Democrats").

d. 95.0 percent of those who favor teaching sex education in public schools are Republican-leaning respondents (including "strong Republicans," "not-strong Republicans," and "independents who are near Republicans").

9. Which of the following is *not* an accurate statement concerning the overall relationship between political party affiliation and views about teaching sex education in public schools?

a. The modal category for all three political categories considered is "Favor teaching sex education in public schools."

b. In general, the number of respondents who opposed teaching sex education in public schools is larger than the number of respondents who favored teaching sex education in public schools.

c. The percentage of Democrats (including "strong Democrats," "not strong Democrats," and "independents who are near Democrats")

who favored teaching sex education in public schools is higher than the percentage of Republicans (including "strong Republicans," "not strong Republicans," and "independents who are near Republicans") who favored teaching sex education in public schools.

d. The weighted number of Democrats (including "strong Democrats," "not strong Democrats," and "independents who are near Democrats") who favored teaching sex education in public schools is higher than the weighted number of Republicans (including "strong Republicans," "not strong Republicans," and "independents who are near Republicans") who favored teaching sex education in public schools.

10. The information presented in Figures 6.8 and 6.9 supports which of the following statements?

a. Democrats are more likely than Republicans to support sex education in the public schools and are also more likely to support young teenagers' access to birth control.

b. Republicans are more likely than Democrats to support sex education in the public schools and are also more likely to support young teenagers' access to birth control.

c. There is no relationship between political party affiliation and views about sex education or birth control for teenagers.

d. Compared with Republicans, Democrats are more likely to have had sex education and are more likely to use birth control.

e. Compared with Democrats, Republicans are more likely to have had sex education and are more likely to use birth control.

ANALYSES & ESSAYS

1. *What socio-demographic characteristics are related to respondents' attitudes about sexuality?* Identify one variable that you think plays a role in determining attitudes about sexuality. Identify three survey questions from the GSS that assess respondents' attitudes about sexuality. Construct three separate cross-tabs that examine how the sociodemographic characteristic you have chosen relates to these three sexuality-related variables. Interpret your

results, being sure to identify and describe the dependent and independent variables in each analysis.

2. *How and to what extent do men and women in the US differ in their beliefs about pornography?* Create four different cross-tab analyses, where SEX is the "Column" variable in each one and where PORNINF, PORNRAPE, PORNOUT, and

PORNMORL are the different "Row" variables. Use a filter to restrict your analysis to the years 1990 through 1994, the most recent years in which these questions were included in the GSS. Interpret your results, giving particular attention to the intersections of gender and sexuality.

3. *To what extent do sexual identities correspond to sexual behaviors?* Create a cross-tab where SEXORNT is the "Row" variable and SEXSEX5 is the "Column" variable. (Note that the variable SEXORNT was first included in the GSS in 2008.) Use a filter to restrict your analysis to men respondents only. Then make a similar cross-tab where your analysis is now restricted to women only. Interpret your results, giving particular attention to the social construction of sexuality.

4. *To what extent do people of different religious affiliations hold different attitudes about young people's sexuality?* Create two different cross-tab analyses where PILLOK and SEXEDUC are the separate "Row" variables and religious affiliation is the independent variable in both. Recode religious affiliation using the command:

RELIG (r:1;2;3;4; 5-13)

Use a filter to restrict your analyses to survey years 2010 through 2014. Interpret your results, making sure to describe what the new categories of religious affiliation represent.

5. *To what extent does condom usage differ across racial/ethnic groups in the US?* Create a cross-tab where RACEHISP is the independent variable and CONDOM is the dependent variables. Use a filter to restrict your analysis to individuals who are currently divorced, separated, or who have never been married; where the data are from survey years from 2010 to 2014; and where the analysis is restricted to men:

MARITAL (3-5) YEAR (2010-2014) SEX (1)

Then create a similar crosstab where you focus on women rather than men. Interpret your results.

NOTES

1. Seidman, Steven. 2009. *The Social Construction of Sexuality*. 2nd ed. New York: W. W. Norton.

2. Ibid., p. x.

3. Foucault, Michel. [1976] 1990. *The History of Sexuality, Vol. 1: An Introduction*, translated by R. Hurley. New York: Vintage Books; Rubin, Gayle. [1984] 1993. "Thinking Sex: Notes for a Radical Theory of the Politics of Sexuality." Pp. 3–44 in *The Lesbian and Gay Studies Reader*, edited by H. Abelove, M. Aina Barale, and D. M. Halperin. New York: Routledge.

4. Plante, Rebecca F. 2006. *Sexualities in Context: A Social Perspective*. Boulder, CO: Westview Press.

5. Lorber, Judith. 1994. *Paradoxes of Gender*. New Haven, CT: Yale University Press, p. 1.

6. See, for example, Kinsey, Alfred C. [1948] 1998. *Sexual Behavior in the Human Male*. Bloomington: Indiana University Press; Kinsey, Alfred C. [1953] 1998. *Sexual Behavior in the Human Female*. Bloomington: Indiana University Press.

7. Erickson, Julia A. 2001. *Kiss and Tell: Surveying Sex in the Twentieth Century*. Cambridge, MA: Harvard University Press.

8. Westbrook, Laurel, and Aliya Saperstein. 2015. "New Categories Are Not Enough: Rethinking the Measurement of Sex and Gender in Social Surveys." *Gender & Society* 29:534–60; Williams, Christine. 2006. "Still Missing? Comments on the Twentieth Anniversary of 'The Missing Feminist Revolution in Sociology.'" *Social Problems* 53:454–58.

9. Ward, Brian W., James M. Dahlhamer, Adena M. Galinsky, and Sarah S. Joestl. 2014. "Sexual Orientation and Health among US Adults: National Health Interview Survey, 2013." National Health Statistics Reports No. 77. Retrieved September 21, 2016 (http://www.cdc.gov/nchs/data/nhsr/nhsr077.pdf). For full survey details, see http://www.cdc.gov/nchs/nhis.htm.

10. Rust, Paula C. 1995. *Bisexuality and the Challenge to Lesbian Politics*. New York: New York University Press; Rupp, Leila J., and Verta Taylor. 2010. "Straight Girls Kissing." *Contexts* 9(3):28–32.

CHAPTER 7

ANALYZING INEQUALITIES IN FAMILIES

INTRODUCTION: FAMILY CHANGE AND FAMILY DIVERSITY

In June 2015, the United States Supreme Court ruled that the US Constitution guarantees same-sex couples the right to marry. After decades of LGBT organization and activism, the decision "set off jubilation and tearful embraces across the country" as same-sex couples and their families were finally recognized with, as Justice Kennedy wrote, "equal dignity in the eyes of the law."[1] While joyful for many, the occasion was, for others, a moment of great concern. Opponents of same-sex marriage saw the decision as one more step in the weakening of marriage and the decline in family values. US Senator Ted Cruz, who had announced his 2016 presidential bid only a few months before, described the day of the ruling as "some of the darkest 24 hours in our nation's history."[2] Despite the ruling, Kim Davis, a county clerk in Kentucky, refused to issue marriage licenses to same-sex couples and was jailed for contempt of court. Her actions were both supported by, among others, presidential candidates Rand Paul and Mike Huckabee, and were overwhelmingly condemned by supporters of same-sex marriage.[3]

Regardless of where you personally stand on this issue, the US Supreme Court's ruling on same-sex marriage marks an important landmark in the movement for LGBT rights and an important moment in the history of marriage and family. It is, perhaps, tempting to view this moment as an unprecedented and fundamental shift in the meaning of marriage, and perhaps to some extent this is true. A sociological perspective, however, emphasizes that families

Learning Objectives

By the end of this chapter, you should be able to:

1. Identify GSS variables related to family.

2. Analyze family change and family diversity using the GSS, paying particular attention to inequalities of race, ethnicity, gender, class and sexuality.

3. Use a variety of analytic techniques appropriately to analyze issues related to families in the US.

4. Interpret these analyses using a social justice framework.

are socially constructed and historically changing. Whether we focus on families in the United States or examine families more globally, families take different forms at different historical moments. And as technology, culture, religion, and political ideas change, these changes affect family forms along with people's ideas about how families *should be*. (Consider, for example, how your own family experiences would be different had you grown up without the Internet, texting, or even a cell phone!) The changes we see in today's families—whether that be state recognition of same-sex marriage, the increasing likelihood that mothers of small children will combine parenting with work outside the home, or the increasing frequency of unmarried couples living together—are connected to changes in the broader social, economic, and political landscape.[4]

Contemporary families are characterized not only by change but also by diversity. While variation in family forms has always existed to some extent, family forms are increasingly diverse in terms of their structure and organization.[5] This chapter draws on the analytic skills covered in Chapters 2 through 6 to examine family change and family diversity over the past four decades. Drawing from the social justice framework presented in Chapter 1, it examines how race, gender, class, and sexuality work together to structure individuals' experiences within families and their ideas about family life.

IDENTIFYING VARIABLES RELATED TO FAMILIES

The General Social Survey includes hundreds of questions about family issues, including questions about respondents' current family life, respondents' family life while growing up, and attitudes and beliefs about family-related issues. A good number of these questions are included in multiple survey years, making the GSS an excellent resource for analyzing how family issues have changed over time.

Searching for Variables Related to Families

When searching for and analyzing variables related to families, it is useful to keep in mind that the meaning of *family* is somewhat subjective. Many times people use the word *family* to mean "immediate family" (parents and their children, for example), and sometimes *family* is used to mean "extended family" (parents, children, grandparents, aunts, uncles, and cousins). Some people include unmarried romantic partners in their definition of family, others include close friends and neighbors, and many others include the family pet![6]

Partly because family can mean different things to different people, social science researchers draw a distinction between *family* and *households*. The US Census describes the difference as follows: "A family consists of two or more people (one of whom is the householder) related by birth, marriage, or adoption residing in the same housing unit. A household consists of all people who occupy a housing unit regardless of relationship. A household may consist of a person living alone or multiple unrelated individuals or families living together."[7] Because households and families can be different things, it is important when analyzing survey data to determine which of these concepts is of most interest to you.

ASKING ABOUT HOUSEHOLD AND FAMILY SIZE

The respondents who take the General Social Survey likely understand family in different ways. And while some respondents probably do understand the difference between households and family, others probably do not. To ensure the most accurate information, the GSS asks multiple questions about respondents' living situation, including:

– Please tell me the names of the people who usually live in this household.

– Have we forgotten anyone: such as babies or small children; roomers; people who usually live here but are away temporarily on business trips, vacations, temporarily in a hospital, and so on?

– Are any of the people we have listed staying somewhere else right now?

IF YES

- Who is staying somewhere else right now?
- Where is (PERSON) living right now: is (PERSON) staying at another household; is (he/she) traveling; is (he/she) in some institution or dormitory like at college, or in a hospital or somewhere; or what?
- Is everyone in the household related to you in some way?

In general, when you "view" the variables on the SDA website, the precise wording of the survey question pops up. This is not the case with some of the basic variables concerning household and family characteristics, as the answers to these questions stem from multiple survey questions. The variable HOMPOP, for example, which is a measure of the number of persons in the respondents' household, is based on the above questions.

Respondents' Current Family Situation

Beyond the number of people living in the household, the GSS asks a number of questions concerning respondents' current family situation. The variable CHILDS indicates the number of children respondents have had, and MARITAL describes respondents' marital status. Those respondents who report that they are currently married or widowed are also asked, "Have you ever been divorced or legally separated?" (DIVORCE), and those who are currently married are asked, "Taking all things together, how would you describe your marriage? Very happy, pretty happy, or not too happy?" From 1972 to 1994 and then again in 2006, the GSS also included a question (AGEWED) that asked about the age at which respondents were first married. From 1994 to 2014, the survey also included a question asking about respondents' age when their first child was born (AGEKDBRN).

Family Life When Respondents Were Growing Up

In addition to questions about respondents' *current* family and living situation, the GSS includes several questions about respondents' life when they were 16 years old. FAMILY16, for example, asks respondents, "Were you living with both your own mother and father around the time you were 16? IF NO: With whom were you living around that time?" The variable INCOM16 asks, "Thinking about the time when you were 16 years old, compared with American families in general then, would you say your family income was far below average, below average, average, above average, or far above average?" And the variable MAWRKGRW, included in survey years 1994 to 2014, asks respondents, "Did your mother ever work for pay for as long as a year, while you were growing up?" These types of variables are particularly valuable for analyzing how respondents' early life experiences help to shape the attitudes, beliefs, and experiences they have in later life.

Attitudes and Beliefs About Families

As is clear from recent debates about same-sex marriage, Americans' views about marriage and family are tremendously diverse and, on some issues, rapidly changing. The GSS has asked a range of questions concerning beliefs about families, including questions related to working mothers, cohabitation, divorce, and same-sex marriage. Multiple questions ask respondents about their "ideal family" forms, such as their ideal number of children (CHLDIDEL) and ideal family arrangement in terms of who should work and who (if anyone) should stay home with the children (FAMWKBST).

Browsing for Variables Related to Families

The codebook on the left-hand side of the SDA website allows users to easily identify clusters of variables about specific topics, such as family. If you are interested in browsing for variables related to family, the following subject headings and subheadings may be especially useful:

- Respondent Background Variables
  - Respondent and Spouse Work Week
  - Respondent's Dwelling
  - Respondent's Household Composition

- Personal and Family Information
  - Marital Status
  - Spouse's Employment
  - Mother's Employment
  - Father's Employment
  - Family Composition
  - Respondent's Background and Childhood
  - Respondent's Current Household Composition

- Societal Concerns
  - Desirable Qualities for Children

- Controversial Social Issues
  - Family Planning, Sex and Contraception

- 1994 Family Mobility Module

- Family – Finances – Donations

- 2002 Topical Module – Adult Transitions

- 2008 Variables
  - Sex/Gay/Marital/Kids

- 2012 ISSP Module: Gender

- 2014 Topical Module: Work and Relationships

- 1986 ISSP Module: Social Support and Networks

- 1988 ISSP Module: Women and Work
  - Working Women and the Family
  - When Should Women Work Outside Home
  - Child Care Arrangements
  - Marriage and Child Bearing
  - Family Size
  - Having Children
  - Divorce
  - Work History – Married Women with Children
  - Work and the Family
  - Family Issues
  - Sexual Issues
  - Household Money and Chore Management
  - Spouse Work Outside Home

- Personal Impact of Public Concerns
  - Parenting
  - Adult Roles in Children's Lives
  - Change in Children's Quality of Life

The previous four chapters presented an overview of how data from the General Social Survey can be used to analyze inequalities of race, gender, class, and sexuality. This chapter draws from the analytic techniques presented in the previous chapters to examine how these inequalities intersect to structure family experiences as well as attitudes and beliefs about family life. The application below shows one approach for examining the intersection of gender, race, ethnicity, and class in the context of beliefs about work-family arrangements.

APPLICATION: HOW DO GENDER, RACE, ETHNICITY, AND CLASS AFFECT RESPONDENTS' VIEWS ABOUT IDEAL WORK-FAMILY ARRANGEMENTS?

The GSS is an excellent source of data for analyzing beliefs and ideals related to family life in the US. Some of these questions (e.g., FEMAM and FECHILD) have been asked regularly over many decades, and others have been introduced in more recent years. One of these recently added variables, FAMWKBST, asks respondents which work-family arrangements they believe are best suited for families with a young child. This application examines how beliefs about work-family arrangements differ for men and women of diverse racial, ethnic, and class-based groups.

Step 1. Restate the research question and identify the independent and dependent variables.

As noted above, the research question is "How do gender, race, ethnicity, and class affect respondents' views about ideal work-family arrangements?" The dependent variable is FAMWKBST, and the independent variables are SEX, DEGREE, and RACEHISP.

Step 2. View each variable to make sure it means what you think it means. In almost all cases, viewing the variable will provide the precise wording of the survey question that corresponds to the variable. When you view the variable, make note of what each response category means as well as the level of measurement for the variable (nominal, ordinal, or interval-ratio).

SEX, RACEHISP, and DEGREE are all variables for which viewing provides incomplete information. Each of these variables are discussed at length in preceding chapters (Chapters 3, 4, and 5, respectively). SEX is a nominal-level variable representing respondent's gender, and DEGREE is an ordinal-level variable corresponding to the highest educational degree the respondent has attained.

RACEHISP is a nominal-level variable indicating the respondent's self-described racial/ethnic identity. Viewing this variable, we see that the category "White" does not include respondents who said they were Hispanic and that Hispanic does not include those who said they were Black. (See Chapter 4 for a more detailed discussion of this and other variables related to race and ethnicity.)

By viewing the variable FAMWKBST, we can see that this is a nominal-level variable that corresponds to the following survey question:

Consider a family with a child under school age. What, in your opinion, is the best way for them to organize their family and work life?

- The mother stays at home and the father works full-time.

- The mother works part-time and the father works full-time.

- Both the mother and father work full-time.

- Both the mother and father work part-time.

- The father works part-time and the mother works full-time.

- The father stays at home and the mother works full-time.

Before moving ahead, take a moment to consider some of the cultural norms that are built into this particular survey question. Perhaps most obviously, the question reflects heteronormative assumptions about families. Each of the scenarios presented assumes a "mother" and "father." How do you think LGBT people might respond to this question? How about heterosexual people who are unmarried, not partnered, and content? Beyond norms pertaining to sexuality, racial/ethnic and class-based biases may also be at work here. Notice that the question assumes a nuclear family, with no explicit mention of grandparents, aunts and uncles, or other extended family. In brief, the question relies upon a narrow understanding of "family," and the family form it centralizes is that found most often among privileged families in the US. These limitations are important to bear in mind throughout the analysis and when interpreting the results.

Step 3. Determine which time period the data are from. Remember that when you view a variable, you are seeing the combined data across all survey years in which the question was included in the GSS. Some questions have been included regularly since 1972, giving us more than four decades of data. Other questions are asked in only one survey year. Either way, it is important to make note of this when conducting and interpreting the analyses.

The easiest way to determine the years in which the variable was included is by creating a cross-tab of the variables in your analysis by the variable YEAR (the variable that corresponds to the survey year). Producing a cross-tab with FAMWKBST in the "Row" field and YEAR in the "Column" field (with the default, COMPWT, selected in the "Weight" field) will result in Figure 7.1.

Producing separate cross-tabs of the variables SEX and DEGREE with the variable YEAR will confirm that these variables have been included in the GSS regularly since 1972. Producing a cross-tab of RACEHISP by YEAR will show that RACEHISP has been included since the 2000 survey. Since the dependent variable, FAMWKBST, is included only in the 2012 survey, all of the analyses that we conduct using this variable will draw only from the 2012 data.

Step 4. Conduct the relevant analysis, such as a cross-tab or a comparison of means. Remember that you may need to include filter and control variables, depending on the research question. Remember too that you may need to recode one or more variables.

Because the dependent variable FAMWKBST is a nominal-level variable, a cross-tab analysis is more appropriate than a comparison of means. Recall that, for nominal-level variables, the mean is meaningless.

Figure 7.1

Frequency Distribution			
Cells contain: -**Column percent** -Weighted N		**YEAR**	
		2012	**ROW TOTAL**
FAMWKBST	1: The mother stays at home and the father works full-time	**39.7** 399.3	**39.7** 399.3
	2: The mother works part-time and the father works full-time	**41.6** 418.2	**41.6** 418.2
	3: Both the mother and father work full-time	**11.3** 113.7	**11.3** 113.7
	4: Both the mother and father work part-time	**6.8** 68.2	**6.8** 68.2
	5: The father works part-time and the mother works full-time	**.2** 1.6	**.2** 1.6
	6: The father stays at home and the mother works full-time	**.5** 5.0	**.5** 5.0
	COL TOTAL	**100.0** 1,006.0	**100.0** 1,006.0

The research question asks us to examine gender, racial/ethnic, and class-based differences in people's ideal work-family arrangements. There are three independent variables in this analysis (SEX, RACEHISP, DEGREE), and there are many different ways to include them in a cross-tab analysis. My approach is to first examine differences in gender to determine if men and women, in general, have different preferences when it comes to their ideal work-family arrangements. Following this general analysis, I will then use gender as a control variable to see how class, race, and ethnicity work with gender to shape respondents' ideals. It would be just as reasonable, however, to start by examining class-based differences, for example, and then to use class as a control variable to see how race, ethnicity, and gender work with class to shape respondents' ideals.

Begin constructing your cross-tabs by entering FAMWKBST in the "Row" field (since it is the dependent variable) and SEX in the "Column" field (since it is the

Figure 7.2

	Frequency Distribution	SEX		
Cells contain: **-Column percent** -Weighted N		1 MALE	2 FEMALE	*ROW* *TOTAL*
FAMWKBST	1: The mother stays at home and the father works full-time	**46.4** 221.7	**33.6** 177.5	*39.7* *399.3*
	2: The mother works part-time and the father works full-time	**37.0** 176.7	**45.7** 241.4	*41.6* *418.2*
	3: Both the mother and father work full-time	**10.9** 51.9	**11.7** 61.8	*11.3* *113.7*
	4: Both the mother and father work part-time	**4.9** 23.5	**8.5** 44.8	*6.8* *68.2*
	5: The father works part-time and the mother works full-time	**.2** .8	**.2** .8	*.2* *1.6*
	6: The father stays at home and the mother works full-time	**.7** 3.3	**.3** 1.7	*.5* *5.0*
	COL TOTAL	*100.0* *477.9*	*100.0* *528.1*	*100.0* *1,006.0*

independent variable). Before running the table, be sure that you have the default, COMPWT, selected in the "Weight" field.

Figure 7.2 shows the resulting cross-tab.

The above figure already shows some significant differences in how people think about ideal work-family arrangements. Among men, the modal category is "The mother stays at home and the father works full-time," and among women, the modal category is "The mother works part-time and the father works full-time." But how do these gender differences intersect with class, race, and ethnicity? To begin answering this question, create an additional cross-tab where DEGREE is the independent variable and SEX is a control variable. Doing so will produce the results shown in Figures 7.3 and 7.4.

Next, create another cross-tab where RACEHISP is the independent variable, SEX remains a control variable, and FAMWKBST remains the dependent variable (in

Figure 7.3

		DEGREE					
Statistics for SEX = 1(MALE)							
Cells contain: **-Column percent** -Weighted N		0 LT HIGH SCHOOL	1 HIGH SCHOOL	2 JUNIOR COLLEGE	3 BACHELOR	4 GRADUATE	*ROW* *TOTAL*
FAMWKBST	1: The mother stays at home and the father works full-time	**58.9** 45.2	**41.5** 101.7	**57.1** 21.9	**44.8** 33.8	**45.5** 19.1	*46.4* *221.7*
	2: The mother works part-time and the father works full-time	**31.2** 24.0	**39.6** 97.2	**34.3** 13.2	**32.6** 24.6	**42.3** 17.8	*37.0* *176.7*
	3: Both the mother and father work full-time	**2.7** 2.1	**13.6** 33.3	**4.3** 1.6	**13.9** 10.5	**10.3** 4.3	*10.9* *51.9*
	4: Both the mother and father work part-time	**6.2** 4.7	**4.1** 10.1	**3.2** 1.2	**8.7** 6.5	**2.0** .8	*4.9* *23.5*
	5: The father works part-time and the mother works full-time	**1.1** .8	**.0** .0	**.0** .0	**.0** .0	**.0** .0	*.2* *.8*
	6: The father stays at home and the mother works full-time	**.0** .0	**1.2** 2.9	**1.1** .4	**.0** .0	**.0** .0	*.7* *3.3*
	COL TOTAL	*100.0* 76.8	*100.0* 245.2	*100.0* 38.4	*100.0* 75.4	*100.0* 42.1	*100.0* 477.9

the "Row" field). Figures 7.5 and 7.6 show how racial/ethnic differences work with gender to structure ideals about work-family arrangements.

Step 5. Interpret your results. There are five basic step to interpreting and communicating your results:

Figure 7.4

Statistics for SEX = 2(FEMALE)						
	DEGREE					
Cells contain: -**Column percent** -Weighted N	0 LT HIGH SCHOOL	1 HIGH SCHOOL	2 JUNIOR COLLEGE	3 BACHELOR	4 GRADUATE	*ROW TOTAL*
FAMWKBST 1: The mother stays at home and the father works full-time	**50.3** 39.0	**34.1** 104.8	**29.0** 10.2	**24.9** 18.6	**14.8** 4.9	*33.6* *177.5*
2: The mother works part-time and the father works full-time	**34.3** 26.6	**45.4** 139.5	**55.6** 19.7	**45.4** 33.8	**65.3** 21.8	*45.7* *241.4*
3: Both the mother and father work full-time	**6.4** 5.0	**11.2** 34.4	**11.9** 4.2	**17.7** 13.2	**14.9** 5.0	*11.7* *61.8*
4: Both the mother and father work part-time	**9.0** 7.0	**8.5** 26.0	**3.5** 1.2	**12.0** 8.9	**4.9** 1.6	*8.5* *44.8*
5: The father works part-time and the mother works full-time	**.0** .0	**.3** .8	**.0** .0	**.0** .0	**.0** .0	*.2* *.8*
6: The father stays at home and the mother works full-time	**.0** .0	**.6** 1.7	**.0** .0	**.0** .0	**.0** .0	*.3* *1.7*
COL TOTAL	**100.0** 77.6	**100.0** 307.2	**100.0** 35.3	**100.0** 74.5	**100.0** 33.4	**100.0** *528.1*

1. Remind your audience of the basics.

    a. Restate your research question.

       The main research question is "How do gender, race, ethnicity, and class affect respondents' views about ideal work-family arrangements?"

Figure 7.5

Cells contain: **-Column percent** -Weighted N		**RACEHISP**				
		1 White	2 Black	3 Hispanic	4 Other	**ROW TOTAL**
FAMWKBST	1: The mother stays at home and the father works full-time	**46.1** 133.5	**38.3** 22.9	**50.9** 48.2	**50.7** 17.2	**46.4** 221.7
	2: The mother works part-time and the father works full-time	**39.3** 113.9	**38.3** 22.9	**28.7** 27.2	**37.7** 12.8	**37.0** 176.7
	3: Both the mother and father work full-time	**11.6** 33.6	**13.4** 8.0	**7.2** 6.8	**10.3** 3.5	**10.9** 51.9
	4: Both the mother and father work part-time	**2.0** 5.8	**10.0** 6.0	**11.9** 11.3	**1.2** .4	**4.9** 23.5
	5: The father works part-time and the mother works full-time	**.3** .8	**.0** .0	**.0** .0	**.0** .0	**.2** .8
	6: The father stays at home and the mother works full-time	**.7** 2.1	**.0** .0	**1.3** 1.2	**.0** .0	**.7** 3.3
	COL TOTAL	**100.0** 289.7	**100.0** 59.7	**100.0** 94.6	**100.0** 33.9	**100.0** 477.9

b. Remind your audience of the data source and the specific variables that you used to answer this question.

This analysis uses a series of cross-tabs to assess how and to what extent respondents' views about ideal work-family arrangements differ for men and women of different racial/ethnic and class groups. The data come from the 2012 General Social Survey.

c. Clearly state how each variable was coded and what each response category represents.

The dependent variable, respondents' views about ideal work-family arrangements, is assessed with the survey question "Consider a family with a child under school age. What, in your opinion, is the best way for them to organize their family and work life? The mother stays at home and the father works

Figure 7.6

Statistics for SEX = 2(FEMALE)						
Cells contain: -**Column percent** -Weighted N		**RACEHISP**				
		1 White	2 Black	3 Hispanic	4 Other	**ROW TOTAL**
FAMWKBST	1: The mother stays at home and the father works full-time	**33.8** 109.8	**30.6** 29.5	**42.4** 32.8	**18.7** 5.5	**33.6** 177.5
	2: The mother works part-time and the father works full-time	**46.8** 152.4	**45.6** 43.9	**36.8** 28.4	**57.5** 16.8	**45.7** 241.4
	3: Both the mother and father work full-time	**9.8** 31.9	**18.9** 18.2	**12.5** 9.7	**7.0** 2.0	**11.7** 61.8
	4: Both the mother and father work part-time	**8.8** 28.7	**4.9** 4.7	**8.3** 6.4	**16.9** 4.9	**8.5** 44.8
	5: The father works part-time and the mother works full-time	**.3** .8	**.0** .0	**.0** .0	**.0** .0	**.2** .8
	6: The father stays at home and the mother works full-time	**.5** 1.7	**.0** .0	**.0** .0	**.0** .0	**.3** 1.7
	COL TOTAL	**100.0** 325.3	**100.0** 96.3	**100.0** 77.3	**100.0** 29.2	**100.0** 528.1

full-time; The mother works part-time and the father works full-time; Both the mother and father work full-time; Both the mother and father work part-time; The father works part-time and the mother works full-time; The father stays at home and the mother works full-time." This is a nominal-level variable. Respondents' gender status (male or female) is recorded by the interviewer, who is instructed not to ask the respondent about their sex or gender identity. Respondents' racial/ethnic identity is assessed with a four-category nominal-level variable, where categories represent self-identification as white (non-Hispanic), African American or Black, Hispanic (non-Black), and other racial/ethnic groups. Respondents' educational attainment is used as a proxy for respondents' social class and is assessed with the variable DEGREE—an ordinal-level variable with categories of less than a high school diploma, a high school diploma, a junior college degree, a bachelor's degree, or a graduate degree.

d. Specify the number of cases included in the analysis. The overall number of valid cases (N) included in the cross-tab is presented in the bottom right corner of each crosstab.

Approximately 478 men and 528 women respondents are included in the analysis.

2. Focus on specifics.

The first step in interpreting cross-tab analyses is to look carefully at the numbers in the tables and interpret them as specifically as you can. When interpreting the results from multiple tables, it's usually best to interpret them one by one. As you interpret a number from a table, be sure to remind the audience of which table the number is coming from.

For example, Figure 7.2 revealed that among men, the most favored arrangement was "The mother stays at home and the father works full-time," and among women, the most favored arrangement was "The mother works part-time and the father works full-time." Figures 7.3 and 7.4, show that, among men and women, views about ideal work-family arrangements are also related to class. At every level of education, the modal category among men is, "The mother stays at home and the father works full-time." Men with less than a high school diploma are the most likely group to favor this type of arrangement, and men with a junior college degree are close behind. Interestingly, it is men whose highest degree is a high school diploma who are least likely to favor this arrangement. Men with a high school education and men with a college-level education are the two groups most likely to favor an arrangement where "both the mother and father work full-time."

Among women, the relationship between class and beliefs about ideal family-work arrangements is slightly different. With every increase in educational attainment, women are significantly less likely to favor the situation where a "mother stays at home and the father works full-time." That said, among women with less than a high school education, this category ("The mother stays at home and the father works full-time") is favored by approximately 50% of respondents. Among women who hold a graduate degree, nearly two thirds (65.3%) favor an arrangement where "The mother works part-time and the father works full-time."

Figures 7.5 and 7.6 show significant racial/ethnic differences in men's and women's beliefs about ideal work-family arrangements for families with a young child. Among white men, Hispanic men, and men who identify with "other" racial/ethnic groups, the modal category is "The mother stays at home and the father works full-time." Among Black men, there are two modal categories: "The mother stays at home and the father works full-time" and "The mother works part-time and the father works full-time." Among the racial/ethnic groups considered here, Black men are the least likely to favor the mother staying at home and the father working full-time and most likely to favor a situation where both the mother and father work full-time.

Figure 7.6 shows that, among the racial/ethnic groups considered here, women who describe themselves as Hispanic (but not Black) are the most likely to favor an arrangement where the mother stays at home and the father works full-time, for families with at least one young child. Among non-Black Hispanic women, "The mother stays at home and the father works full-time" is the modal category. Gender remains important, though. While 50.9% of non-Black Hispanic men favor this arrangement (Figure 7.5), only 42.4% of non-Black Hispanic women do (Figure 7.6). For women of all other racial/ethnic groups considered here, the modal category is mothers working part-time and fathers working full-time. Black women are significantly more likely than women of other racial/ethnic groups to favor both the parents working full-time. Nearly 19% of Black women favor this option, as opposed to 9.8% of non-Hispanic white women, 12.5% of non-Black Hispanic women, and 7% of women who identify with other racial/ethnic groups.

3. Consider the big picture.

After examining individual means or percentages within the table, it is important to step back and take a larger view of the overall relationship presented in the tables. When examining each table individually, can you see any patterns or trends in the column percentages, or do the numbers seem to go up and down at random? If you see clusters of dark blue or dark red cells in the table, then there is probably an identifiable pattern. If there are very few darkly colored cells or if they seem randomly scattered across the table, then there may not be an easily identifiable pattern. It's also important to think about how the individual analyses work together. Do they all point to the same overall conclusion, or are the results more mixed? If the individual analyses seem to point to different conclusions, how do you make sense of these results? Remember that having mixed results is not wrong. Results without identifiable patterns can be just as important and interesting as results with an identifiable pattern—especially if the pattern you expected is not apparent.

What, in general, can be said about how gender, class, race, and ethnicity structure individuals' beliefs about ideal work-family arrangements for families with at least one small child? In 2012, regardless of gender, regardless of educational attainment, and regardless of racial/ethnic identity, very few respondents favored an arrangement where the mother works full-time and the father works part-time or stays at home. In cases where there is a child under school age, respondents clearly favor fathers working full-time and mothers working either part-time or not at all.

Comparing the top rows of data presented in Figure 7.3 with the top row of data presented in Figure 7.4, we can see that, at every level of education, men are more likely to favor mothers "staying at home." Moreover, the gap between men's and women's preferences tends to increase as educational attainment increases. Figure 7.7 below is created by graphing (in Excel) the difference between the values presented in the top row of Figure 7.4 and the values presented in the top row of Figure 7.3. You can see that at higher levels of education, there is a greater difference in the percentage of men who favor the "mother stays home/father works full-time" approach as compared to the percentage of women who favor this approach.

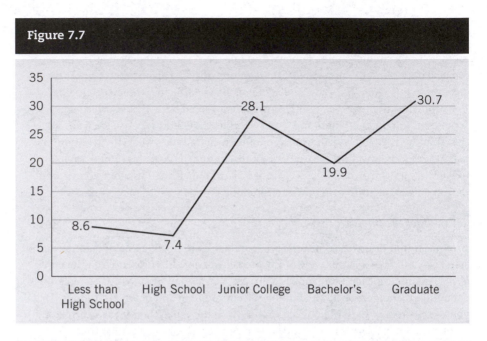

Figure 7.7

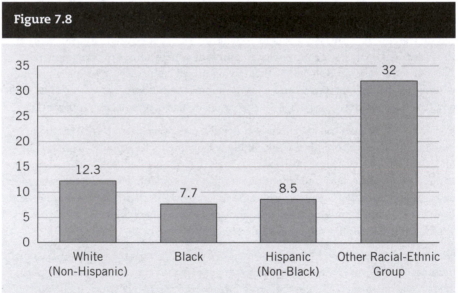

Figure 7.8

Figure 7.8 shows a similar analysis in the gender gap but examines it across racial/ethnic groups. This figure was also created in Excel, using the information presented in the top rows of Figures 7.5 and 7.6. You can see that, among Black and Hispanic respondents, there is a smaller difference (7.7 and 8.5 percentage points, respectively), in the percentage of men who favor the "mother stays home/father works full-time" approach as compared to the percentage of women who favor this approach. There is a noticeably large gender gap for respondents who identify with "other" racial/ethnic groups, though it is difficult to interpret what this means, due to the ambiguity of and diversity within this particular category.

There are many other legitimate ways to interpret the "big picture." The statistics presented in Figures 7.3 through 7.6 can be analyzed together in multiple different ways, and different approaches may yield an interpretation with a slightly different emphasis.

4. Consider limitations.

An important part of all scientific research is to be clear about the limitations of the research. Every research project has limitations, some more than others, and it is important to make these clear when interpreting the results. It is also important to consider potential confounding variables—variables that are not included in the analyses but might be affecting the relationship between the independent and dependent variables. Finally, while it is crucial to explain what the analyses reveal about the larger research question, it is often useful to clarify what the analyses do *not* tell us about the research question. Anticipate possible misinterpretations.

When considering the limitations of any survey research project, it is important to consider issues of survey design, possible sample biases, and generalizability. In the current analysis the results apply only to adults in the US who are aged 18 and older. Respondents include English- and Spanish-speaking adults, but adults in the US who are not able to speak either language are not included in the analysis. Nor are those living in institutions such as prisons or mental institutions included in this analysis.

As previously mentioned, the dependent variable is heteronormative and maybe culturally biased as well. If multigenerational family forms were presented among the "best" options, we might see different results. The cross-tab of the variables SEXORNT and FAMWKBST presented in Figure 7.9 shows that the favored family form of gay and lesbian respondents is most likely to be "Both the mother and father work full-time," whereas bisexual respondents favor the mother staying at home and the father working full-time, but the tiny number of gay, lesbian, and bisexual respondents makes these patterns unreliable. We might wonder, too, if same-sex family forms were presented alongside "mother-and-father" scenarios, might the responses of lesbian, gay, and bisexual respondents differ?

Finally, a number of other variables, such as religious affiliation, political party, and age, likely play an important role in shaping beliefs about work-family arrangements and are not considered in this analysis.

5. Summarize your conclusions.

Interpreting your results within a social justice framework requires thinking through issues of power and inequality, socially constructed differences, and links between the micro and macro levels of society as well as the importance of intersecting inequalities.

Figure 7.9

		SEXORNT			
Cells contain: **-Column percent** -Weighted N		1 Gay, lesbian, or homosexual	2 Bisexual	3 Heterosexual or straight	*ROW* *TOTAL*
FAMWKBST	1: The mother stays at home and the father works full-time	.0 .0	50.8 8.1	38.2 322.6	37.8 330.7
	2: The mother works part-time and the father works full-time	35.5 4.7	28.5 4.5	43.1 364.0	42.7 373.2
	3: Both the mother and father work full-time	51.2 6.7	13.0 2.1	11.6 97.7	12.2 106.5
	4: Both the mother and father work part-time	13.3 1.7	5.2 .8	6.6 55.4	6.6 58.0
	5: The father works part-time and the mother works full-time	.0 .0	.0 .0	.2 1.6	.2 1.6
	6: The father stays at home and the mother works full-time	.0 .0	2.6 .4	.4 3.8	.5 4.2
	COL TOTAL	*100.0* *13.2*	*100.0* *15.9*	*100.0* *845.2*	*100.0* *874.2*

Frequency Distribution

While the focus of this chapter is on family, respondents' beliefs about the "ideal" family life are intertwined with gender, sexuality, and class. Working-class respondents might be more inclined to favor an arrangement where the "mother stays at home and the father works full-time," because the low wages earned by many working-class men and women make this arrangement unattainable. Beyond their preferences about work and family arrangements, respondents who favor an arrangement where "the mother stays at home and the father works full-time" are simultaneously favoring a situation where fathers' earnings are sufficient for supporting a family. Moreover, the "mother stays at home and the father works full-time" arrangement conforms to societal constructions of heterosexual masculinity and femininity.

Despite the recent attention to family change and diversity within the United States, the results presented here highlight the strength of gender norms surrounding work and home life. Though "family" is a socially constructed concept and one that has changed dramatically over the past few decades, the overwhelming majority of GSS respondents in 2012 provided responses that associated women with the home and men with the world of work. Sexuality, age, religion, and region likely all complicate these general patterns, and further analyses of GSS data, in combination with research that is qualitative, historical, comparative, and theoretical, will be important to move this research forward.

EXERCISES

Whether they embrace these changes or oppose them, most people have a general sense that family life in the United States has been changing over the past several decades. Far fewer people, however, know precisely *how and to what extent* family life has changed. It may be common knowledge, for example, that adults in the US are generally postponing the age at which they marry and the age at which they have their first child. But, in addition to knowing this general trend, it is useful to know *how much* the average age of marriage has increased over the past 40 years. We might also want to know if diverse racial/ethnic and social class groups are all postponing marriage to the same extent. Analyzing data from the General Social Survey can help to demonstrate some of the ways in which family life has changed and the extent to which this change is structured by social inequalities.

To determine the general extent to which family forms in the US have changed over the past four decades, create a cross-tab with the variable MARITAL in the "Row" field and YEAR in the "Column" field, being sure to keep the "Weight" selection at COMPWT.

1. According to the resulting cross-tab, approximately what percentage of GSS respondents were married in 1972?

   a. 84%

   b. 74%

   c. 63%

   d. 53%

2. According to the resulting cross-tab, approximately what percentage of GSS respondents were married in 2014?

   a. 63%

   b. 53%

   c. 44%

   d. 34%

3. According to the resulting cross-tab, approximately what percentage of respondents to the 1972 survey said that they had never been married?

   a. 1%

   b. 5%

   c. 10%

   d. 15%

4. According to the resulting cross-tab, approximately what percentage of respondents to the 2014 survey said that they had never been married?

   a. 15%

   b. 25%

   c. 35%

   d. 45%

Questions 1 through 4 were based on an analysis of all respondents, but to what extent do these differences vary for respondents of different racial groups? To answer this question, rerun the cross-tab above, but this time include a "control" for race. To do this, simply enter the variable RACE in the

"Control" field. (Note: In this instance, RACE is preferable to RACEHISP, because RACEHISP was not included prior to the 2000 survey.)

5. In the 1972 survey, ____% of white respondents said they were currently married, compared with ____% of black respondents.

   a. 91; 77

   b. 86; 72

   c. 81; 67

   d. 76; 62

6. By 2014, about ____% of white respondents said they were currently married, compared with about ____% of black respondents.

   a. 58; 29

   b. 63; 35

   c. 68; 39

   d. 60; 50

In addition to differences in marital status, the past four decades have seen significant changes in child-bearing patterns. The age at which individuals are having children has shifted, as has the average number of children born to people in the US.

7. What is the survey question that corresponds to the variable AGEKDBRN?

   a. "How old was your spouse when your first child was born?"

   b. "How old were you when your first child was born?"

   c. "What is the best age for people to be when their first child is born?"

   d. "How old was your mother when you were born?"

8. Make a cross-tab with the variables AGEKDBRN and YEAR. In what year was the variable AGEKDBRN first included in the GSS?

   a. 1972

   b. 1986

   c. 1994

   d. 2000

To examine changes in the ages at which people are having their first child, run a comparison of means with the variable AGEKDBRN as the dependent variable and YEAR as the "Row" variable. (Recall that, in order to do this, you will need to select the "Means" tab on the right portion of the page.)

9. In the first year for which there are data, what was the mean of the variable AGEKDBRN?

   a. 20.97

   b. 21.48

   c. 23.84

   d. 24.26

10. By 2014, the mean value of the variable AGEKDBRN had increased to:

    a. 23.84.

    b. 24.51.

    c. 25.83.

    d. 28.03.

To examine the extent to which the average number of children has changed for the overall US adult population, now run a comparison of means with the variable CHILDS as the dependent variable and YEAR as the "Row" variable. The resulting table will show the average number of children born to GSS respondents in each year.

11. Based on your comparison of means, respondents to the 1972 GSS had, on average, how many children?

    a. 1.58 children

    b. 1.94 children

    c. 2.34 children

    d. 3.2 children

12. Respondents to the 2014 GSS had, on average:

    a. 1 fewer child.

    b. 0.5 fewer children.

    c. the same number of children.

    d. 0.5 more children.

    e. 1 more child.

In addition to examining how family forms have changed over time, the GSS offers a window into how beliefs about family issues have changed over time. The next several questions examine ideas about gender and sexuality. Begin by viewing the variable FECHLD, and then create a cross-tab of the variable FECHLD with the variable YEAR.

13. Someone who scores a 4 on the variable FECHLD believes that:

    a. a working mother can establish just as warm and secure a relationship with her children as a mother who does not work.

    b. a working mother cannot establish just as warm and secure a relationship with her children as a mother who does not work.

    c. a working father can establish just as warm and secure a relationship with his children as a father who does not work.

    d. a working father cannot establish just as warm and secure a relationship with his children as a father who does not work.

14. In 1977, the percentage of people who strongly agreed with the idea that mothers working doesn't hurt children was approximately:

    a. 5%.

    b. 10%.

    c. 15%.

    d. 20%.

15. In 2014, the percentage of people who strongly agreed with the idea that mothers working doesn't hurt children increased to approximately:

    a. 30%.

    b. 35%.

    c. 40%.

    d. 45%.

ANALYSES & ESSAYS

Use the data analysis skills you learned in the previous chapters to answer the questions below.

1. How do individuals' race and class statuses affect the likelihood of their owning a home? Construct cross-tabs using the variables RACEHISP, DEGREE, CLASS, and DWELOWN and interpret your results.

2. How and to what extent does age affect the likelihood that individuals will support same-sex marriage? Construct a cross-tab using the variables AGE and MARHOMO to answer this question. Before running your analysis, recode age into three categories: 18–35, 36–55, and 56 and older.

3. Do married women and married men differ in their assessments of how happy their marriages are? Use the variables SEX and HAPMAR to answer this question. Restrict your analysis to data from years 2010 and later.

4. Analyze three variables from the 2012 Special Module on Gender to assess the extent to which household responsibilities differ for men and women.

5. How do race, gender, and class affect respondents' views about having children?

NOTES

1. Liptak, Adam. 2015. "Supreme Court Ruling Makes Same-Sex Marriage a Right Nationwide." *New York Times*, June 26. Retrieved September 18, 2016 (http://www.nytimes.com/2015/06/27/us/supreme-court-same-sex-marriage.html).

2. E. W. 2015. "Stuck on the Wrong Side." *The Economist*, July 3. Retrieved September 18, 2016 (http://www.economist.com/blogs/democracyinamerica/2015/07/opponents-same-sex-marriage).

3. Weigel, David. 2015. "Rand Paul Says KY Clerk's Gay Marriage Protest Is 'Part of the American Way.'" *Washington Post*, September 1. Retrieved September 18, 2016 (https://www.washingtonpost .com/news/post-politics/wp/2015/09/01/rand-paul-says-ky-clerks-gay-marriage-protest-is-part-of-the-american-way/).

4. Baca Zinn, Maxine, D. Stanley Eitzen, and Barbara Wells. 2014. *Diversity in Families*. New York: Pearson; Coontz, Stephanie. 2008. *The Way We Really Are: Coming to Terms with America's Changing Families*. Basic Books; Risman, Barbara J., ed. *Families as They Really Are*. New York: W. W. Norton, 2010.

5. The US Census Bureau has many graphs, charts, and reports that document the increasing diversity of family forms over that past century. See, for example, https://www.census.gov/hhes/families/ data/households.html.

6. See Powell, Brian, Catherine Bolzendahl, Claudia Geist, and Lala Carr Steelman. 2012. *Counted Out: Same-Sex Relations and Americans' Definitions of Family*. Washington, DC: American Sociological Association.

7. US Census Bureau. n.d. "Income." Retrieved September 18, 2016 (https://www.census.gov/hhes/ www/income/about/faqs.html).

CHAPTER 8

ANALYZING INEQUALITIES IN EDUCATION

INTRODUCTION: INEQUALITIES IN EDUCATION

Quality public education is foundational to democracy. Without an informed and educated public, without citizens who can understand and evaluate different arguments and various sorts of evidence, a truly democratic system is not possible. In addition, quality public education is a necessary precondition for achieving—or even approaching—societal ideals of meritocracy and equal opportunity. The "American Dream"—the idea that, in the US, those who are talented and work hard can get ahead—is also dependent on a system of quality public education in which those who are talented and are willing to work hard are given the educational resources (such as experienced and knowledgeable teachers, textbooks, technological equipment, reasonable class sizes, and a comfortable learning environment) that allow them to succeed.[1]

Despite these ideals, the US education system remains marked by tremendous inequalities. Nationwide, in school year 2011–2012, the four-year high school graduation rate for students at public high schools was 80%. This statistic, provided by the National Center for Education Statistics, tells us that one out of every five students attending a public high school did not earn a high school degree within four years.[2] But this graduation rate masks significant differences in race, ethnicity, class, and gender. Compared with men, women had a higher likelihood of graduating in four years: 85% of women students graduated within four years, compared to only 78% of men. Racial/ethnic differences are even more pronounced. Among students who identified as

Learning Objectives

By the end of this chapter, you should be able to:

1. Identify GSS variables related to education.

2. Analyze education as an indication of social class, as a predictor of other inequalities, and as an outcome of inequality.

3. Analyze education as it intersects with race, gender, class, and sexuality.

4. Use a variety of analytic techniques appropriately to analyze issues related to education.

5. Interpret these analyses using a social justice framework.

American Indian or Alaska Native, the four-year graduation rate was 67%. Among Black students nationwide, it was 69%, and among white students, it was 86%. Students who were economically disadvantaged, regardless of racial/ethnic group, had a four-year graduation rate of 72%, and students with disabilities had a four-year graduation rate of only 61%. In some states, such as Georgia, Mississippi, Oregon, and Louisiana, the four-year graduation rate for students with disabilities was less than 40%, while in others, such as Pennsylvania, Texas, and Kansas, the four-year graduation rate for students with disabilities was 70% or higher. These inequalities continue at higher levels of education.[3]

Tremendous gains have been made with respect to gender inequality in education. In 1970, for example, women represented 40% of college students enrolled in degree-granting institutions in the US, and by 2007, this percentage had increased to more than half (55%).[4] Fifty-seven percent of bachelor's degrees conferred in the 2012–2013 school year were awarded to women, up from 43% in 1969–1970.[5] At every degree level (e.g., high school, bachelor's, master's), the percentage of women earning degrees is higher than the percentage of men, but significant gender inequality remains. Though there were more women enrolled in college than men from 2008 to 2013, only 35% of bachelor's degrees awarded in the fields of science, technology, engineering, and mathematics (STEM fields) were awarded to women.[6] The increasing media attention to issues of sexual harassment and sexual assault on college campuses also suggests that, while attending school, men's and women's experiences may differ dramatically.[7] And, while women graduates outnumber men, women's earnings upon graduation are significantly less. One recent study found that, in 2009, "women one year out of college who were working full time earned, on average, just 82% of what their male peers earned."[8]

This chapter uses the statistical skills covered in Chapters 2 through 6 to examine inequalities in education. Guided by the social justice framework presented in Chapter 1, it examines how race, gender, class, and sexuality work together to structure individuals' educational experiences, the correlates of respondents' educational attainment, and respondents' beliefs about education.

IDENTIFYING VARIABLES RELATED TO EDUCATION

Searching for Variables Related to Education

Since 1972, the General Social Survey has asked hundreds of questions about issues related to education, including questions about respondents' educational attainment, respondents' major in college (if applicable), the educational attainment of respondents' parents, and the educational attainment of respondents' spouses (if they are currently married). The survey also includes lots of question concerning respondents' attitudes and beliefs about a variety of education-related issues. A good number of these questions are included in multiple survey years, making the GSS an excellent resource for analyzing how inequalities related to education have changed over time. When searching for variables related to education, try key words such as *education*, *school*, and *major*. By searching with just these three terms, you will find more than 300 variables related to education.

Respondents' Education

Respondents' educational attainment is typically measured by one of two variables: EDUC, which represents the number of years of formal schooling the respondent has had, and DEGREE, which represents the highest degree the respondent has attained. Since 2006, the GSS has asked respondents about whether they have taken any college-level science courses (COLSCI), and those who indicate that they have taken a college-level science course are then asked to specify the number of college-level science courses they have taken (COLSCINM). In 2012 and 2014, respondents were also asked to specify their "major course of study" when they received their highest degree (MAJOR1).

Educational Attainment of Respondents' Families

In addition to analyzing the educational attainment of GSS respondents, it can also be useful to analyze the educational attainment of respondents' parents. MAEDUC represents the number of years of formal schooling the respondent's mother has had, and MADEG represents the respondent's mother's highest degree. Similarly, PAEDUC corresponds to the number of years of formal schooling the respondent's father has had, and PADEG corresponds to the respondent's father's highest degree. In addition, the variable SPEDUC corresponds to the number of years of formal schooling the respondent's spouse has had.

Attitudes and Beliefs About Education

Beyond asking questions about educational attainment, the GSS includes a number of questions that assess respondents' views about education, such as their confidence in educational institutions (CONEDUC). Also included are questions related to respondents' beliefs about inequality and diversity in educational institutions. NOBILING, a variable included in the 2000 GSS, asked respondents whether they strongly agreed, agreed, disagreed, or strongly disagreed with the idea that "bilingual education programs should be eliminated in American public schools." BUSING, a variable asked from 1972 to 1996, corresponds to the question "In general, do you favor or oppose the busing of (negro/black/African-American) and white school children from one school district to another?" (Note that the language of negro/black/African-American changed over time, reflecting changes in how Americans talk about racial issues.)

In addition, the GSS includes questions about what respondents believe should be taught in public schools. Respondents are asked, "Would you be for or against sex education in the public schools?" (SEXEDUC). From 1974 to 2014, respondents were also asked about their views of religion in public school. "The United States Supreme Court has ruled that no state or local government may require the reading of the Lord's Prayer or Bible verses in public schools. What are your views on this—do you approve or disapprove of the court ruling?" (PRAYER).

Browsing for Variables Related to Education

The codebook on the left-hand side of the SDA website allows users to look for clusters of variables about a variety of specific topics. Unfortunately, the variables related to education are scattered throughout the GSS, and most do not fall neatly into particular subheadings. As a result, searching for variables is much more efficient than browsing through multiple topical headings.

In addition to questions concerning education in general, the GSS has in recent years included a number of special modules that focus specifically on science, and many of these variables are also related to education. Browsing through the topics below, you will find variables related to respondents' knowledge of scientific ideas, their science coursework, and beliefs about science and scientists.

- 2006/2008/2010 Topical Module: Science

- 2010 Science (New)

- 2012 Topical Module: Science

ANALYZING INEQUALITIES RELATED TO EDUCATION

In general, there are three different ways in which to assess the relationship between education and intersecting inequalities of race, gender, sexuality, and class. One approach is to use education as an indicator of social class. People with higher levels of education typically have a higher level of social class, other things being equal. A second approach is to conceptualize respondents' educational attainment as an outcome of gender, racial/ ethnic, and other types of inequalities. In this way, education is analyzed as the dependent variable. A third approach is to think about educational attainment as a predictor of other forms of inequality. In this last approach, education is used as an independent variable, but not necessarily as a proxy for social class. Analyzing education through each of these approaches can yield important insights into the intersecting inequalities.

Educational Attainment as an Indicator of Social Class

The level of education that the respondent has, along with the educational attainment of the respondent's parents, can be used as a proxy for the respondent's social class. As discussed in Chapter 5, there are many dimensions of social class, such as financial resources, cultural capital, and social capital, but educational attainment is highly correlated with each of these.

EDUCATION AND RESPONDENTS' AGE

The GSS is administered to people who are 18 years and older, and some of the GSS respondents are currently in school and have not yet finished their schooling. You can check this by examining the variable WRKSTAT, which is meant to assess respondents' labor force status but includes a category for currently being in school.

In addition to GSS respondents who are currently in school, some respondents may not be in school at the time of the survey but may return to school in later years. For this reason, when analyzing educational attainment as a dependent variable, you may want to include a filter that restricts the analyses to respondents who are 25 and older.

Respondents' educational attainment is also closely related to respondents' subjective class identification, as shown in Figure 8.1. This table shows the relationship between respondents' subjective class identification (CLASS) and their highest educational degree (DEGREE) using data from the 2014 GSS. As shown in Figure 8.1, nearly 90% of all respondents (47.0% + 42.4% = 89.4%) describe themselves as either "working class" or "middle class," and very few (7.9%) self-identify as "lower class." Even fewer (2.7%) describe themselves as "upper class." Within this overall pattern, it is also clear that respondents with less than a college education are more likely to identify as lower class or working class than are those with higher levels of educational attainment. Similarly, respondents who hold a bachelor's degree or higher are more likely than those with lower levels of educational attainment to describe themselves as middle or upper class.

Analyzing education as an indicator of social class, one might ask: Are people of different social classes equally likely to participate in political processes such as voting or volunteering for political campaigns? Do people of different social classes feel differently about the government's responsibility for helping poor people? Does social class shape one's support for paid parental leave policies? In answering each of these questions, one could use respondents' educational attainment (EDUC or DEGREE) as an approximate indicator of respondents' social class.

Educational Attainment as a Predictor of Other Forms of Inequality

Beyond being an indicator of respondents' social class, educational attainment is a key predictor of a number of social inequalities, including personal and family income, occupational prestige, the likelihood of owning a home, and a variety of physical and mental health outcomes. Educational attainment can also be used to predict individuals' attitudes and beliefs about a wide range of social justice issues.

Figure 8.1

Frequency Distribution							
		DEGREE					
Cells contain: **-Column percent** -Weighted N		0 LT HIGH SCHOOL	1 HIGH SCHOOL	2 JUNIOR COLLEGE	3 BACHELOR	4 GRADUATE	*ROW TOTAL*
CLASS	1: LOWER CLASS	**19.7** *62.4*	**9.1** *117.3*	**4.1** *7.4*	**1.8** *8.6*	**1.7** *4.3*	**7.9** *200.1*
	2: WORKING CLASS	**51.9** *164.8*	**55.4** *717.9*	**62.2** *113.6*	**31.0** *145.1*	**16.4** *42.2*	**47.0** *1,183.7*
	3: MIDDLE CLASS	**26.9** *85.5*	**34.6** *448.5*	**32.5** *59.4*	**61.1** *285.5*	**74.1** *191.1*	**42.4** *1,070.0*
	4: UPPER CLASS	**1.4** *4.5*	**.9** *11.3*	**1.2** *2.3*	**6.1** *28.3*	**7.9** *20.4*	**2.7** *66.9*
	COL TOTAL	*100.0* *317.2*	*100.0* *1,295.0*	*100.0* *182.7*	*100.0* *467.5*	*100.0* *258.0*	*100.0* *2,520.6*

Education as an Outcome of Existing Inequalities

In addition to using educational attainment as an indicator of social class and a predictor of other types of inequality, it is possible to analyze respondents' educational attainment as an outcome of social inequality. It is well established that throughout the history of the United States and continuing to this day, inequalities of race, class, and gender have structured education. Racial and ethnic disparities are significant, with non-Hispanic whites, on average, having higher levels of education compared with African Americans, Latinos/Latinas, and Hispanics.[9] Class differences matter too, as individuals whose parents have a college degree are much more likely than individuals whose parents lack a college degree to go on to obtain a college degree themselves.[10]

When analyzing education as an *outcome* of existing inequalities, it is important to remember that most people finish their schooling in the early part of their lives. When thinking about the factors that shape respondents' educational attainment as well as their coursework and major choice (when applicable), it is crucial to use predictors that occurred *before* respondents completed their education. Variables such as parents' educational attainment (MADEG, PADEG), the type of family in which the respondent grew up (INCOM16, FAMILY16), the respondent's number of siblings (SIBS), the respondent's race/ethnicity (RACE, RACEHISP, ETHNIC), and the respondent's gender (SEX) are all good candidates, because, for the most part, these are stable characteristics that are "in place" before an individual finishes her or his schooling.[11]

Chapters 3 through 6 presented an overview of how data from the General Social Survey can be used to analyze inequalities of race, gender, class, and sexuality. This chapter draws from the analytic techniques presented in the previous chapters to examine how these inequalities intersect with education. As you work through the following application and exercises, refer back to previous chapters for more information on the topics, concepts, and techniques presented here.

APPLICATION: HOW DO GENDER, RACE, ETHNICITY, AND CLASS AFFECT RESPONDENTS' VIEWS ABOUT EDUCATION EXPENDITURES?

The GSS is an excellent source of data for analyzing patterns of educational attainment, the correlates of educational attainment, and beliefs about education. One of the variables that has been included regularly since its inception is NATEDUC, which asks respondents whether they think we, as a country, are spending the right amount on improving the nation's education system. This application examines how beliefs about educational expenditures are structured by gender, racial/ethnic group, and class.

Step 1. Restate the research question and identify the independent and dependent variables.

As noted above, the research question is "How do gender, race, ethnicity, and class affect respondents' views about education expenditures?" The dependent variable is NATEDUC, and the independent variables are SEX, INCOME06, and RACEHISP.

Step 2. View each variable to make sure it means what you think it means. In almost all cases, viewing the variable will show the precise wording of the survey question that corresponds to the variable. When you view the variable, make note of what each response category means as well as the level of measurement for the variable (nominal, ordinal, or interval-ratio).

Viewing the variable NATEDUC shows that this is an ordinal-level variable, where respondents are told:

> We are faced with many problems in this country, none of which can be solved easily or inexpensively. I'm going to name some of these problems, and for each one I'd like you to tell me whether you think we're spending too much money on it, too little money, or about the right amount. . . . [i]mproving the nation's education system.

INCOME06 is an ordinal-level variable corresponding to the respondent's family income. It ranges from 1 to 25, where 1 indicates a total family income of below $1,000 and 25 indicates a family income of $150,000 or more. SEX and RACEHISP are both variables where viewing the variable provides incomplete information. Each of these variables is discussed at length in preceding chapters (Chapters 3 and 4, respectively). SEX is a nominal-level variable representing the respondent's gender, categorized as "male" or "female."

RACEHISP is a nominal-level variable indicating the respondent's self-described racial/ethnic identity. By viewing this variable, we see that the category "White" does not include respondents who said they were Hispanic and that Hispanic does not include those who said they were Black.

Step 3. Determine which time period the data are from. Remember that when you view a variable, you are seeing the combined data across all survey years in which the question was included in the GSS. Some questions have been included regularly since 1972, giving us more than four decades of data. Other questions are asked in only one survey year. Either way, we must be careful to make note of this when conducting and interpreting the analyses.

The easiest way to determine the years in which the variable is included is by creating a cross-tab of the variables in the analysis by the variable YEAR (the variable that corresponds to the survey year). Producing a cross-tab with NATEDUC in the "Row" field and YEAR in the "Column" field (with COMPWT selected in the "Weight" field) will result in a large table with data from 1973 to 2014. Producing separate cross-tabs of the variables SEX and INCOME06 with the variable YEAR will show that the variable SEX has been included in the GSS regularly since 1972 and that INCOME06 has been included since 2006. Producing a cross-tab of RACEHISP by YEAR will reveal that RACEHISP has been included since the 2000 survey.

To focus our analysis on relatively recent data, let's restrict further analysis to survey years 2010 to 2014 using the filter "YEAR (2010-2014)." For more information on using filters in SDA, see Chapters 4 and 6.

Step 4. Conduct the relevant analysis, such as a cross-tab or a comparison of means. Remember that you may need to include filter and control variables, depending on the research question. Remember too that you may need to recode variables.

The research question asks us to examine gender, racial/ethnic, and class-based differences in respondents' beliefs about educational expenditures. There are three independent variables in this analysis (INCOME06, SEX, and RACEHISP), and there are many different approaches to conducting this analysis. My approach is to use cross-tabs to first examine the extent to which racial/ethnic groups differ in their beliefs about educational expenditures. Following this general analysis, I will use gender as a control variable to see how gender works with class, race, and ethnicity to shape respondents' beliefs. It would be just as appropriate, however, to start by examining class-based differences, for example, and then to use class as a control variable to see how race, ethnicity, and gender work with class to shape respondents' ideals.

Begin constructing your cross-tabs by entering NATEDUC in the "Row" field (since it is the dependent variable) and RACEHISP in the "Column" field (since it is the independent variable). Before running the table, be sure that you have the default,

COMPWT, selected in the "Weight" field, and that you filter the data for survey years 2010 to 2014. Figure 8.2 shows the resulting cross-tab. Across all racial/ethnic groups considered, the modal category is "too little," and only a small proportion of respondents answered "too much."

But how might respondents' gender work with race and ethnicity to shape views about educational expenditures? Keeping NATEDUC in the "Row" field and RACEHISP in the "Column" field and using a filter for survey years 2010 through 2014, now add a control for respondents' gender by entering the variable SEX in the "Control" field. Running the table should produce three cross-tabs: one for men respondents (shown in Figure 8.3), one for women respondents (shown in Figure 8.4), and one summary table identical to that shown in Figure 8.2.

Figures 8.3 and 8.4 show that, when controlling for respondents' gender, the modal category for every racial/ethnic group remains "too little," and very few respondents, men or women, answer that "too much" money is currently being put toward improving the nation's education system. By comparing percentages across the two tables, we can also see some interesting gender differences begin to emerge. These are discussed in Step 5 below.

Now let's examine how class helps to shape respondents' views about national educational expenditures. A number of different variables, such as DEGREE, CLASS, RINCOM06, and REALINC, could be used as a proxy for respondents' class. Here I am using INCOME06, which corresponds to respondents' family income. INCOME06 has 25 categories and, as a result, would be difficult to interpret in a cross-tab without recoding. To make things more manageable, I will recode the variable into four categories, where 1 represents family incomes under

Figure 8.2

Frequency Distribution						
Cells contain: -**Column percent** -Weighted N		**RACEHISP**				
		1 White	2 Black	3 Hispanic	4 Other	*ROW* *TOTAL*
NATEDUC	1: TOO LITTLE	**73.5** 1,555.1	**77.3** 367.0	**64.3** 324.3	**72.7** 117.8	72.6 *2,364.2*
	2: ABOUT RIGHT	**18.6** 392.9	**20.9** 99.2	**30.7** 154.7	**22.2** 36.0	21.0 *682.8*
	3: TOO MUCH	**7.9** 166.7	**1.8** 8.8	**5.0** 25.2	**5.1** 8.2	6.4 *208.9*
	COL TOTAL	*100.0* *2,114.7*	*100.0* *475.1*	*100.0* *504.2*	*100.0* *162.0*	*100.0* *3,255.9*

Figure 8.3

<table>
<tr><th colspan="7">Statistics for SEX = 1(MALE)</th></tr>
<tr><td rowspan="2">Cells contain:
-**Column percent**
-Weighted N</td><td rowspan="2"></td><th colspan="4">RACEHISP</th><td rowspan="2">**ROW
TOTAL**</td></tr>
<tr><th>1
White</th><th>2
Black</th><th>3
Hispanic</th><th>4
Other</th></tr>
<tr><td rowspan="8">**NATEDUC**</td><td rowspan="2">1: TOO LITTLE</td><td>**67.8**</td><td>**78.7**</td><td>**64.9**</td><td>**69.5**</td><td>**68.7**</td></tr>
<tr><td>679.0</td><td>143.5</td><td>162.7</td><td>55.7</td><td>1,040.8</td></tr>
<tr><td rowspan="2">2: ABOUT RIGHT</td><td>**22.6**</td><td>**18.4**</td><td>**30.9**</td><td>**26.1**</td><td>**23.6**</td></tr>
<tr><td>226.1</td><td>33.5</td><td>77.5</td><td>20.9</td><td>357.9</td></tr>
<tr><td rowspan="2">3: TOO MUCH</td><td>**9.6**</td><td>**2.9**</td><td>**4.1**</td><td>**4.4**</td><td>**7.6**</td></tr>
<tr><td>96.3</td><td>5.3</td><td>10.4</td><td>3.5</td><td>115.5</td></tr>
<tr><td rowspan="2">*COL TOTAL*</td><td>*100.0*</td><td>*100.0*</td><td>*100.0*</td><td>*100.0*</td><td>*100.0*</td></tr>
<tr><td>*1,001.4*</td><td>*182.3*</td><td>*250.6*</td><td>*80.1*</td><td>*1,514.3*</td></tr>
</table>

Figure 8.4

<table>
<tr><th colspan="7">Statistics for SEX = 2(FEMALE)</th></tr>
<tr><td rowspan="2">Cells contain:
-**Column percent**
-Weighted N</td><td rowspan="2"></td><th colspan="4">RACEHISP</th><td rowspan="2">**ROW
TOTAL**</td></tr>
<tr><th>1
White</th><th>2
Black</th><th>3
Hispanic</th><th>4
Other</th></tr>
<tr><td rowspan="8">**NATEDUC**</td><td rowspan="2">1: TOO LITTLE</td><td>**78.7**</td><td>**76.3**</td><td>**63.7**</td><td>**75.8**</td><td>**76.0**</td></tr>
<tr><td>876.2</td><td>223.5</td><td>161.6</td><td>62.1</td><td>1,323.4</td></tr>
<tr><td rowspan="2">2: ABOUT RIGHT</td><td>**15.0**</td><td>**22.5**</td><td>**30.4**</td><td>**18.4**</td><td>**18.7**</td></tr>
<tr><td>166.8</td><td>65.8</td><td>77.2</td><td>15.1</td><td>324.9</td></tr>
<tr><td rowspan="2">3: TOO MUCH</td><td>**6.3**</td><td>**1.2**</td><td>**5.8**</td><td>**5.7**</td><td>**5.4**</td></tr>
<tr><td>70.3</td><td>3.5</td><td>14.8</td><td>4.7</td><td>93.4</td></tr>
<tr><td rowspan="2">*COL TOTAL*</td><td>*100.0*</td><td>*100.0*</td><td>*100.0*</td><td>*100.0*</td><td>*100.0*</td></tr>
<tr><td>*1,113.3*</td><td>*292.8*</td><td>*253.6*</td><td>*81.9*</td><td>*1,741.6*</td></tr>
</table>

$24,999; 2 represents family incomes of $25,000 to $49,999; 3 represents family incomes of $50,000 to $89,999; and 4 indicates family incomes of $90,000 and higher. In constructing these new categories, I have aimed to make the first three approximately equal while ensuring that each category also has a relatively large number of respondents.

Figure 8.5

Frequency Distribution						
Cells contain: -**Column percent** -Weighted N		**INCOME06**				
		1 1-14	2 15-18	3 19-21	4 22-25	**ROW** **TOTAL**
NATEDUC	1: TOO LITTLE	**68.8** 502.9	**73.5** 496.7	**74.4** 589.3	**77.1** 525.2	**73.4** 2,114.2
	2: ABOUT RIGHT	**25.4** 185.5	**20.1** 135.7	**20.3** 160.8	**15.5** 105.4	**20.4** 587.5
	3: TOO MUCH	**5.8** 42.4	**6.4** 43.0	**5.3** 41.7	**7.4** 50.3	**6.2** 177.4
	COL TOTAL	**100.0** 730.8	**100.0** 675.4	**100.0** 791.8	**100.0** 681.0	**100.0** 2,879.0

To assess the relationship between respondents' social class and beliefs about national educational expenditures, create a cross-tab by entering NATEDUC in the "Row" field. In the "Column" field, type:

INCOME06 (R: 1-14; 15-18; 19-21; 22-25)

Restrict the analysis to recent survey years by filtering the data for survey years 2010 to 2014. Figure 8.5 shows the resulting cross-tab.

Next, create another cross-tab analysis to examine how class works with gender to structure views on educational expenditures. Use the recoded INCOME06 as the independent variables, and use SEX as a control variable. NATEDUC should remain the dependent variable (in the "Row" field), and keep the filter for years 2010 to 2014 in the "Filter" field. Figures 8.6 and 8.7 show how class-based differences work with gender to structure ideals about educational expenditures.

Step 5. Interpret your results. There are five basic step to interpreting and communicating your results:

1. *Remind your audience of the basics.*

    a. Restate your research question.

        The main research question is "How do gender, race, ethnicity, and class affect respondents' views about education expenditures?"

Figure 8.6

Statistics for SEX = 1(MALE)						
Cells contain: -**Column percent** -Weighted N		**INCOME06**				
		1 1-14	2 15-18	3 19-21	4 22-25	**ROW TOTAL**
NATEDUC	1: TOO LITTLE	**65.4** 184.8	**71.3** 225.0	**69.1** 278.3	**72.3** 252.0	**69.6** 940.1
	2: ABOUT RIGHT	**28.1** 79.2	**22.9** 72.2	**24.1** 97.1	**18.9** 65.8	**23.3** 314.3
	3: TOO MUCH	**6.5** 18.4	**5.9** 18.6	**6.8** 27.5	**8.9** 30.9	**7.1** 95.5
	COL TOTAL	**100.0** 282.5	**100.0** 315.8	**100.0** 402.9	**100.0** 348.8	**100.0** 1,349.9

Figure 8.7

Statistics for SEX = 2(FEMALE)						
Cells contain: -**Column percent** -Weighted N		**INCOME06**				
		1 1-14	2 15-18	3 19-21	4 22-25	**ROW TOTAL**
NATEDUC	1: TOO LITTLE	**71.0** 318.1	**75.6** 271.7	**80.0** 311.0	**82.2** 273.2	**76.8** 1,174.1
	2: ABOUT RIGHT	**23.7** 106.3	**17.7** 63.5	**16.4** 63.7	**11.9** 39.6	**17.9** 273.1
	3: TOO MUCH	**5.3** 24.0	**6.8** 24.4	**3.6** 14.1	**5.8** 19.4	**5.4** 81.9
	COL TOTAL	**100.0** 448.3	**100.0** 359.6	**100.0** 388.9	**100.0** 332.2	**100.0** 1,529.0

b. Remind your audience of the data source and the specific
variables that you used to answer this question.

This analysis uses a series of cross-tabs to assess how and to what
extent respondents' views about educational expenditures differ
for men and women of different racial/ethnic and class groups.
The data come from the 2010 to 2014 General Social Surveys.

c. Clearly state how each variable was coded and what each response category represents.

The dependent variable, respondents' views about educational expenditures, is assessed with the survey question "We are faced with many problems in this country, none of which can be solved easily or inexpensively. I'm going to name some of these problems, and for each one I'd like you to tell me whether you think we're spending too much money on it, too little money, or about the right amount. . . . [i]mproving the nation's education system." This is an ordinal-level variable with three categories. The respondent's gender status (male or female) is recorded by the interviewer, who is instructed not to ask the respondent about their sex or gender identity. The respondent's racial/ethnic identity is assessed with a four-category nominal-level variable, where categories represent self-identification as white (non-Hispanic), African American or Black, Hispanic (non-Black), or part of some other racial/ethnic group. Respondents' family income is used as a proxy for respondents' social class. Family income was recoded into four categories: under $24,999; $25,000 to $49,999; $50,000 to $89,999; and $90,000 and higher.

d. Specify the number of cases included in the analysis. The overall number of valid cases (N) included in the cross-tab is presented in the bottom right corner of each cross-tab.

The analyses focusing on race and ethnicity include approximately 3,256 respondents (1,514 men and 1,712 women). The analyses focusing on respondents' family income have more missing data, and consequently a smaller number of respondents (2,879 total, 1,350 men and 1,529 women).

2. Focus on specifics.

The first step in interpreting a cross-tab or a comparison of means is to examine the specific numbers in the tables and interpret them in a detailed way. When interpreting the results from multiple tables, it is usually best to interpret them one by one.

For example, Figure 8.2 shows that, for all racial/ethnic groups considered here, the modal category is "too little." Most people surveyed, regardless of their racial/ethnic identity, believe that we are spending too little on improving the nation's education system. Figure 8.2 also suggests some important differences in people's perception of educational expenditures. Approximately three quarters of non-Hispanic whites, Blacks, and "other" (non-Hispanic) racial/ethnic groups believe we are spending too little on improving education. Non-Black Hispanic respondents are relatively less likely to answer "too little" and are more likely than the other racial/ethnic groups considered here to believe that our current expenditures are "about right."

Figures 8.3 and 8.4 show how these racial/ethnic differences intersect with gender. Interestingly, the percentage of non-Hispanic white women who believe we are spending too little on improving education (78.7%) is much higher than the corresponding percentage of non-Hispanic white men (67.8%). Among Black and Hispanic respondents, there is much greater similarity between men and women; 78.7% of Black men respondents and 76.3% of Black women respondents answered that we are spending too little on improving the nation's education system. Among Hispanic respondents, 64.9% of men and 63.7% of women reported that we are spending too little. Nearly one in 10 non-Hispanic white men surveyed (9.6%) answered that we are currently spending too much on improving education.

Figure 8.5 examines the relationship between family income and beliefs about educational expenditures. Across all the income categories considered here, the majority of respondents believe that we are spending "too little" on improving the nation's education system. Interestingly, and perhaps unexpectedly, respondents with lower family incomes are less likely than respondents with higher family incomes to believe we are spending too little on education. As family income increases, the percentage of respondents who believe we are spending too little on education increases. Compared to respondents with family incomes above $90,000 per year (category 4), respondents with family incomes under $25,000 (category 1) are much more likely to believe that we are spending about the right amount on improving the nation's education system.

Figures 8.6 and 8.7 show how class and gender combine to influence perceptions of educational expenditures. Among men (Figure 8.6) and among women (Figure 8.7), respondents with higher family incomes are more likely to answer that we are spending too little on improving the nation's education system. Among the highest income group, more than four in five women surveyed (82.2%) answered that we are spending too little on improving the nation's education system. Men in the highest income group were somewhat less likely to provide this response, but still nearly three quarters (72.3%) responded that we are spending too little on improving the nation's education system.

3. Consider the big picture.

After examining individual statistics within the analyses, it is important to step back and take a larger view of the overall relationship presented in the tables. When examining each table individually, can you see any patterns or trends in the column percentages, or do the numbers seem to go up and down at random? If you see clusters of dark blue or dark red cells in the table, then there is probably an identifiable pattern. If there are very few darkly colored cells or if they seem randomly scattered across the table, then there may not be an easily identifiable pattern. It's also important to think about how the individual analyses work together. Do they all point to the same overall conclusion, or are the results more mixed? If the individual analyses seem to point to different conclusions, how do you make sense of these results? Remember that having mixed results is not wrong. Results without identifiable patterns can be just as important and interesting as results with an identifiable pattern—especially if the pattern you expected is not apparent.

What, in general, can be said about how gender, class, race, and ethnicity structure individuals' beliefs about educational expenditures? From 2010 to 2014, regardless of gender, regardless of family income, and regardless of racial/ethnic identity, very few respondents answered that we are spending too much on improving education. Among every racial/ethnic, gender, and class group considered, the majority answered that we are spending too little on improving the nation's education system.

Comparing the top rows of data presented in Figure 8.6 with the top row of data presented in Figure 8.7, we can see that, at every level of family income, women are more likely than men to answer that we are spending too little. Moreover, the gap between men's and women's preferences is particularly large among men and women with high family incomes. Figure 8.8 is created by graphing (in Excel) the difference between the values presented in the top row of Figure 8.6 and the values presented in the top row of Figure 8.6. You can see that at higher levels of family incomes, there is a larger difference in the percentage of women who respond "too little" and the percentage of men who respond "too little."

There are many other legitimate ways to interpret the "big picture." The statistics presented above can be analyzed together in multiple different ways, and some approaches may yield an interpretation with a slightly different emphasis. There are multiple combinations and multiple correct answers.

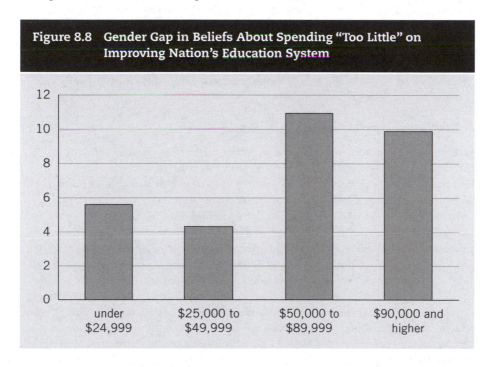

Figure 8.8   Gender Gap in Beliefs About Spending "Too Little" on Improving Nation's Education System

4. Consider limitations.

An important part of all scientific research is to be clear about the limitations of the research. Every research project has limitations, and it is important to make these clear when interpreting the results. It is also important to consider potential confounding variables, variables that are not included in the analyses but may be affecting the relationship between the independent and dependent variables. Finally, while it is crucial to explain what the analyses reveal about the larger research question, it is often useful to clarify what the analyses do *not* tell us about the research question. Anticipate possible misinterpretations.

When considering the limitations of any survey research project, it is important to consider the issues of survey design, possible sample biases, and generalizability. In the current analysis, the results apply only to adults in the US who are aged 18 and older. Respondents include English- and Spanish-speaking adults, but adults in the US who are not able to speak either language are not included in the analysis. Nor are those living in institutions such as prisons or mental institutions included in this analysis.

A second limitation concerns the ways in which gender and race/ethnicity are measured. As indicated previously, the GSS does not ask respondents directly about their gender identity and instead relies on interviewers' perceptions. Respondents are asked about their racial/ethnic identities, but in the variable used here (RACEHISP), the identities that respondents report are then grouped together into broad categories that may or may not be comfortable for many respondents. In addition, by grouping together respondents under these broad racial/ethnic categories, the variation within any one of these categories is obscured.

Finally, a number of other variables, such as region of the country, political party, and age, likely play an important role in shaping beliefs about educational expenditure and are not considered in this analysis.

5. Summarize your conclusions.

Interpreting these results within a social justice framework requires thinking through issues of power and inequality, socially constructed differences, and links between the micro and macro levels of society as well as the importance of intersecting inequalities. Given the fact that the overwhelming majority of individuals surveyed responded that we are spending too little on improving the nation's education system, why are we, as a nation, not spending more on this problem? Beyond the level of individual attitudes and beliefs, what are the macro-level processes, institutions, and power dynamics that are working against further funding of education? What do the gender differences we see in the above analyses reveal about the social construction of gender and its relation to race, ethnicity, and class? And what other inequalities might work with race, ethnicity, class, and gender to shape individuals' beliefs about these issues? These questions can be answered by combining further analyses of GSS data with research that is qualitative, historical, comparative, and theoretical.

EXERCISES

The following 10 questions examine how race, class, ethnicity, and gender help to structure educational outcomes for individuals in the US. First let's look at the extent to which respondents' fathers' educational attainment is related to their children's educational attainment. On the SDA website, create a cross-tab with the variable PADEG in the "Column" field and DEGREE in the "Row" field and with a filter for survey years 2010 to 2014. Be sure to keep the weight selection at COMPWT.

1. When arguing that respondents' educational attainment is likely affected by their fathers' educational attainment, respondents' educational attainment is best described as the:

    a. dependent variable.

    b. independent variable.

    c. control variable.

    d. filter variable.

2. Of those respondents whose fathers had less than a high school diploma, what percentage of respondents also had less than a high school diploma?

    a. 9.8

    b. 26.5

    c. 52.6

    d. 42.9

3. Among respondents whose fathers had a graduate degree, ___% of survey respondents had less than a high school diploma and ___% had a graduate degree.

    a. 2.2; 25.8

    b. 5.8; 26.5

    c. 10.4; 42.9

    d. 52.6; 64.5

4. In general, as fathers' educational attainment increases, the likelihood of respondents themselves having a graduate degree:

    a. increases.

    b. decreases.

    c. stays about the same.

To examine the extent to which racial/ethnic and gender differences shape educational attainment, now produce a cross-tab with the variable DEGREE as the "Row" variable, RACEHISP as the "Column" variable, and SEX as the control variable. Use a filter to restrict the analysis to data from 2010 to 2014.

5. According to the resulting cross-tab, which of the following racial/ethnic groups has the highest percentage of men respondents with less than a high school diploma?

    a. non-Hispanic white respondents

    b. Black respondents

    c. non-Black Hispanic/Latino respondents

    d. respondents from other racial/ethnic groups

6. According to the resulting cross-tab, the percentage of Black men respondents whose highest degree was a bachelor's degree is ____. In contrast, ___% of non-Hispanic white men surveyed indicated that they had earned a bachelor's degree (but not higher than a bachelor's degree).

    a. 11.5; 22.2

    b. 9.3; 21.8

    c. 11.7; 20.2

    d. 18.6; 25.9

7. According to the resulting cross-tab, which of the following racial/ethnic groups has the highest percentage of women respondents with less than a high school diploma?

    a. non-Hispanic white respondents

    b. Black respondents

    c. non-Black Hispanic/Latina respondents

    d. respondents from other racial/ethnic groups

8. According to the resulting cross-tab, the percentage of Latina/Hispanic women respondents whose highest degree was a graduate degree is ____. In contrast, ___% of non-Hispanic white women surveyed indicated that they had earned a graduate degree.

    a. 3.1; 11.1

    b. 5.6; 11.6

    c. 18.5; 9

    d. 11.8; 51.5

To examine the extent to which race and ethnicity shape the differences in college-level coursework, run a comparison of means with the variable COLSCINM as the dependent variable and RACEHISP as the "Row" variable. (Remember that you need to select the "Means" tab to move from the cross-tab page to the comparison of means page.) Use a filter to restrict the analysis to data from 2010 to 2014. The resulting table will show the average number of college-level science courses for respondents who have indicated that they have taken at least one college-level science course.

9. Of those respondents who had taken at least one college-level science course, non-Hispanic white respondents had, on average, completed _____ courses.

   a. 6.35

   b. 4.73

   c. 4.2

   d. 9.47

10. Of those respondents who had taken at least one college-level science course, Black respondents had, on average, completed _____ courses.

    a. 6.35

    b. 4.73

    c. 4.2

    d. 9.47

The previous questions examined how various inequalities shape GSS respondents' educational experiences. The next five questions focus on educational attainment as a predictor of social inequalities.

To what extent is educational attainment related to attitudes about same-sex marriage? View the variable MARHOMO to determine the precise wording of this question as well as the level of measurement. Next, construct a cross-tab with MARHOMO as the "Row" variable and DEGREE as the "Column" variable, and use a filter of "YEAR (2010-2014)." Be sure to keep the "Weight" selection as COMPWT. (Remember that you may have to click on the "Tables" analysis tab if you are currently on the "Means" analysis tab.)

11. The variable MARHOMO is best described as:

    a. a categorical-level variable.

    b. an ordinal-level variable.

    c. an interval-ratio-level variable.

    d. a dummy variable.

12. Among respondents with less than a high school diploma, the modal category for MARHOMO is:

    a. strongly agree with the idea that "homosexual couples should have the right to marry one another."

    b. agree with the idea that "homosexual couples should have the right to marry one another."

    c. neither agree nor disagree with the idea that "homosexual couples should have the right to marry one another."

    d. disagree with the idea that "homosexual couples should have the right to marry one another."

    e. strongly disagree with the idea that "homosexual couples should have the right to marry one another."

13. Among respondents who reported that their highest degree was a high school diploma, approximately ___ either strongly agreed or agreed with the idea that homosexual couples should have the right to marry one another.

    a. 40%

    b. 50%

    c. 60%

    d. 70%

14. Among respondents who reported that their highest degree was a bachelor's degree, approximately ___ either strongly agreed or agreed with the idea that homosexual couples should have the right to marry one another.

    a. 40%

    b. 50%

    c. 60%

    d. 70%

15. Among respondents with a graduate degree, the modal category for MARHOMO is:

    a. strongly agree with the idea that "homosexual couples should have the right to marry one another."

    b. agree with the idea that "homosexual couples should have the right to marry one another."

    c. neither agree nor disagree with the idea that "homosexual couples should have the right to marry one another."

    d. disagree with the idea that "homosexual couples should have the right to marry one another."

    e. strongly disagree with the idea that "homosexual couples should have the right to marry one another."

ANALYSES & ESSAYS

Use the data analysis skills you learned in the previous chapters to answer the questions below.

1. How and to what extent is respondents' mothers' educational attainment related to respondents' educational attainment? Does this relationship differ for men and women respondents? Construct cross-tabs using the variables MADEG and DEGREE, using SEX as a control variable, to answer this question. Use the filter "YEAR (2010-2014) AGE (25-95)." Interpret your results.

2. How and to what extent does respondents' perception of their financial status when they were growing up relate to their educational attainment? Construct cross-tabs using the variables INCOM16 and DEGREE, using SEX as a control variable, to answer this question. Use the filter "YEAR (2010-2014) AGE (25-95)." Interpret your results.

3. How have racial-ethnic disparities in educational attainment changed since 2000? Construct a cross-tab using the variables RACEHISP and DEGREE, using SEX as a control variable, using the filter "YEAR (2000) AGE (25-95)." Then create a second cross-tab using the variables RACEHISP and DEGREE, using SEX as a control variable, using the filter "YEAR (2014) AGE (25-95)." Interpret your results.

4. To what extent is education related to beliefs about immigration? Construct cross-tabs using the variables DEGREE, IMMCULT, IMMEDUC, and LETIN1A. Interpret your results.

5. Analyze three variables from the 2012 Special Module on Gender to assess the extent to which views about children differ for people with different levels of educational attainment.

NOTES

1. Weber, Lynn. 2010. *Understanding Race, Class, Gender and Sexuality: A Conceptual Framework*. New York: Oxford University Press, p. 145.

2. National Center for Education Statistics. N.d. "Public High School Four-Year On-Time Graduation Rates and Event Dropout Rates: School Years 2010–11 and 2011–12." Retrieved September 23, 2016 (http://nces.ed.gov/pubs2014/2014391/findings.asp).

3. See Massey, Douglas S., Camille Z. Charles, Garvey F. Lundy, and Mary J. Fischer. 2003. *The Source of the River: The Social Origins of Freshmen at America's Selective Colleges and Universities*. Princeton, NJ: Princeton University Press.

4. National Center for Education Statistics. 2008. "Table 190. Total Fall Enrollment in Degree-Granting Institutions, by Sex, Age, and Attendance Status: Selected Years, 1970 through 2017." Retrieved March 3, 2010 (http://nces.ed.gov/programs/digest/d08/tables/dt08_190.asp).

5. National Center for Education Statistics. 2016. "Digest of Education Statistics: 2014." Retrieved May 9, 2016 (http://nces.ed.gov/programs/digest/d14/).

6. National Center for Education Statistics. 2015. "Table 318.45. Number and Percentage Distribution of Science, Technology, Engineering, and Mathematics (STEM) Degrees/Certificates Conferred by Postsecondary Institutions, by Race/

Ethnicity, Level of Degree/Certificate, and Sex of Student: 2008–09 through 2012–13." Retrieved May 24, 2016 (https://nces.ed.gov/programs/digest/d14/tables/dt14_318.45.asp).

7. See Hill, Catherine, and Elena Silva. 2005. "Drawing the Line: Sexual Harassment on Campus." Washington, DC: AAUW Educational Foundation. Retrieved May 22, 2016 (http://www.aauw.org/files/2013/02/drawing-the-line-sexual-harassment-on-campus.pdf).

8. Corbett, Christianne, and Catherine Hill. 2012. "Graduating to a Pay Gap: The Earnings of Women and Men One Year after College Graduation." Retrieved May 24, 2016 (http://www.aauw.org/files/2013/02/graduating-to-a-pay-gap-the-earnings-of-women-and-men-one-year-after-college-graduation.pdf).

9. Kao, Grace, and Jennifer S. Thompson. 2003. "Racial and Ethnic Stratification in Educational Achievement and Attainment." *Annual Review of Sociology* 29:417–42.

10. Kerbo, Harold R. 2009. *Social Stratification and Inequality*. 7th ed. New York: McGraw-Hill.

11. Of course, the racial, ethnic, and gender identities of some GSS respondents will change over time, including during the school-aged years. Significant, categorical changes in these characteristics are likely to occur within a minority of respondents and thus are unlikely to affect the overall pattern of results in a major way.

CHAPTER 9

ANALYZING INEQUALITIES IN THE ECONOMY AND AT WORK

INTRODUCTION: INEQUALITIES IN THE ECONOMY AND AT WORK

Writing in the 1950s, sociologist C. Wright Mills described the "sociological imagination" as the quality of mind that allows one to "grasp the interplay of man and society, of biography and history, of self and world."[1] Mills argued that the sociological imagination enables its possessor to understand how macro-level institutions, policies, and processes shape the lives of individual people—their experiences, their beliefs, and even their desires and feelings.

In addition, he believed that the social sciences, and sociology in particular, could help people to distinguish "personal troubles"—those problems arising primarily from individual qualities or from bad luck—from "issues," by which he meant problems rooted in the larger social structure.

As Mills explains:

> When, in a city of 100,000, only one person is unemployed, that is their personal trouble, and for its relief we properly look to the character of the person, their skills, and their immediate opportunities. But when in a nation of 50 million employees, 15 million people are unemployed, that is an issue, and we may not hope to find its solution within the range of opportunities open to any one individual. The very structure of opportunities has collapsed. *Both the correct statement of the problem*

Learning Objectives

By the end of this chapter, you should be able to:

1. Identify GSS variables related to work and the economy.

2. Analyze various dimensions of work and the economy as they relate to racial, gender, class, and sexuality.

3. Use a variety of analytic techniques appropriately to analyze issues related to the economy and work.

4. Interpret these analyses using a social justice framework.

and the range of possible solutions require us to consider the economic and political institutions of the society, and not merely the personal situation and character of a scatter of individuals.[2,3]

Being able to differentiate personal troubles from public issues is important for two reasons. First, as Mills explains, it can help individual people to better understand their own lives and to make sense of the problems they themselves, their families, and their friends experience. Second, Mills believed that determining whether a problem was an individual trouble or a social issue was the first step, and arguably the most important, in addressing a problem. Personal troubles are isolated events, and, when a resolution is in fact possible, these troubles can be resolved at the individual level. If, for example, Jennifer is the one person in the city of 100,000 who lacks a job, we might try to solve Jennifer's problem by improving her education, helping her to format her résumé, or perhaps even helping her with motivation or self-esteem. If, on the other hand, Jennifer is one among many millions of people who are unemployed, and especially if unemployment is patterned in such a way that it is certain groups of people (for example, young people, those with low levels of education, or racial/ethnic minorities) who are most likely to be unemployed or underemployed, then focusing on Jennifer as an isolated individual is unlikely to solve her problem. A real solution to this type of problem requires a broader, more macro-level approach.

In 2007–2009, a financial recession and home mortgage crisis rocked the US economy—and indeed the economy around the world. The official US unemployment rate, which had been 5.0% in December of 2007, doubled to 10% in October 2009.[4] The number of home foreclosures in the US tripled from 717,522 in 2006 to 2,330,483 in 2008.[5] But the pain of the great recession was not distributed evenly across all groups in society. While the unemployment rate for non-Hispanic whites peaked below 10%, among African Americans, the unemployment rate was above 15%. Young people and those with low levels of education felt the effects of the crisis particularly painfully. By 2010, after the recession officially ended, young adults (aged 20–24) who had less than a high school education had an employment rate of only 44%.[6]

If there was ever a time in recent history where the unemployed and underemployed Americans should not have felt alone in their troubles, where all Americans—regardless of their economic well-being—were positioned to see the ways in which the hardships of individuals, as well as their successes, were intertwined with the broader political and economic institutions, then this was it. The very structure of opportunities had, in many ways, collapsed, and many people saw the results of this collapse—in real, economic, and material terms—in their lives. We might wonder, though: Did this economic collapse fundamentally shift the ways in which people understand success and failure? Did the collapse of the economic system help individuals to, as Mills writes, "define the troubles they endure in terms of historical change and institutional contradiction"?[7] Or did the ideology of individualism and meritocracy endure?

This chapter uses the statistical skills covered in Chapters 2 through 6 to examine inequalities in work and the broader economy. Guided by the social justice framework presented in Chapter 1, it examines how inequalities of gender, race, ethnicity, and class work together to structure individuals' beliefs about work and the economy as well as their work-related experiences.

IDENTIFYING VARIABLES RELATED TO WORK AND THE ECONOMY

Over the past four decades, the General Social Survey has asked hundreds of questions about work-related issues, including questions about respondents' current workforce status, the type of work they do, the financial and emotional rewards they take from their job, questions about work-family balance, and a variety of other topics. A good number of these questions are included in multiple survey years, making the GSS an excellent resource for analyzing diversity and inequalities related to work and the broader economy, and how these have changed over time.

Searching for Variables Related to Work and the Economy

When searching for and analyzing variables related to work, it is important to remember that GSS respondents range in age from 18 into their 80s and above. People at different life stages are often differently situated with respect to the workforce: Some have yet to enter the labor force, some are in their peak work years, and others have long since retired. Many of the GSS variables related to work (e.g., respondents' income: RINCOM06; respondents' workforce status: WRKSTAT) are asked to all respondents, regardless of whether they are currently working in the paid labor force. Other variables (e.g., how often respondents feel ignored at work: IGNORWK) are asked only to those respondents who are active in the workforce—either working full time, working part time, or temporarily not working.

GENDER, CLASS, AND WORK

Though it may not seem so at first, work is a sensitive topic. Even a basic question like "Last week were you working full time, part time, going to school, keeping house, or what?" (WRKSTAT) is more complicated than it may first appear. Much of the complexity stems from the intersection of gender and class within dominant American culture.

The American Dream—the promise that all individuals can, through hard work, persistence, and creative problem-solving, work their way up to a comfortable middle- or upper-class position—is a central part of American culture.[8] And while the historical record demonstrates that some individuals born into poverty have indeed managed to overcome significant obstacles and have "made it" to the upper class, the historical record also demonstrates that cases of significant class mobility in the US are the exception, not the rule.[9]

(Continued)

(Continued)

Work status can be a sensitive topic for individuals who find themselves unemployed or underemployed. In a society where successes and failures are viewed primarily as resulting from individual characteristics (e.g., intelligence and determination) rather than from structural conditions and macro-level processes (e.g., globalization, financial recessions, shifts from a manufacturing to a service-based economic system), those who are unemployed or underemployed may not report their work status accurately in the context of a survey.

Among men, American ideals of masculinity further underscore the importance of work. Having a "good job"—a job that can support not only oneself but also one's family—is often equally important to both men and women. US culture emphasizes work as a central part of masculinity—what it means to be a "real man."[10] Cultural notions of femininity—what it means to be a "real woman"—do just the opposite. While fatherhood and work are seen as compatible and synergistic, dominant ideals in the contemporary US pit motherhood and work against each other.[11]

In brief, it is important to think carefully about how gender, along with class and other social statuses, may influence respondents' answers to questions about work. How likely is it that men would respond that they were "keeping house," for example, even if they hadn't worked in years and were in fact performing the majority of the domestic work? Cultural ideas about gender can potentially bias how respondents answer questions about their work lives, and when this happens, it is important to make note of this when interpreting your results.

Respondents' Current Work Life

The GSS includes a number of variables related to respondents' current work situation. Among the most commonly analyzed questions are "Last week were you working full time, part time, going to school, keeping house, or what?" (WRKSTAT) and "If working, full or part time: how many hours did you work last week, at all jobs?" (HRS1); the variable PRESTG80 is included in years 1988 to 2010 and is an indication of the prestige associated with one's occupation (see Chapter 5 for more detailed information on occupational prestige).

SKIP PATTERNS IN WORK-RELATED QUESTIONS

Some of the questions in the GSS are asked to respondents only if they respond in a particular way to a previous question. The question "How many hours did you work last week, at all jobs?" (HRS1), for example, is asked only to those respondents who indicated in a prior question (WRKSTAT) that last week they were working full time or part time.

Similarly, the variable SPHRS1, which corresponds to the question "How many hours did [your spouse] work last week, at all jobs?" is asked only to respondents who are married and who in a previous question (SPWRKSTA) indicated that their spouse was working either full or part time the previous week.

In most cases, viewing a variable will help you to determine whether all respondents were asked a question or whether a skip pattern in the survey design means that some types of respondents were not asked the question. In the event that skip patterns were used and some groups of respondents (e.g., those not currently working or those not currently married) were not asked the question, it is important to make note of this when interpreting your results.

Respondents' Work Environment

In the 2002, 2006, 2010, and 2014 surveys, there are a number of questions about respondents' workplace experiences and respondents' overall assessment of their work environment. The variable SATJOB1, for example, corresponds to the question "All in all, how satisfied would you say you are with your job?" The variable JOBSECOK concerns respondents' perception of their job security, and PROUDEMP assesses whether respondents are proud they work for their current employer. Surveys in these years also include a number of questions about workplace mistreatment. WKSEXISM corresponds to the question "Do you feel in any way discriminated against on your job because of your gender?" WKRACISM and WKAGEISM ask about racial discrimination and age-based discrimination, respectively, and WKHARSEX asks respondents whether, in the last 12 months, they were sexually harassed by anyone while on the job.

Workforce Participation of Respondents' Families

In addition to asking questions about respondents' personal experiences in the workforce, the GSS also includes a number of questions that ask respondents about the work experiences of their family members. For those respondents who are currently married, the variable SPWRKSTA includes information about their spouses' labor force participation: "Last week was your (wife/husband) working full time, part time, going to school, keeping house, or what?" SPHRS1 asks respondents who are currently married and whose spouses are working, full or part time, how many hours their spouse worked last week, at all jobs.

The variable MAWRKGRW asks respondents, "Did your mother ever work for pay for as long as a year, while you were growing up?" Survey years 1988 to 2010 include a variable (PAPRES80) that indicates the respondent's father's occupational prestige; survey years 1994 to 2010 also include a variable corresponding to the respondent's mother's occupational prestige (MAPRES80).

Attitudes and Beliefs About Work and the Economy

In addition to asking questions about respondents' work life and that of their families, the GSS also includes a number of questions concerning respondents' beliefs about work and the economy. The variable GETAHEAD has been included in the GSS regularly since 1973 and assesses respondents' beliefs about whether success is generally a result of hard work or if it stems from lucky breaks or help from other people. The variable CONBIZ was included in the 1991, 1998, and 2008 surveys and corresponds to the survey question "How much confidence do you have in Business and Industry?" In four survey years (1985, 1990, 1996, and 2006), the GSS also included questions about whether respondents were in favor of the government financing projects to create new jobs (MAKEJOBS) and whether respondents were in favor of less governmental regulation of business (LESSREG).

In addition to these questions, the GSS also includes questions about the relationship between work and family. FAMWKBST, included at this point only in the 2012 survey and discussed at greater length in Chapter 7, asks respondents about the ideal family-work structure for families with small children. MAPAID, which was included in the 1994 and 2002 surveys, asks respondents if they believe "working women should receive paid maternity leave when they have a baby." The 2012 ISSP Module on Gender includes multiple questions related to work and family, including questions about paid leave, child care, and elder care.

Browsing for Variables Related to the Economy and Work

The codebook on the left-hand side of the SDA website allows users to easily identify clusters of variables related to work and the broader economy. If you are interested in browsing for variables related to respondents' beliefs about the economy, work, and their work-related experiences, the following subject headings and subheadings may be especially useful:

- Respondent Background Variables
  - Respondent and Spouse Work Week

- Personal and Family Information
  - Respondent's Employment
  - Spouse's Employment
  - Mother's Employment
  - Father's Employment

- Workplace and Economic Concerns
  - Job Security and Satisfaction
  - Class and Financial Needs
  - Job Supervision
  - Standard of Living

- Controversial Social Issues
  - o Working Mothers
  - o Important Life Aspects

- 1991 Topical Module – Work Organizations

- 2002 Topical Module – Quality of Working Life

- 2002 Topical Module –Employee Compensation

- 2004 Topical Module – Work Environment

- 2008 Variables
  - o Business Owners
  - o Past Employment

- 2012 Topical Module – Workplace Violence

- 2012 ISSP Module – Gender

- 2014 Topical Module – The Quality of Working Life

- 2014 Topical Module – Employee Compensation

- 2014 Topical Module – Work and Relationships

- 1988 ISSP Module: Women and Work
  - o Working Women and the Family
  - o When Should Women Work Outside Home
  - o Work History – Married Women with Children
  - o Work and the Family
  - o Spouse Work Outside Home

APPLICATION: HOW AND TO WHAT EXTENT DO BELIEFS ABOUT THE IMPORTANCE OF HARD WORK FOR "GETTING AHEAD" DIFFER FOR RESPONDENTS OF DIFFERENT RACIAL/ETHNIC AND CLASS BACKGROUNDS? AND HOW, IF AT ALL, DID THESE BELIEFS CHANGE DURING THE GREAT RECESSION?

Over the past four decades, the GSS has included literally hundreds of questions that relate to work life and the economy more generally. One of the variables that has been asked regularly since the 1973 survey is GETAHEAD, which asks respondents whether they believe that people get ahead by their own hard work or whether lucky breaks or help from other people are more important. This application examines how these beliefs intersect with race, ethnicity, and class in the contemporary US and how they have changed from 2004 to 2014.

Step 1. Restate the research question and identify the independent and dependent variables.

In this case, the research question is, "How do race, ethnicity, and class affect respondents' beliefs about how people "get ahead," and to what extent did these beliefs change in the years surrounding the Great Recession?" The dependent variable is GETAHEAD, and the independent variables are DEGREE, RACEHISP, and YEAR.

Step 2. View each variable to make sure you understand what it means. In almost all cases, viewing the variable will give the precise wording of the survey question that corresponds to the variable. When you view the variable, make note of what each response category means as well as the level of measurement for the variable (categorical, ordinal, or interval ratio).

By viewing the variable GETAHEAD, we can see that this is an ordinal-level variable, with three categories, that corresponds to the following survey question:

> Some people say that people get ahead by their own hard work; others say that lucky breaks or help from other people are more important. Which do you think is most important?

YEAR is an interval-ratio-level variable that corresponds to the year from which the data were collected. RACEHISP is a nominal-level variable that corresponds to respondents' self-described racial/ethnic identity. Viewing this variable, we see that the category "White" does not include respondents who said they were Hispanic and that Hispanic does not include those who said they were Black. (Chapter 4 provides a more detailed discussion of this and other variables related to respondents' race and ethnicity.) DEGREE is an ordinal-level variable corresponding to respondents' highest degree earned. (See Chapters 5 and 8 for a more detailed discussion of this and other variables related to class and education.)

Step 3. Determine the time period for which the data are available. Remember that viewing a variable shows you the combined data across all possible survey years. Some questions have been included regularly since 1972, while others are asked in only one or two survey years.

To determine the years in which the variables are included, create a cross-tab of each variable in your analysis by the variable YEAR. Create a cross-tab with GETAHEAD in the "Row" field and YEAR in the "Column" field (with COMPWT selected in the "Weight" field). The resulting table should have data from 1973 to 2014, showing that, while not included in every survey year, the variable GETAHEAD has been asked throughout the history of the GSS.[12]

Producing a cross-tab of RACEHISP by YEAR will show that RACEHISP has been included since the 2000 survey. Creating a cross-tab of DEGREE by YEAR will show that this variable has been included in every year of the GSS.

Step 4. Conduct the relevant analysis, such as a cross-tab or a comparison of means. Remember that you may need to include filter and control variables, depending on the research question. Remember too that you may need to recode one or more variables.

The research question asks us to examine how race, ethnicity, and class affect respondents' beliefs about the importance of hard work for "getting ahead" and to assess how these beliefs have changed in the years surrounding the Great Recession. There are many possible approaches to answer this question. My approach is to begin by examining how and to what extent respondents' beliefs about getting ahead have changed over time. Following this general analysis, I will focus my analysis on recent years, examining how race, ethnicity, and class shape views about how people get ahead.

Begin constructing your cross-tabs by entering GETAHEAD in the "Row" field (since it is the dependent variable) and YEAR in the "Column" field (since we are interested in knowing how these beliefs have changed over time). Before running the table, be sure that you have the default, COMPWT, selected in the "Weight" field. Running the table should produce a large cross-tab, which is shown in Figure 9.1.

Though there is some variation from year to year, Figure 9.1 shows that, over time, respondents' beliefs about how people get ahead have remained remarkably stable. Even from 2006 to 2010, the years immediately surrounding the Great Recession, respondents overwhelmingly reported that getting ahead is largely a result of hard work. Very few people—in any survey year—responded that getting ahead was primarily a result of good luck or help from other people.

Let's now focus on data from recent years and examine how racial/ethnic and class-based inequalities shape views about the role that hard work, luck, and social networks play in getting ahead. Begin by creating a new cross-tab, where the dependent variable GETAHEAD is in the "Row" field and the independent variable DEGREE is in the "Column" field. To make things simpler, recode DEGREE into a variable that has just two categories: those who have less than a bachelor's degree and those who have a bachelor's degree or higher.

DEGREE (R: 0-2; 3-4)

To restrict the analysis to data from the past decade, use the filter:

YEAR (2004-2014)

The resulting analysis is presented in Figure 9.2.

Figure 9.2 shows that, during the survey years 2004 to 2014, respondents with high educational attainment (at least a bachelor's degree) were less likely than respondents with lower levels of education to believe that getting ahead was due primarily to hard work.

Figure 9.1

Frequency Distribution

Cells contain:
- **Column percent**
- Weighted N

GETAHEAD		YEAR												
		1973	1974	1976	1977	1980	1982	1984	1985	1987	1988	1989	1990	1991
1: HARD WORK		**64.5** 963.9	**60.6** 892.0	**62.1** 921.9	**60.6** 918.5	**64.3** 937.6	**61.1** 1,125.1	**66.8** 974.6	**66.7** 1,017.0	**66.1** 1,191.7	**67.6** 658.9	**66.8** 685.9	**65.8** 594.0	**66.9** 658.0
2: BOTH EQUALLY		**24.3** 364.0	**29.2** 430.6	**24.7** 367.0	**28.8** 437.3	**27.8** 405.8	**25.7** 473.6	**17.4** 254.2	**18.1** 275.2	**18.3** 330.8	**20.4** 198.7	**18.7** 192.0	**21.1** 190.8	**21.0** 206.6
3: LUCK OR HELP		**10.0** 149.5	**8.8** 130.0	**13.2** 196.1	**10.6** 160.6	**7.9** 115.0	**13.1** 241.5	**15.8** 231.1	**15.2** 231.9	**15.6** 280.6	**12.0** 116.9	**14.4** 148.1	**13.1** 118.0	**12.1** 119.5
4: OTHER		**1.2** 17.4	**1.4** 20.0	**.0** .0	**.0** .0	**.0** .0	**.0** .0	**.0** .0	**.0** .0	**.0** .0	**.0** .0	**.0** .0	**.0** .0	**.0** .0
COL TOTAL		**100.0** 1,494.7	**100.0** 1,472.7	**100.0** 1,485.0	**100.0** 1,516.3	**100.0** 1,458.4	**100.0** 1,840.2	**100.0** 1,459.8	**100.0** 1,524.1	**100.0** 1,803.0	**100.0** 974.5	**100.0** 1,026.1	**100.0** 902.7	**100.0** 984.1

Frequency Distribution

Cells contain:
- **Column percent**
- Weighted N

GETAHEAD		YEAR												ROW TOTAL
		1993	1994	1996	1998	2000	2002	2004	2006	2008	2010	2012	2014	
1: HARD WORK		**66.9** 708.2	**70.2** 1,408.8	**69.3** 1,310.7	**67.9** 1,266.9	**65.8** 1,212.7	**64.7** 600.7	**66.4** 579.3	**68.8** 1,862.7	**67.1** 904.2	**69.6** 881.1	**69.9** 903.2	**70.7** 1,203.9	**66.4** 24,388.6
2: BOTH EQUALLY		**20.8** 219.9	**19.6** 392.9	**18.8** 355.8	**21.7** 405.9	**23.9** 441.1	**25.8** 239.9	**24.3** 211.8	**19.9** 538.7	**20.8** 260.1	**20.4** 258.6	**20.1** 261.5	**19.6** 333.6	**22.0** 8,066.2
3: LUCK OR HELP		**12.4** 131.1	**10.2** 205.7	**11.9** 226.0	**10.4** 194.2	**10.2** 188.4	**9.5** 88.1	**9.3** 81.2	**11.3** 306.8	**12.1** 163.6	**10.0** 126.1	**10.0** 130.1	**9.8** 166.5	**11.6** 4,246.4
4: OTHER		**.0** .0	**.0** .0	**.0** .0	**.0** .0	**.0** .0	**.0** .0	**.0** .0	**.0** .0	**.0** .0	**.0** .0	**.0** .0	**.0** .0	**.1** 37.4
COL TOTAL		**100.0** 1,059.2	**100.0** 2,007.5	**100.0** 1,892.5	**100.0** 1,869.0	**100.0** 1,842.1	**100.0** 928.7	**100.0** 872.3	**100.0** 2,708.2	**100.0** 1,347.9	**100.0** 1,265.8	**100.0** 1,299.8	**100.0** 1,704.0	**100.0** 36,738.6

Color coding:

< -2.0	< -1.0	< 0.0	> 0.0	> 1.0	> 2.0	Z

Figure 9.2

Frequency Distribution				
Cells contain: -**Column percent** -Weighted N		**DEGREE**		
		1 0-2	2 3-4	**ROW TOTAL**
GETAHEAD	1: HARD WORK	**70.6** 4,744.6	**64.3** 1,592.1	**68.9** 6,336.7
	2: BOTH EQUALLY	**18.7** 1,255.6	**25.3** 627.6	**20.5** 1,883.2
	3: LUCK OR HELP	**10.7** 718.0	**10.3** 256.2	**10.6** 974.2
	COL TOTAL	**100.0** 6,718.2	**100.0** 2,476.0	**100.0** 9,194.2

Figure 9.3

Statistics for DEGREE = 1(0-2)								
Cells contain: -**Column percent** -Weighted N		**YEAR**						
		2004	2006	2008	2010	2012	2014	**ROW TOTAL**
GETAHEAD	1: HARD WORK	**66.7** 421.6	**70.4** 1,435.8	**68.2** 681.0	**71.8** 647.8	**72.7** 682.1	**72.6** 876.3	**70.6** 4,744.6
	2: BOTH EQUALLY	**24.1** 152.5	**18.2** 371.6	**18.8** 188.0	**18.2** 163.9	**16.7** 156.5	**18.5** 223.0	**18.7** 1,255.6
	3: LUCK OR HELP	**9.2** 58.3	**11.4** 231.5	**13.0** 130.0	**10.1** 91.1	**10.6** 99.2	**8.9** 108.0	**10.7** 718.0
	COL TOTAL	**100.0** 632.4	**100.0** 2,038.9	**100.0** 998.9	**100.0** 902.9	**100.0** 937.8	**100.0** 1,207.3	**100.0** 6,718.2

But how, if at all, did the beliefs of respondents with higher and lower levels of education change in response to the Great Recession of 2007–2009? To answer this question, create a new cross-tab where GETAHEAD remains the "Row" variable and YEAR is now the "Column" variable. Use DEGREE (with the same recoding described above) as a control variable, and keep the filter restricting

Figure 9.4

Statistics for DEGREE = 2(3-4)								
Cells contain: **-Column percent** -Weighted N		**YEAR**						
		2004	2006	2008	2010	2012	2014	**ROW TOTAL**
GETAHEAD	1: HARD WORK	**65.6** 156.8	**63.7** 425.1	**64.2** 223.3	**64.3** 233.3	**62.5** 226.1	**66.0** 327.6	*64.3* *1,592.1*
	2: BOTH EQUALLY	**24.8** 59.3	**25.0** 167.1	**26.2** 91.0	**26.1** 94.6	**29.0** 105.0	**22.3** 110.5	*25.3* *627.6*
	3: LUCK OR HELP	**9.6** 22.9	**11.3** 75.3	**9.7** 33.6	**9.6** 35.0	**8.5** 30.9	**11.8** 58.5	*10.3* *256.2*
	COL TOTAL	*100.0* *239.0*	*100.0* *667.5*	*100.0* *348.0*	*100.0* *362.9*	*100.0* *362.0*	*100.0* *496.7*	*100.0* *2,476.0*

the analysis to survey years 2004 to 2014. The resulting analysis is presented in Figures 9.3 and 9.4.

Figure 9.3 shows the results for the approximately 6,718 individuals who answered these questions on the 2004 to 2014 surveys and who held less than a bachelor's degree. Figure 9.4 shows the results for the 2,476 respondents who held a bachelor's degree or higher.

Reading across the top row of Figure 9.3, we can see that 66.7% of respondents with lower levels of education reported that getting ahead was primarily due to individuals' hard work. This percentage increases to 70.4% in 2006 and then falls slightly in 2008, only to increase again in the following years. Overall, there is relatively little change during this time period. Figure 9.4, which examines responses of those with higher levels of education, shows largely the same result: Though there is variation from year to year, there is no clear pattern to the variation and no significant change in responses in the years surrounding the Great Recession.

The second part of the research question asks us to examine the extent of racial/ethnic differences in beliefs about how people get ahead. To do this, we can rerun the above analyses, substituting the variable RACEHISP for the variable DEGREE. Create a cross-tab where the dependent variable, GETAHEAD, is in the "Row" field and the independent variable, RACEHISP, is in the "Column" field. Use a filter to restrict the analysis to data from 2004 to 2014. Figure 9.5 shows the resulting analysis.

Figure 9.5 reveals that, in each of the racial/ethnic groups examined here, the majority of respondents report believing that getting ahead is largely a result of hard work. For each racial/ethnic group, "hard work" is the modal category in the dependent variable. To assess how these patterns have changed over the past decade, produce a new cross-tab where GETAHEAD remains the "Row" variable and YEAR

Figure 9.5

Frequency Distribution						
Cells contain: -**Column percent** -Weighted N		**RACEHISP**				
		1 White	2 Black	3 Hispanic	4 Other	*ROW TOTAL*
GETAHEAD	1: HARD WORK	**69.2** 4,315.8	**64.6** 794.8	**73.7** 946.7	**62.6** 282.1	*68.9* *6,339.4*
	2: BOTH EQUALLY	**20.6** 1,284.3	**21.4** 263.1	**17.3** 222.4	**25.4** 114.5	*20.5* *1,884.3*
	3: LUCK OR HELP	**10.1** 632.2	**14.1** 173.0	**9.0** 115.0	**12.0** 54.1	*10.6* *974.2*
	COL TOTAL	*100.0* *6,232.3*	*100.0* *1,230.8*	*100.0* *1,284.1*	*100.0* *450.7*	*100.0* *9,197.9*

is now the "Column" variable. Use RACEHISP as a control variable, and keep the filter restricting the analysis to survey years 2004 to 2014.

The resulting analysis is presented in Figures 9.6 through 9.9. Each table focuses on one racial/ethnic group: Figure 9.6 on non-Hispanic whites, Figure 9.7 on Black respondents, Figure 9.8 on non-Black, Hispanic/Latino respondents, and Figure 9.9 on respondents who identify with other racial/ethnic groups. When examining the results within these figures, note that the sample size differs dramatically across these groups.

Figure 9.6

Statistics for RACEHISP = 1(White)								
Cells contain: -**Column percent** -Weighted N		**YEAR**						
		2004	2006	2008	2010	2012	2014	*ROW TOTAL*
GETAHEAD	1: HARD WORK	**66.0** 428.8	**69.6** 1,289.9	**67.5** 623.3	**69.7** 619.4	**69.0** 570.5	**71.9** 783.9	*69.2* *4,315.8*
	2: BOTH EQUALLY	**24.9** 161.8	**19.2** 355.6	**21.0** 194.1	**21.1** 187.8	**21.6** 178.8	**18.9** 206.3	*20.6* *1,284.3*
	3: LUCK OR HELP	**9.2** 59.5	**11.2** 207.7	**11.5** 106.6	**9.1** 81.0	**9.4** 77.7	**9.1** 99.6	*10.1* *632.2*
	COL TOTAL	*100.0* *650.1*	*100.0* *1,853.2*	*100.0* *924.0*	*100.0* *888.3*	*100.0* *827.1*	*100.0* *1,089.8*	*100.0* *6,232.3*

Figure 9.7

<table>
<tr><th colspan="9" style="text-align:center">Statistics for RACEHISP = 2(Black)</th></tr>
<tr><td rowspan="2">Cells contain:
-Column percent
-Weighted N</td><td></td><th colspan="6" style="text-align:center">YEAR</th><td rowspan="2">ROW
TOTAL</td></tr>
<tr><td></td><td>2004</td><td>2006</td><td>2008</td><td>2010</td><td>2012</td><td>2014</td></tr>
<tr><td rowspan="8">GETAHEAD</td><td>1: HARD
WORK</td><td>63.9
66.2</td><td>63.0
210.4</td><td>59.4
108.7</td><td>64.8
112.9</td><td>69.1
137.3</td><td>67.0
159.3</td><td>64.6
794.8</td></tr>
<tr><td>2: BOTH
EQUALLY</td><td>25.5
26.4</td><td>21.9
73.0</td><td>22.6
41.4</td><td>21.0
36.6</td><td>19.1
37.9</td><td>20.1
47.8</td><td>21.4
263.1</td></tr>
<tr><td>3: LUCK OR
HELP</td><td>10.7
11.1</td><td>15.1
50.4</td><td>18.0
32.9</td><td>14.2
24.7</td><td>11.8
23.4</td><td>12.9
30.6</td><td>14.1
173.0</td></tr>
<tr><td>COL TOTAL</td><td>100.0
103.6</td><td>100.0
333.8</td><td>100.0
183.0</td><td>100.0
174.2</td><td>100.0
198.6</td><td>100.0
237.7</td><td>100.0
1,230.8</td></tr>
</table>

Figure 9.8

<table>
<tr><th colspan="9" style="text-align:center">Statistics for RACEHISP = 3(Hispanic)</th></tr>
<tr><td rowspan="2">Cells contain:
-Column percent
-Weighted N</td><td></td><th colspan="6" style="text-align:center">YEAR</th><td rowspan="2">ROW
TOTAL</td></tr>
<tr><td></td><td>2004</td><td>2006</td><td>2008</td><td>2010</td><td>2012</td><td>2014</td></tr>
<tr><td rowspan="8">GETAHEAD</td><td>1: HARD
WORK</td><td>76.0
58.8</td><td>70.1
282.2</td><td>72.7
130.8</td><td>84.5
120.7</td><td>75.8
141.3</td><td>72.1
212.8</td><td>73.7
946.7</td></tr>
<tr><td>2: BOTH
EQUALLY</td><td>18.0
13.9</td><td>21.2
85.4</td><td>19.3
34.7</td><td>8.7
12.4</td><td>11.5
21.5</td><td>18.5
54.6</td><td>17.3
222.4</td></tr>
<tr><td>3: LUCK OR
HELP</td><td>6.0
4.7</td><td>8.6
34.8</td><td>8.1
14.5</td><td>6.8
9.6</td><td>12.6
23.6</td><td>9.4
27.8</td><td>9.0
115.0</td></tr>
<tr><td>COL TOTAL</td><td>100.0
77.4</td><td>100.0
402.3</td><td>100.0
180.0</td><td>100.0
142.7</td><td>100.0
186.3</td><td>100.0
295.2</td><td>100.0
1,284.1</td></tr>
</table>

Step 5. Interpret your results. There are five basic steps to interpreting and communicating your results:

1. Remind your audience of the basics.

    a. Restate your research question.

        The main research question is "How do race, ethnicity, and class structure respondents' beliefs about how people

Figure 9.9

<table>
<tr><td colspan="9">Statistics for RACEHISP = 4(Other)</td></tr>
<tr><td rowspan="2">Cells contain:
-Column percent
-Weighted N</td><td rowspan="2"></td><td colspan="6">YEAR</td><td rowspan="2">*ROW TOTAL*</td></tr>
<tr><td>2004</td><td>2006</td><td>2008</td><td>2010</td><td>2012</td><td>2014</td></tr>
<tr><td rowspan="8">**GETAHEAD**</td><td>1: HARD WORK</td><td>**62.0**
25.5</td><td>**67.4**
80.1</td><td>**68.0**
41.5</td><td>**46.4**
28.1</td><td>**67.3**
59.1</td><td>**58.8**
47.8</td><td>*62.6*
282.1</td></tr>
<tr><td>2: BOTH EQUALLY</td><td>**23.5**
9.7</td><td>**20.8**
24.8</td><td>**16.3**
10.0</td><td>**36.0**
21.8</td><td>**26.5**
23.3</td><td>**30.7**
24.9</td><td>*25.4*
114.5</td></tr>
<tr><td>3: LUCK OR HELP</td><td>**14.4**
5.9</td><td>**11.8**
14.0</td><td>**15.6**
9.5</td><td>**17.6**
10.7</td><td>**6.1**
5.4</td><td>**10.6**
8.6</td><td>*12.0*
54.1</td></tr>
<tr><td>*COL TOTAL*</td><td>*100.0*
41.2</td><td>*100.0*
118.9</td><td>*100.0*
60.9</td><td>*100.0*
60.6</td><td>*100.0*
87.8</td><td>*100.0*
81.3</td><td>*100.0*
450.7</td></tr>
</table>

'get ahead,' and how did these beliefs change in the years surrounding the Great Recession of 2007–2009?"

b. Remind your audience of the data source and the specific variables that you used to answer this question.

To answer this question, this analysis uses a series of cross-tabs that examine the relationship between respondents' beliefs and their social class as well as their racial/ethnic identities. The data come from the 2004–2014 General Social Surveys.

c. Clearly state how each variable was coded and what each response category represents.

The dependent variable, respondents' views about the importance of hard work for people getting ahead, is assessed with the survey question "Some people say that people get ahead by their own hard work; others say that lucky breaks or help from other people are more important. Which do you think is most important?" This is an ordinal-level variable with three categories. Respondents' racial/ethnic identity is assessed with a four-category nominal-level variable, where categories represent self-identification as white (non-Hispanic), African American or Black, Hispanic (non-Black), or other racial/ethnic groups. Respondents' educational attainment is used as a proxy for respondents' social class and is assessed with the variable DEGREE—an ordinal-level variable with categories of less than a high school diploma, a high school diploma, a junior college degree, a bachelor's degree, or a graduate degree. In the present analysis, educational attainment is recoded into a variable with two categories: those with less than a bachelor's degree and those with a bachelor's degree or higher.

d. Specify the number of cases included in the analysis. The overall number of valid cases (N) included in the cross-tab is presented in the bottom right corner of each cross-tab.

The first analysis presented here (Figure 9.1) shows an overview of the data from 1973 to 2014 and includes data from approximately 36,739 respondents. Subsequent analyses include a smaller subset of data from the 2004 to 2014 surveys. Analyses of class differences include approximately 9,194 respondents. Analyses of racial/ethnic differences include approximately 9,198 people, 6,232 of whom ([6,232 / 9,198] * 100 = 67.8%) self-identify as non-Hispanic and white. As shown in Figure 9.5 and again in Figure 9.9, approximately 450 respondents in the analysis are grouped into the "other racial ethnic group."

2. Focus on specifics.

The first step in interpreting the results is to look carefully at the numbers in the tables and interpret them as specifically as you can. When interpreting the results from multiple tables, begin by interpreting them one by one. As you interpret a number from a table, be sure to remind the audience of which table the number is coming from.

For example, as stated above, Figure 9.1 provides an overview of respondents' beliefs about how people get ahead and shows that, from 1973 to 2014, most people have answered that they believe getting ahead is largely the result of hard work. Figure 9.2 breaks this down by respondents' educational attainment and shows that, from 2004 to 2014, respondents with lower levels of education were slightly more likely to endorse this view than were those with higher levels of education. Of those respondents who held less than a bachelor's degree, 70.6% answered that they believed getting ahead was largely a result of hard work. Of those with a bachelor's degree or higher, 64.3% of respondents expressed this view.

Figures 9.3 and 9.4 break this down even further, showing how respondents with higher and lower levels of education changed in their views from 2004 to 2014. Overall, the percentages do not change very much from one year to the next. Looking at Figure 9.3, we can see that the percentage of respondents who expressed the belief that luck or help from others was the most important determinant of success rose slightly from 2006 to 2008, but then fell again from 2010 onward. Even this change, however, is relatively small.

Figure 9.5 examines racial/ethnic differences in respondents' beliefs about how people get ahead, again using data from the 2004 to 2014 surveys. The row totals in Figures 9.7 and 9.9 show that approximately fourteen percent of Black respondents and 12% of those who identified with racial/ethnic groups other than Hispanic, Black, or African American responded that luck and help from other people are most important for getting ahead. Respondents who identified as Hispanic (but not Black) and those who identified as white (but not Hispanic) were somewhat less likely to support this view.

Analyzing racial/ethnic differences over time shows some interesting variation. As shown in Figure 9.6, the majority of non-Hispanic white respondents identify hard work as the most important factor in getting ahead. This figure ranges from 66% of non-Hispanic white respondents expressing this view in 2004 to a high of 71.9% in 2014. In almost every one of these years, a slightly lower percentage of Black respondents expressed this view, but the majority of Black respondents also emphasized the importance of hard work. In every survey year, the percentage of Black respondents who attributed getting ahead to luck or help from others was higher than the percentage of non-Hispanic whites who expressed this view.

Of the four racial/ethnic groups considered here, non-Black Hispanics were the most likely to report believing that hard work is the most important driver of success. The percentage of non-Black Hispanics who supported this view spiked dramatically in 2010 and in later years fell back to pre-recession levels. Finally, in most survey years, respondents who identified with other, non-Black, non-Hispanic racial/ethnic groups expressed beliefs about getting ahead that were close to those of Black and non-Hispanic white respondents. This changed dramatically in 2010, however, when only 46.4% of respondents identifying with other racial/ethnic groups supported the idea that hard work was the most important factor in getting ahead.

3. Consider the big picture.

After examining the specific numbers within the table and describing each table individually, it is important to step back and take a larger view of the overall relationship presented in the analysis. How do the individual analyses work together? Do they all point to the same overall conclusion, or are the results more mixed? If the individual analyses seem to point to different conclusions, how do you make sense of these results? Remember that results without identifiable patterns can be just as important and interesting as results with an identifiable pattern—especially if the pattern you expected is not apparent.

What can be said about how race, ethnicity, and class affect respondents' beliefs about how people "get ahead"? And how, if at all, did these beliefs change from 2004 to 2014? The analyses presented here are surprising in a few ways. First, as shown in Figures 9.2 through 9.4, respondents with higher levels of educational attainment are less likely than those with lower levels of education to believe that getting ahead is attributable primarily to hard work. Another way of saying this is that respondents with lower levels of education were more likely to believe in a meritocratic ideal of hard work resulting in success. Unemployment rates soared during the Great Recession, but respondents to the 2004–2014 General Social Surveys showed remarkable consistency in their answers despite the economic turmoil surrounding them.

Figures 9.6 through 9.9 show some evidence of racial/ethnic group variation, but also a great deal of similarity. In every year considered, for every racial/ethnic group considered, the modal category for getting ahead is "work hard." In every year, fewer than one in five respondents reported believing that luck and help from other people were the most important factors in getting ahead. Though some fluctuation occurred in 2010, the beliefs after the recession were very similar to beliefs prior to the recession.

4. Consider limitations.

An important part of all scientific research is to be clear about the limitations. Every project has limitations, some more than others, and it is important to make these clear when interpreting the results. It is also important to consider potential confounding variables—variables that are not included in the analyses but might be affecting the relationship between the independent and dependent variables. Finally, while it is crucial to explain what the analyses reveal about the larger research question, it is often useful to clarify what the analyses do *not* tell us about the research question. Anticipate possible misinterpretations.

When considering the limitations of any survey research project, it is always important to consider the issues of survey design, possible sample biases, and generalizability. In the current analysis, the results apply only to adults in the US who are aged 18 and older. From 2006 onward, respondents include English- and Spanish-speaking adults, but prior to this year, the survey is representative of only those who are able to speak English. Adults in the US who are not able to speak either language are not included in the analysis. Nor are those living in institutions such as prisons or mental institutions included in this analysis.

One of the strengths of the GSS, particularly now that it includes Spanish-speaking individuals, is the diversity of its sample. Despite this diversity, the number of respondents who identify with racial/ethnic groups other than white, Hispanic, or Black is small. Because there are so few respondents in this group and because there is also great diversity within this group, the findings from the "other racial ethnic" group should be interpreted with extra caution.

Finally, a number of other variables, such as age, gender, respondents' current employment status, political party, and income, likely play an important role in shaping beliefs about how people get ahead and are not considered in this analysis.

All of these variables, and the role they play in shaping respondents' beliefs about how people get ahead, could be assessed using data from the GSS.

5. Summarize your conclusions.

Earlier in this chapter, the ideal of the "American Dream" was described as the promise that all individuals can, through hard work, persistence, and creative problem-solving, work their way up to a comfortable middle- or upper-class position. Taken together, the analyses presented in this application show that the majority of respondents endorse at least some elements of this ideal. Overwhelmingly, GSS participants respond that hard work, not luck or help from others, is what drives success. By examining these beliefs over time, the analyses underscore the tenacity of these beliefs. Even in the midst of economic collapse, GSS respondents cling to their belief in the importance of hard work. Some groups (e.g., those with lower levels of education) were more likely to believe in the importance of hard work after the recession than they were before.

Interpreting these results within a social justice framework requires thinking through issues of power and inequality, socially constructed differences, and links between the micro and macro levels of society as well as the importance of intersecting inequalities. We might ask, for example, whose interests are served when people with lower levels of education believe hard work yields success? What structural, geographical, and ideological factors help to explain the racial/ethnic differences—and similarities—found in Figures 9.6 through 9.9? How do we explain the fact that a severe macro-level economic meltdown didn't appear to generate a more structural understanding of success in the minds of GSS respondents? And how might other axes of inequality, such as gender, (dis)ability, age, citizenship, and sexuality, work with race, ethnicity, and class to structure individuals' beliefs? These questions can be answered by combining further analyses of GSS data with research that is qualitative, historical, comparative, and theoretical.

EXERCISES: ANALYZING INEQUALITIES AT WORK

Chapters 3 through 6 presented an overview of how data from the General Social Survey can be used to analyze inequalities of race, gender, class, and sexuality. This chapter draws from the analytic techniques presented in the previous chapters to examine how race, gender, class, and sexuality intersect to structure work-related experiences as well as attitudes and beliefs about work life.

Over the past four decades, one of the biggest changes with respect to the world of work has been the increased participation of women—and particularly women with small children—in the paid labor force. To examine this trend, create a cross-tab of WRKSTAT by YEAR, and use SEX as a control variable. When you run the analysis, you should see two tables: one showing changes in men's workforce participation over time and the other showing women's workforce participation over time. When you create these tables, be sure to keep the default weight of COMPWT selected.

1. The variable WRKSTAT is best described as:

    a. a categorical-level variable.

    b. an ordinal-level variable.

    c. an interval-ratio-level variable.

    d. a dummy variable.

2. In 1972, the percentage of women respondents who indicated that they were "working full time" was approximately:

    a. 8.2%.

    b. 13.6%.

    c. 25.0%.

    d. 20.8%.

3. In 2014, the percentage of women respondents who indicated that they were "working full time" was approximately:

    a. 26.7%.

    b. 42.7%.

    c. 52.7%.

    d. 74.9%.

4. In 2014, the percentage of men respondents who indicated that they were "working full time" was approximately:

    a. 57.6%.

    b. 64.0%.

    c. 72.7%.

    d. 81.5%.

5. In 1972, the percentage of women respondents who indicated that they were "keeping house" was approximately:

    a. 15.7%.

    b. 27.6%.

    c. 53.3%.

    d. 88.5%.

6. In 2014, the percentage of women respondents who indicated that they were "keeping house" was approximately:

    a. 17.5%.

    b. 22.3%.

    c. 27.2%.

    d. 33.6%.

In 2012, the GSS included a special topical module on workplace violence. The next several questions consider how respondents' social class shapes their experiences at work. Produce a cross-tab between the variable RUDEWK and CLASS, putting RUDEWK in the "Row" field and CLASS in the "Column" field. In the "Filter" field, type "YEAR (2012)."

7. In arguing that respondents' social class shapes their workplace experiences, the variable CLASS is being used as the:

    a. dependent variable.

    b. independent variable.

    c. intervening variable.

    d. dummy variable.

8. Among respondents who describe themselves as lower class, ____ indicate that they are "sometimes" treated rudely at work.

    a. 3.6%

    b. 8.3%

    c. 13.9%

    d. 19.7%

9. Among respondents who describe themselves as middle class, ____ indicate that they are "sometimes" treated rudely at work.

    a. 4.4%

    b. 8.3%

    c. 23.5%

    d. 39%

10. For both lower- and working-class respondents, the modal category for RUDEWK is:

    a. often.

    b. sometimes.

    c. rarely.

    d. never.

11. For both middle- and upper-class respondents, the modal category for RUDEWK is:

    a. often.

    b. sometimes.

    c. rarely.

    d. never.

Now produce a cross-tab that examines the relationship between the variables IGNORWK and CLASS. Put IGNORWK in the "Row" field and CLASS in the "Column" field. In the "Filter" field, type "YEAR (2012)."

12. Of those respondents who answered questions about their class identity and who also provided a valid response to the question about feeling ignored, excluded, or isolated from others at work, approximately what percent described themselves as "upper class"?

    a. 25%

    b. 30%

    c. 39%

    d. 45%

13. Approximately what percent of respondents who described themselves as "upper class" also reported that they "often" felt ignored, excluded, or isolated from others at work?

    a. 0%

    b. 9%

    c. 14%

    d. 30%

14. Among respondents who described themselves as "lower class," _____ reported "never" feeling ignored, excluded, or isolated from others at work.

    a. 3.3%

    b. 20.5%

    c. 43.1%

    d. 54.7%

15. Among respondents who describe themselves as "middle class," _____ reported "never" feeling ignored, excluded, or isolated from others at work.

    a. 43.1%

    b. 54.7%

    c. 65.1%

    d. 72.6%

ANALYSES & ESSAYS

Use the data analysis skills you learned in the previous chapters to answer the questions below.

1. How and to what extent do people of different racial/ethnic and gender groups perceive workplace discrimination? Produce three different cross-tabs that assess the relationship between (1) respondents' racial/ethnic group (RACEHISP) and perceived racial discrimination in the workplace (WKRACISM); (2) respondents' gender (SEX) and perceptions of gender discrimination in the workplace (WKSEXISM); and (3) respondents' gender (SEX) and perceptions of sexual harassment in the workplace (WKHARSEX). Interpret your results.

2. How and to what extent do men and women with different levels of educational attainment differ in terms of the hours they typically work? Analyze a comparison of means using the variables HRS1, SEX, and DEGREE. Interpret your results.

3. How and to what extent does gender shape the extent to which work responsibilities interfere with home life? Use the variables SEX, JOBVSFA1, and TIREDHM1 to answer this question.

4. How and to what extent do gender and racial/ethnic inequalities work together to shape the time that people have available for relaxation after work? Analyze a comparison of means using HRSRELAX as the dependent variable, with RACEHISP in the "Column" field and SEX in the "Row" field. Interpret your results.

5. How and to what extent do gender, race, and ethnicity work together to shape the extent to which individuals use technology in their jobs? Run a comparison of means with the variable USETECH as the dependent variable, RACEHISP in the "Row" field, and SEX in the "Column" field. Interpret your results.

NOTES

1. Mills, C. Wright. [1959] 2000. *The Sociological Imagination.* New York: Oxford University Press, p. 4.

2. Ibid., p. 9. Italics added for emphasis.

3. Writing in the 1950s, Mills relies on masculine pronouns when referring to men and women. Mills's insights here apply equally well to people of all genders, and I have modified the first two sentences of this quotation so that it is more gender inclusive.

4. US Bureau of Labor Statistics. 2012. "The Recession of 2007–2009." Retrieved May 26, 2016 (http://www.bls.gov/spotlight/2012/recession/pdf/recession_bls_spotlight.pdf).

5. Kocchar, Rakesh, Ana Gonzalez-Barrera, and Daniel Dockterman. 2009. "V. Foreclosures in the U.S. in 2008." Pew Research Center. Retrieved July 3, 2016 (http://www.pewhispanic.org/2009/05/12/v-foreclosures-in-the-u-s-in-2008).

6. This figure comes from the National Center for Education Statistics' report "Employment and Unemployment Rates by Educational Attainment." The employment rate is defined as "the number of persons in that age group who are employed as a percentage of the civilian population in that age group. Data exclude persons enrolled in school [at the time of the survey]." Retrieved May 26, 2016 (http://nces.ed.gov/programs/coe/indicator_cbc.asp).

7. Mills, *Sociological Imagination*, p. 3.

8. Weber, Lynn. 2010. *Understanding Race, Class, Gender, and Sexuality.* 2nd ed. New York: Oxford University Press.

9. Kerbo, Harold R. 2009. *Social Stratification and Inequality.* 7th ed. New York: McGraw-Hill.

10. Townsend, Nicholas W. 2002. *The Package Deal: Marriage, Work and Fatherhood in Men's Lives.* Philadelphia: Temple University Press; Connell, R. W. 1995. *Masculinities.* Cambridge, UK: Polity Press.

11. Budig, Michelle J., and Paula England. 2001. "The Wage Penalty for Motherhood." *American Sociological Review* 66:204–25; Glenn, Evelyn Nakano, Grace Change, and Linda Rennie Forcey. 1994. *Mothering: Ideology, Experience, and Agency.* New York: Routledge.

12. GETAHEAD is not included in years 1972, 1975, 1983, and 1986.

ABOUT THE AUTHOR

Catherine E. Harnois is Associate Professor in the Departments of Sociology and Women's, Gender, and Sexuality Studies at Wake Forest University, where she teaches courses on social inequality and research methods. Her work on the intersection of gender and racial discrimination received the *2012 Outstanding Contribution to Scholarship Article Award* from the American Sociological Association Section on Race, Gender, and Class. Her research has appeared in the journals *Gender & Society, Ethnic and Racial Studies, Sociological Forum, Social Psychology Quarterly, Sociology of Race and Ethnicity,* and the *National Women's Studies Association Journal,* in addition to other scholarly outlets.